USING THE IBM 1130

USING THE IBM 1130

ALFRED M. BORK
University of California
Irvine

ADDISON-WESLEY PUBLISHING COMPANY
Reading, Massachusetts
Menlo Park, California/London/Don Mills, Ontario

1521330

This book concerns programming and using the
IBM 1130, a recently designed small digital computer.
No previous acquaintance with digital computers or
their function is assumed, so the material is
suitable for a novice, either as an introduction to
this computer, or to computers in general. It will also
serve readers already acquainted with other computers
who desire an introduction to the IBM 1130 and
its programming facilities. All the major programming
systems of the 1130—the monitor, FORTRAN, and
the assembler—are described.

The organization of the book merits some discussion.
Books on computers and programming language
are often organized, I believe, much too logically.
Covering every topic systematically is not necessarily
suited to best learning. The pedagogical approach
used here yields a much messier structure; topics are
occasionally repeated, and neat, logical subdivision
is sacrificed. I have tried to present the material in a
natural learning sequence, rather than in a logical
sequence. Thus, for example, some of the
middle chapters group related facilities of FORTRAN
and the monitor system, because these are used
together. FORTRAN is the first language presented,
because it is usually the easiest way for the
beginner to gain access to the computer.

The book attempts no complete description of
the programming and functioning of the 1130. To be
complete would require a book many times this
size, and because any computer system changes as
new hardware and programming developments
are announced, even a book complete when initially
published would soon fail to reflect all the
current details of the system. The rational attitude
is that the final source of information concerning
the system will be the IBM published manuals.

I assume that the advanced user will have access to such information. These manuals are frequently revised to reflect the day-to-day progress of the system in a way not possible with a bound book.

The manuals for a computer system are often maligned as being unreadable. Although some manuals are difficult to read, I feel that this criticism is primarily due to a misunderstanding. The purpose of the manuals for a computer system is not to teach people about the system, but rather to define all the components of the system carefully. They are intended for reference and definition rather than for introducing the system.

This book, intended for anyone becoming acquainted with the 1130 system, can be much more free in its organization, grouping topics that naturally fit together for a person first learning the system. But it cannot replace the manuals. I believe that some of the IBM 1130 manuals are quite readable, while others are difficult to understand without previous computer experience. For example, learning the assembler language from the IBM 1130 assembler manual would not be easy, since this very brief manual was written presumably for people already somewhat acquainted with assembler languages.

I hope that the book will be useful in a modular fashion. A person who wants to write and run simple FORTRAN programs will probably find the description in Chapters 1 and 2 sufficient for his immediate needs. These chapters should enable him to learn by beginning to write and run his own programs. If a reader then wants to become acquainted with more details of the FORTRAN language, the next two chapters will be useful. Many readers may stop at this point, but others will want to continue the study of the assembler and machine-language facilities of the 1130.

It is *not* assumed that every reader will read the book from beginning to end. Those already familiar with FORTRAN for other machines, for example, can jump in at the chapters on coding and the assembler language and study these facilities without having worked through the previous chapters, or they can read the sections which particularly concern the monitor system.

Each of the programming languages is introduced primarily through examples. I have found this approach to be faster for my students and, for most students, more satisfying than the usual FORTRAN treatments proceeding through grammatical considerations, though undoubtedly some students will learn the language faster through direct study of its syntax. My experience shows the approach through examples to be the simplest procedure for the majority, even though the arrangement is less satisfying logically.

The tables in the Appendix section of the book are intended to satisfy a special need. Some of this material is useful while reading the rest of the book, and consequently it is referenced at appropriate points; but more important, these tables and charts are intended for the active programmer, who needs a brief collection of reference material concentrated for convenience in a single place. Some of the tables are reprinted by permission from the IBM 1130 manuals or are modifications of tables in those manuals. Others have been developed particularly for this book. To make this section complete and self-contained, the information tables occasionally overlap material in the body of the book.

My experience with the IBM 1130, reflected in this book, has been with the version 1 Disk Monitor System which supported the original 1130 configuration. As the manuscript was about to go to the publisher, the version 2 system was announced; the new version should be available at about the time this book is published. The version 2 system is an extension of the version 1 system, keeping the facilities already available and adding support for additional input/output equipment and multiple disks. As with all computer systems, there may be some modifications in its final form. It seems likely that in the near future both versions will be in use, version 1 on smaller and version 2 on larger configurations. Eventually the additional version 2 facilities will probably be available on all 1130 computers.

The reader should keep in mind that the descriptions of the version 2 monitor may be modified in future development. I have isolated the statements that refer just to version 2 to forewarn the reader.

The writing of this book involved assistance from many others. My immediate impetus was the acquisition of an IBM 1130 by the computer center at Reed College in the fall of 1966. Several of us, faculty and students, took it upon ourselves to become as acquainted as possible with the machine in advance, through reading the manuals, and then to aid in educating others in the community in its use. Like other computer centers, the Reed computer center has an innovative group of very capable student programmers. This book reflects my deep indebtedness in many ways to that small group of students who worked with me in learning how to program and use the machine when it first arrived.

Two students in particular, Peter Langston and David Raich, were especially helpful in guiding my learning processes, and on several occasions they gave me important assistance in the writing of early programs. They read drafts of parts of the book and made many useful suggestions. For their effective contributions I wish to thank them.

My wife Annette read the manuscript—some sections of it in several drafts—and made invaluable contributions to the readability of the final product.

Cambridge, Massachusetts   A.M.B.
April, 1968

CONTENTS

INTRODUCTION TO FORTRAN
AND TO THE COMPUTER

CHAPTER 1

There are several ways to study a new language. Here we are interested in learning FORTRAN, a rather specialized language intended for the communication of a problem to a digital computer. Learning FORTRAN is not too different from learning any other language. We can approach it through its grammatical structure and vocabulary or through examples of its use, as people learn their native languages. Both methods may lead to the same result, but each begins quite differently. We shall follow the second method, becoming acquainted with FORTRAN, or at least a part of FORTRAN, by studying some examples. The particular FORTRAN dialect we shall study is that used on the IBM 1130, but much of the discussion will be applicable to other versions of FORTRAN.

We begin, as in all computer programs, with a problem. Our strategy is first to discuss the problem we want to solve and then to develop the FORTRAN program to solve it, discussing the steps in the program as we proceed. We shall choose a problem not requiring specialized knowledge but one that is a genuine computer problem. Even from the beginning it is reasonable to ask just which problems should be run on computers and which problems should not. To get a "feel" for the types of problems suitable for computer solution, we want our first example to be a problem difficult to solve by hand calculation. In other words, the computer should be used to work a problem that would present real difficulties without it.

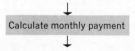

FIG. 1–1. The loan calculation, first stage.

THE LOAN PROBLEM

Let us consider the calculation of a loan. A person goes to a bank to borrow money for a house. He may negotiate concerning interest rate or he may accept a fixed rate. He may have a choice about the length of the loan: some housing loans are for 20 years, others for 30.

Although we are specifying a house loan in this example, we want a program which will work for any loan; it should accept the amount of money to be borrowed, the interest rate, and the period of the loan, and then calculate all the payments, interest, etc., on the loan.

In writing this program we need to know how to compute the monthly payments. If you think a little about it, you may realize that this calculation is not trivial. We cannot simply divide the loan by the number of months in the period to find the monthly payment, because part of each one will go to interest instead of decreasing the amount owed. We shall not develop the full mathematical structure for computing these monthly payments. Many books on banking or related topics contain a formula for calculating the monthly payments on a loan, and we intend to borrow this result. Here is the formula,

$$P = \frac{AR(1 + R)^N}{(1 + R)^{N-1}},$$

in which A is the amount of the loan, N is the number of months for which the loan is extended, R is the interest rate per month (that is, the interest rate for the year divided by 12), and P is the monthly payment. If N is a large number, because the loan is for a long period of time, then raising quantities to the Nth power is a complicated calculation. (Anyone familiar with logarithms may know how to compute the result.) To make our calculations easier, we propose to get the computer to carry them out by writing a FORTRAN program to instruct the computer what to do. Figure 1–1 shows the first stage in developing a diagram of the program.

The FORTRAN statement describing the calculation of the monthly payment does not look much different from the formula just expressed in everyday algebra:

```
P = (A*R*(1. + R)**N)/((1. + R)**N - 1.)
```

The names A, R, and N are those previously used. Comparing this with the algebraic formula, we can readily see that "*" (asterisk) is the FORTRAN multiplication sign and that "/" means division. A FORTRAN statement may use parentheses which in algebra would be redundant, and spaces can be put anywhere for clarity. By comparing the FORTRAN statement of the formula with the algebraic formula, we can see that the double asterisk, "**," means "to the power." Because of limitations on the input-output machines, FORTRAN programs have only linear strings of characters, and raised exponents may not be used. The decimal points after the 1's are not essential in 1130 FORTRAN, but (as we shall see) lead to faster execution of the program.

ENTERING THE BASIC INFORMATION

One FORTRAN statement, or sentence, does not make a program. Since the loan calculation can be carried out for many different loans, we want to be able to give the computer the loan description before each calculation. Therefore a part in the FORTRAN program must describe these initial conditions. This stage is added to the diagram (Fig. 1–2.) One way to give information to the 1130 is through the typewriter keyboard built into the console of the computer.

Here is a possible introductory section of the program designed to accomplish the input of this information:

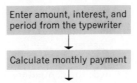

FIG. 1–2. The loan calculation, first and second stages.

```
    WRITE (1,2)
2   FORMAT ( 'LOAN PROGRAM - ENTER AMOUNT IN FORM XXXXX.XX' )
    READ (6,3 ) A
3   FORMAT (F8.2)
    WRITE (1,4)
4   FORMAT ( 'ENTER INTEREST RATE PER YEAR IN FORM XX.XX' )
    READ (6,5 ) RY
5   FORMAT (F5.2)
    WRITE (1,6)
6   FORMAT ( 'ENTER NUMBER OF MONTHS IN FORM XXX' )
    READ (6,7 ) N
7   FORMAT (I3)
```

Our strategy is to enter the amount of the loan, the interest, and the period of the loan at the console keyboard, in response to messages typed by the console printer, or typewriter. This program fragment contains WRITE statements alternating with READ statements. Each WRITE or READ statement is followed by a FORMAT statement. READ is an input command; it asks the computer to accept some data from the outside world. WRITE is an output command instructing the computer to give us some information, in either printed or punched form.

A computer usually has several devices for input and output of information. In this program we will be using three input-output devices. The first two have just been mentioned, the console printer and keyboard. We intend to enter the initial data from the keyboard. This is a standard electric typewriter keyboard with a slightly altered arrangement of some of the control keys. The console printer is the printing part of an IBM Selectric typewriter. The third output device, used later in this program, is a physically separate unit, the 1132 Printer,

a *line printer* because it appears to print a whole line at one time. The 1132 is a relatively slow line printer, producing eighty lines of output per minute, little more than one per second. A faster printer, the 1403, is also available. Larger computers have line printers generating more than a thousand lines per minute.

If you look at the READ and WRITE statements in our program fragment, you may note that the word READ or WRITE is always followed by parentheses containing two numbers separated by a comma. The first number identifies the input-output device used; the second is the statement number identifying an associated FORMAT statement. Every 1130 READ or WRITE has a FORMAT statement associated with it. We have put the FORMAT statements right after the READ and WRITE statements, but they could occur anywhere in the program. FORMAT statements are not executed; they only furnish information for the associated READ and WRITE statements.

Numbers used in the READ and WRITE statements to specify devices are determined by the programs supplied with the computer. The identifying numbers assumed by the 1130 FORTRAN compiler (including a device not yet discussed) are as follows:

Console Printer	1
Card Read Punch	2
Line Printer	3
Console Keyboard	6

In our FORTRAN program fragment, the three WRITE statements contain nothing after the close of the parentheses. In each case the associated FORMAT sentence contains a message to be typed; the computer is told to WRITE the message found in single quotes in the FORMAT statement. Each of these three messages, typed on the console printer when the program is run, tells the *operator* the quantity to be entered next, as well as the form to be followed in typing.

Each READ statement is followed by a letter or collection of letters. These letters are FORTRAN variable names, just as P, A, R, and N were in the FORTRAN formula. Each variable is used elsewhere within the FORTRAN program. Thus the third READ statement instructs the computer to read the variable N, the number of months. This value is to be entered from the console keyboard when the READ statement is encountered, and then stored in the memory of the computer. Later in the calculation when the computer needs the number of months, it knows where to find that figure stored in memory for use in the calculation.

FORTRAN variables are much like those you are familiar with in ordinary algebra. However, a group of up to five letters or numbers can be used as a single variable name, provided that the first symbol in the group is a letter. Thus RY, in the second READ, is an acceptable variable. Usually all variables starting with the letters I through N are special variables which can hold only integral values. The differences between real and integer variables are significant and will be discussed in more detail later.

The FORMAT statement associated with each READ statement through its statement number specifies the structure of the information to be entered. Thus the I3 in FORMAT statement 7 indicates that N should be entered as a three-position integer, such as 123. (The present 1130 system demands that the number be right-justified when entered. For example, if 42 is typed, it must either be 042 or preceded by one space.) In FORMAT statement 3, the F8.2 indicates that eight places (including decimal point and sign, if any) are to be allowed for input of the variable A; if no decimal point is entered, the computer is to assume that two of the places are to the right of the point. FORMAT specifications are a little messy to learn, but you will begin to understand them better with use. We shall see more details later.

THE FULL LOAN PROGRAM

At this point, instead of looking at more pieces of the program, we shall present the full program. We want our program to do more than simply compute the monthly payment. For income tax purposes, it is necessary to know how much of the payment is interest and how much is a deduction from the balance owed, since interest on a loan is an allowable deduction. It is also useful to know the monthly balance. For example, the borrower may want to know the balance if he is considering paying the remainder of the loan in one payment. Therefore we want the output of the program to contain the payment, the interest paid each month, and the remaining balance.

With this rather vague description, we present the 1130 FORTRAN program for carrying out the load calculation in Fig. 1–3. The full loan program can be represented by a diagram (Fig. 1–4) like those shown in Figs. 1–1 and 1–2. Diagrams of the type shown in Fig. 1–4 provide a convenient way of following the flow of the calculation.

A FORTRAN program is a series of FORTRAN statements, usually written one per line. For input to the computer, each line of the program will correspond to one punched card. The physical order of the FORTRAN sentences on the page (the order of the cards) is the order in which the instructions are normally executed, although certain instructions can modify this execution order.

The program in Fig. 1–3 begins with the WRITE and READ statements already examined. These three pairs of WRITE—READ statements are followed by another WRITE statement. The device number, 3, indicates that the material is to be written on the line printer. The FORMAT statement (9) associated with this WRITE statement has several new aspects. First, note the several slashes (the symbol "/"). These slashes could not mean division, since a FORMAT statement does not specify an arithmetic operation. A slash in a FORMAT specification indicates a new line on the output device, the line printer. If the output device were the card punch, the slash would indicate that a new card is to be punched.

The second interesting thing about this FORMAT statement is that it is too long for a single card. A punch card has 80 columns; the body of a FORTRAN statement can use columns 7 through 72. The line following the 9 has a 1 in a column that none of the earlier statements used, and the next line has a 2 in the same column. This column, number 6 on a punched card, is called the continuation column. Customarily a FORTRAN statement does not use this column, but if the sentence is too long for one card, a number of continuation cards can be used by putting any nonzero character in the continuation column. In 1130 FORTRAN up to five cards are allowable for a statement. Here our statement is continued on two

```
      REAL I
      WRITE (1,2)
 2 FORMAT ( 'LOAN PROGRAM - ENTER AMOUNT IN FORM XXXXX.XX' )
      READ (6, 3 ) A
 3 FORMAT (F8.2)
      WRITE ( 1,4)
 4 FORMAT ( 'ENTER INTEREST RATE PER YEAR IN FORM XX.XX' )
      READ (6,5 ) RY
 5 FORMAT ( F5.2)
      WRITE (1,6)
 6 FORMAT ('ENTER NUMBER OF MONTHS IN FORM XXX' )
      READ (6,7) N
 7 FORMAT (I3)
      WRITE(3, 9) A, RY, N
 9 FORMAT ( ' INTEREST CALCULATION ON A LOAN' / ' AMOUNT = ' F10.2
 1/ ' INTEREST RATE PER YEAR = 'F5.2 / ' NUMBER OF MONTHS = ' I4 //
 2'  PAYMENT' 13X 'INTEREST' 12X 'BALANCE' )
      R = (RY/12.) / 100.
      P = (A * R * (1. + R ) ** N ) / ( (1. + R) ** N - 1)
      K = 0
76 K = K + 1
      I = R * A
      A = A - P + I
      WRITE (3, 8)    P, I, A
 8 FORMAT  (' $'F8.2, 11X'$'F8.2, 11X '$' F9.2 )
      IF ( N - K ) 84, 84, 76
84 CALL EXIT
      END
```

FIGURE 1-3

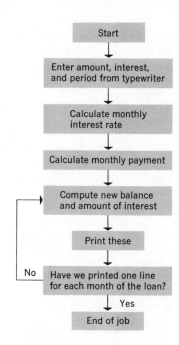

FIGURE 1-4

Flowchart:
Start → Enter amount, interest, and period from typewriter → Calculate monthly interest rate → Calculate monthly payment → Compute new balance and amount of interest → Print these → Have we printed one line for each month of the loan? (No → back to Compute new balance; Yes → End of job)

successive cards. This use of continuation cards is a matter of convenience rather than necessity, for it is almost always possible to break up a statement into a series of smaller entities. However, breaking up a statement is not always convenient. Although continuation is used here in a FORMAT statement, it can be used with any FORTRAN statement.

FORMAT statement 9 is complicated. Its first line is simply a heading line, ordering that INTEREST CALCULATION ON A LOAN be printed. This heading identifies the output page, telling what is happening. The second line of output will contain the printed expression AMOUNT=; this will be followed by the *value* of the variable A, the amount of the loan. The format specification, F10.2, allows 10 places for printing the value and demands two places to the right of the decimal point. The 10 places include the decimal point and possible sign. The next line will start with INTEREST RATE PER YEAR=, followed by the value of R. Five places are allowed, including a decimal point and, if necessary, a sign, with two digits to the right of the point. The next line allows four spaces to print the number of months of the loan, again following an identifying message. The last number (months of the loan) was stored as an integer, and thus must be printed under an *integer* format specification, in this case I 4; i.e., no decimal point is printed.

It may seem a little silly to print on the line printer the same information we have just entered from the keyboard.

This output serves two functions: First, the heading assures us that we entered the information that we *thought* we entered and thus did not make a typing error; and second, the messages printed identify the output. The information on the typewriter and the information on the line printer will be on two separate sheets of paper, and there is some advantage in having all the information together.

Finally, our long FORMAT statement prints another line, the heading for the table we intend to print. In addition to the three quoted words, we have the first occurrence of an *X specification*. The format specification 13X indicates that 13 blank spaces are to be left between the words PAYMENT and INTEREST in the printed output. Similarly, 12 blank spaces between INTEREST and BALANCE are specified by the 12X.

One further aspect of this FORMAT statement should be noted. It concerns the fact that the line printer rather than another output device is used. The operation of the line printer involves establishing an area (a *buffer*) in the memory of the computer where the information to be printed is stored. The first character in the buffer is *not* to be printed out, but is rather to control the carriage on the line printer. In each of our messages, the first character inside the quote at the beginning of the line is a blank. This is the control character for single spacing before the printing of that line. It is possible to enter a double-space character, or a character which would begin a new page before printing. Carriage control characters are used only by the line printer and should not appear in FORMAT statements associated with either the typewriter or the card punch.

The two lines following FORMAT statement 9 calculate the monthly payment. The second of these is our complicated formula for the payment; the first one does a little bookkeeping. We enter the interest in the usual percent form, such as 6.5. This is a yearly rate, not expressed as a decimal, while the formula for the payment assumes a monthly decimal rate. Hence we must first divide by 12 to get the monthly rate and then divide by 100 to convert to decimal form. The result of this calculation, the monthly interest rate, is stored as the variable R, and is available when we calculate the monthly payments in the next statement.

The arithmetic statement in Fig. 1–3, $K = 0$, setting a variable K to zero, may seem mysterious. K is to be the month during the calculation; each time we compute a new balance we increment K by 1, so we initially set it to zero months. We shall compare this variable with the total number of months to determine when we are finished.

The next statement, labeled 76, also involves K:

$$K = K + 1$$

At first glance this statement may seem strange to someone not familiar with an algebraic computer language such as FORTRAN. If you saw such a relation in an algebra book, you would think that something was wrong: canceling *K* would leave the odd result $0 = 1$. However, a FORTRAN statement is not to be treated in this way; it is a specification for a calculation. K will correspond to a location in the memory of the computer. An arithmetic statement such as 76 instructs the computer to find the current value of K, add 1 to it, and store the result in the same location K. Thus it has the effect of incrementing K by 1 each time it is executed. We shall see in a moment that this statement will be executed over and over again.

The next line computes the interest by the simple expedient of multiplying the rate per month by the amount.

The calculation of the new balance is straightforward. We cannot simply take away the monthly payment, P, from the old balance, because part of that payment does not reduce the balance but represents interest, I. Hence the new balance is found by subtracting $(P - 1)$ from the old balance. We could have written

$$A = A - (P - I)$$

in the FORTRAN program, but rather arbitrarily we

decided to eliminate the parentheses and write I as a positive quantity.

The following WRITE statement and its associated FORMAT statement (8) print the monthly information: the principal, the interest, and the balance. This statement does not contain much that is new, although it does perform the slight trick of instructing the computer to print the dollar sign before each of the quantities, making the output slightly fancier. Note again the space before the first dollar sign, needed for carriage control on the line printer. The first two variables are allowed eight places each, with two digits to the right of the decimal point, while the third variable, the amount, is to be allowed nine places. The count of places used by a number must always include the decimal point and any needed sign; if insufficient space is allotted, 1130 FORTRAN suppresses the number and prints a row of asterisks!

The IF statement immediately following FORMAT statement 8 is new for us. It represents one way of altering the flow of the program in FORTRAN. The facility to *branch* in a program, and thus to be able to execute a group of instructions many times, is an important aspect of computer programming. In general, the computer continues with the next statement after finishing the current one, but the IF statement is a conditional branching statement, generating a change in order which depends on conditions at the time the IF statement is reached. (We shall later encounter other branching statements.)

IF statements have this meaning: *if* the entity in the parentheses is negative, control is transferred to the first statement named; *if* the entity in the parentheses is zero, control is transferred to the second statement; *if* the entity in the parentheses is positive, control is transferred to the third statement. In this case the IF statement assures us that we will calculate just the right number of months before considering the computation finished. The expression $(N - K)$ is the difference between the total number of months the loan is to run and the number of months already reached in the calculation. So long as K is less than N, i.e., so long as more computation is necessary, $N - K$ will be a positive number. Then control will be transferred to the last statement referred to by the list following the condition $N - K$, i.e., back to statement 76 where we again increment K, compute the new interest and the new balance, and print this information. Thus we repeat or, in computer terminology, *loop* through this part of the program N times. But as soon as K becomes equal to or greater than N, then $N - K$ will become negative or zero, and we proceed to the first or second statement in the list, both 84 in this case. You can see from its name that statement 84 is the *exit* from the program, instructing the computer to transfer control to another computer program.

Let us return to the first statement in the program:

REAL I.

This refers to an aspect of FORTRAN variables mentioned only briefly before. FORTRAN recognizes two types of variables and numbers. Some of the variables and constants are called *integer*, or *fixed point*, variables. Integers are the familiar counting numbers of everyday life, numbers without decimal point or fractional part. FORTRAN usually assumes that if the variable name begins with I, J, K, L, M, or N, it is an integer variable. Thus the number of months, K, in our program is an integer variable, and the 1 we add to it an integer constant. Any variable beginning with any other letter of the alphabet is considered to be a *real*, or *floating point*, variable. A real variable or number contains an explicit decimal point; e.g., 2.734 and 3.974×10^{17} are real.

These two kinds of numbers and variables, integer and real, correspond to two different methods of internal storage of numbers. Beginners should be cautioned that integer arithmetic does not necessarily produce the results one might expect, since the answers are also integers. Thus the statement I = 5/10 will set the variable I to zero! Hence, except for counting, it might be best for the beginner to use real variables and numbers. If an expression contains a mixture of reals and integers, the integers are converted to real numbers when necessary; but this conversion takes time, and so it is best to include decimal points, as in the constants in the calculation for P. In some varieties of FORTRAN, mixture of modes is not allowed.

Sometimes it is convenient to override the variable type. In the present problem I is a convenient variable to denote interest, because it is the first letter of the corresponding word. However, I would usually be an integer, not suitable for expressing dollars and cents. Hence we override the specification by the REAL I statement at the beginning of the FORTRAN program. This statement expresses our intention that I is to be a real variable. The opposite procedure is possible; by an INTEGER or REAL specification, we can override the initial-letter specification of a variable of either type. A single specification statement can refer to several variables.

Finally, we come to the END statement. The very last statement of every FORTRAN program must be an END statement. However, this statement has nothing to do with the calculation; rather it is needed for other purposes we shall note later. For the moment, you can simply accept it as a rule that such a statement must end any program.

RUNNING THE PROGRAM

We have completed the discussion of the FORTRAN loan program. You might be curious to see the result of running the program for one case, to see whether our discussion of what should happen predicts what did happen. The program is first punched on cards, and then the card deck is fed to the computer via the card reader. After some delay (the details will concern us later) the typewriter types the first messages. We enter the three requested numbers at the console keyboard, pressing EOF (End Of Field) after each. One resultant output from the line printer is shown in Fig. 1–5. You should compare this output with the discussion of the program and see that they agree. The spacing and information in the output correspond to the specifications in the FORMAT statements. It is comforting to see that the balance is zero after the final payment. This final balance is a reasonable assurance of the validity of the calculation, since a check on the method of computation shows that we did not simply juggle the numbers to make the balance zero at the end. It is always desirable, whenever possible, to have such a check in a calculation; it ensures that the program is doing what we *think* it is doing.

```
INTEREST CALCULATION ON A LOAN
AMOUNT =    5000.00
INTEREST RATE PER YEAR =   8.00
NUMBER OF MONTHS =   24
```

PAYMENT	INTEREST	BALANCE
$ 226.13	$ 33.33	$ 4807.19
$ 226.13	$ 32.04	$ 4613.10
$ 226.13	$ 30.75	$ 4417.72
$ 226.13	$ 29.45	$ 4221.04
$ 226.13	$ 28.14	$ 4023.04
$ 226.13	$ 26.82	$ 3823.72
$ 226.13	$ 25.49	$ 3623.08
$ 226.13	$ 24.15	$ 3421.10
$ 226.13	$ 22.80	$ 3217.77
$ 226.13	$ 21.45	$ 3013.08
$ 226.13	$ 20.08	$ 2807.03
$ 226.13	$ 18.71	$ 2599.61
$ 226.13	$ 17.33	$ 2390.80
$ 226.13	$ 15.93	$ 2180.61
$ 226.13	$ 14.53	$ 1969.01
$ 226.13	$ 13.12	$ 1756.00
$ 226.13	$ 11.70	$ 1541.57
$ 226.13	$ 10.27	$ 1325.71
$ 226.13	$ 8.83	$ 1108.41
$ 226.13	$ 7.38	$ 889.66
$ 226.13	$ 5.93	$ 669.46
$ 226.13	$ 4.46	$ 447.78
$ 226.13	$ 2.98	$ 224.63
$ 226.13	$ 1.49	$ -0.00

FIGURE 1–5

MORE ON THE LOAN CALCULATION

CHAPTER 2

THE DO STATEMENT

So far we have discussed one FORTRAN loan program in detail and have seen the results for one set of input values. However, this program represents neither the beginning nor the end of the work on this problem. We want now to look at some of the missing details.

After a program is written, the programmer may see ways to improve it or "clean it up." Some of these changes are trivial variations, but others modify the program to make it more effective. Figure 2-1 shows another program functionally identical to the one just discussed but using a FORTRAN statement not yet mentioned.

If you compare this program with the previous loan program (Fig. 1-3), you can see that some of the statements involving K are no longer present; rather we have two new ones, DO 99 . . . and CONTINUE. These two statements perform the same task as those they replace. They provide a convenient way of setting up a loop, going through the same part of the program a number of times. A DO statement, like an IF, is a way of constructing a branch in a program.

As you might suspect, looking at the program, the 99 in the DO statement refers to statement 99. Statement 99, CONTINUE, is a dummy statement, that is, a statement which leads to no instructions for the computer but simply marks a place in the program, the end of the DO

loop. When the DO loop is first entered through the DO 99 statement, the variable K is set equal to 1. (Any integer variable could be used.) When the end of the loop, statement 99, is reached, K is increased by 1; then it is compared with N to see whether K has exceeded N; if not, control is returned to the next statement after the DO 99 statement. This continues until K exceeds the value N, at which point the statement after the CONTINUE statement is executed. The DO loop is not doing anything we could not accomplish with an IF statement, but it is slightly neater. In some situations it has advantages over other ways to create loops. Although it is not necessary to end a DO loop with a CONTINUE statement, it is convenient, particularly if you may want to modify the program and alter the range of the DO loop. Many experienced programmers routinely end DO loops in this manner.

DO statements can be *nested*, but they cannot be overlapping: one cannot, in the middle of the execution of one DO loop, start another DO loop with a terminal statement (CONTINUE in our example is the terminal statement) outside the first loop. As long as the nest is truly an enclosure, or the loops end at the same statement, there is no difficulty (Fig. 2-2). There are restrictions on the number of DO loops allowable in a nest and on the ways these may be combined, but this is unlikely to concern the beginning programmer.

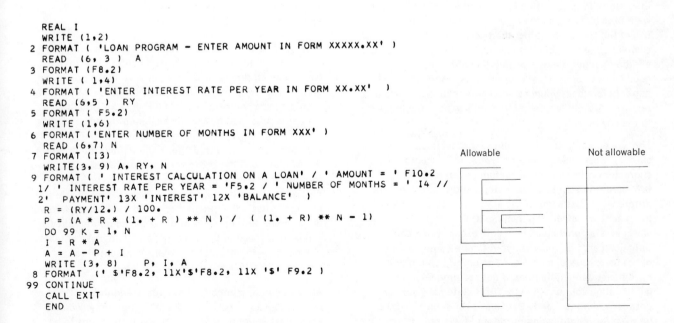

```
      REAL I
      WRITE (1,2)
    2 FORMAT ( 'LOAN PROGRAM - ENTER AMOUNT IN FORM XXXXX.XX' )
      READ (6, 3 )  A
    3 FORMAT (F8.2)
      WRITE ( 1,4)
    4 FORMAT ( 'ENTER INTEREST RATE PER YEAR IN FORM XX.XX'  )
      READ (6,5 )  RY
    5 FORMAT ( F5.2)
      WRITE (1,6)
    6 FORMAT ('ENTER NUMBER OF MONTHS IN FORM XXX' )
      READ (6,7) N
    7 FORMAT (I3)
      WRITE(3, 9) A, RY, N
    9 FORMAT ( ' INTEREST CALCULATION ON A LOAN' / ' AMOUNT = ' F10.2
     1/ ' INTEREST RATE PER YEAR = 'F5.2 / ' NUMBER OF MONTHS = ' I4 //
     2' PAYMENT' 13X 'INTEREST' 12X 'BALANCE'  )
      R = (RY/12.) / 100.
      P = (A * R * (1. + R ) ** N ) / ( (1. + R) ** N - 1)
      DO 99 K = 1, N
      I = R * A
      A = A - P + I
      WRITE (3, 8)    P, I, A
    8 FORMAT  (' $'F8.2, 11X'$'F8.2, 11X '$' F9.2 )
   99 CONTINUE
      CALL EXIT
      END
```

FIGURE 2-1

Allowable   Not allowable

FIG. 2-2. Nesting of DO loops.

```
// JOB              LOAN CALCULATION
// FOR
*IOCS(TYPEWRITER, KEYBOARD, 1132 PRINTER)
*EXTENDED PRECISION
*LIST SOURCE PROGRAM
      REAL I
      WRITE (1,2)
    2 FORMAT ( 'LOAN PROGRAM - ENTER AMOUNT IN FORM XXXXX.XX' )
      READ (6, 3 ) A
* A IS THE AMOUNT OF THE LOAN
    3 FORMAT (F8.2)
      WRITE ( 1,4)
    4 FORMAT ( 'ENTER INTEREST RATE PER YEAR IN FORM XX.XX' )
      READ (6,5 ) RY
    5 FORMAT ( F5.2)
      WRITE (1,6)
    6 FORMAT ('ENTER NUMBER OF MONTHS IN FORM XXX )
      READ (6,7) N
    7 FORMAT (I3)
      WRITE(3, 9) A, RY, N
    9 FORMAT ( ' INTEREST CALCULATION ON A LOAN' / ' AMOUNT = ' F10.2
     1/ ' INTEREST RATE PER YEAR = 'F5.2 / ' NUMBER OF MONTHS = ' I4 //
     2'  PAYMENT' 13X 'INTEREST' 12X 'BALANCE'  )
      R = (RY/12.) / 100.
      P = (A * R * (1. + R ) ** N ) /  ( (1. + R) ** N - 1)
      DO 99 J = 1, N
      I = R * A / 100.
      A = A - P + I
      WRITE (3, 8)     P, I, A
    8 FORMAT  (' $'F8.2, 11X'$'F8.2, 11X '$' F9.2 )
   99 CONTINUE
      CALL EXIT
      END
```

FIGURE 2–3

WRITING AND RUNNING THE PROGRAM

Now I should like to go back to the beginning of the work on this program and recount my experience in writing it. First, of course, I had to decide what problem might be interesting for people first learning to use FORTRAN; I wanted to choose a problem which made some effective use of the computer, rather than performing trivial calculation. I had seen the loan problem used to introduce another computer language and thought it might be a good choice here. Usually a program is roughed out on paper before being punched on cards. Since this was a relatively simple program, however, I went immediately to the key punch.

The key punch is an instrument for producing punched cards; it works like an electric typewriter, except that each character is punched in one column of an 80-column IBM card, the standard card you probably know. Another difference is that some of the keys move cards through the machine instead of punching. One FORTRAN statement is punched on one card, except when continuation cards are necessary. A C for a comment card, not to be executed, may occupy column 1; columns 2–5, have the statement number, if any; column 6 is the continuation column; the FORTRAN statement appears between columns 7 and 72 inclusive; columns 73–80 can be used for identification purposes, if desired. Correction of typing errors is relatively easy on the key punch, since

error-free portions of a card can be duplicated without retyping. We shall not comment in detail on key-punch operations; with just a few minutes' practice you will find the key punch easy to use, particularly if you first watch someone use it for a short time.

After getting the loan calculation program on cards, I was in a position to try it. I should confess that my first punched program was *not* either of those presented so far. The program first entered, with no embellishments, is shown in Fig. 2–3. The FORTRAN program proper is preceded by cards which identify this as a new job, announce that the language is going to be FORTRAN, and give certain auxiliary information about the program. We will not consider these cards in detail, but only indicate that their purpose is to communicate with programs stored on the computer *disk*, a form of internal storage. These disk programs, called the *monitor system*, are an important element in using the computer; they will be discussed in the next chapter. The disk contains, among other things, all the materials essential for running FORTRAN programs.

At this point it is important to understand that a FORTRAN program given directly to a digital computer, *any* digital computer, would be useless. All the instructions to be carried out by the 1130 must eventually be in 1130

of error is given by a code, necessitating the use of a FORTRAN error code sheet. The error codes, contained in an IBM manual for the 1130, are given in Appendix A–6.

The three errors cited in Fig. 2–4 can be identified by referring to the Appendix A–6 listing of error codes; however, one can often find the error more quickly just by inspecting the erroneous statement. For example, look at FORMAT statement 6 of the program in Fig. 2–3. You will see that the single quote at the right-hand end has been omitted; the computer is complaining that I have not set off the entire message in single quotes. We confirm this analysis by looking up C 29 in the error code listing, where we find

Field width specification > 145.

The compiler thinks that the message to be printed does not stop, because it cannot locate the second single quote. In other words, it believes that we want to print too many characters. Thus we have probably found the error in this statement, and we can repunch the card.

Sometimes error messages are less informative. One cannot expect the compiler to be able to take into account all possible kinds of errors, so the messages may be misleading. For example, we are told that the statement printed two statements past number 9 is invalid. This is the statement beginning P =. (Remember that the continuation cards are all part of statement 9.) The error code explanation,

Invalid integer constant,

seems meaningless, since there are *no* integer constants on this card! Inspecting the listing of the program, however, we discover that the D0 statement immediately following is out of line; it has the letter 0 sitting in the continuation column. This is a typical punching mistake. So the FORTRAN compiler considers the D0 statement part of the arithmetic statement defining P! It cannot make any sense of the D0 material as part of the statement on calculating P and therefore an error message is produced. This error also led to the comment that 99 was an unreferenced statement number.

The first of the errors caught by the compiler is of slightly different but related type. STATEMENT NUMBER 2 + 001 refers to the READ sentence. Since it is very simple, we can quickly see that it contains no error. Therefore we go on to the next sentence. Here I had intended to write a comment sentence, but instead of the C in the first column, I typed an asterisk. Hence the compiler does not interpret that sentence as a comment, but, since an S occupies column 6, considers it a continuation of the previous sentence. This produced nonsense, and I received an error message.

```
UNREFERENCED STATEMENTS
 99

UNDEFINED VARIABLES
 P

INVALID STATEMENTS
 C 07 ERROR AT STATEMENT NUMBER 2      +001
 C 29 ERROR AT STATEMENT NUMBER 6
 C 24 ERROR AT STATEMENT NUMBER 9      +002

OUTPUT HAS BEEN SUPPRESSED

END OF COMPILATION
```

FIGURE 2–4

machine language, a coding form which looks very different from a FORTRAN program. But as part of the monitor system the 1130 is equipped with a program called the FORTRAN *compiler* which *translates* any valid 1130 FORTRAN program into an 1130 machine-language program. The FORTRAN compiler is essential if we are to run a FORTRAN program. The // FOR card tells the supervisor program, part of the monitor, that the following cards hold a FORTRAN program and that the FORTRAN compiler should be made available. The process of translating is complex; the FORTRAN compiler is a much larger program than any you are likely to write.

Figure 2–4 shows the output I received from the line printer when I used this program. The rude remarks on this printout may surprise you. Beginning programmers usually do not realize that programs almost never work when first written. New programs, particularly if complex, are almost certain to contain errors. Much of the job of programming is not the initial writing of the program, but the finding of errors and correcting them. This process, known as *debugging*, is partly done by the FORTRAN compiler. The output lists three error messages in three statements in the program, identified by number. In each case the sum added after the statement number indicates how many statements one must go past the identified statement to find the defective one. The type

```
VARIABLE ALLOCATIONS
 I    =0000  A    =0002  RY  =0004  R    =0006  P    =0008  N    =0010  K    =0012

STATEMENT ALLOCATIONS
 2    =001D  3    =0035  4    =0037  5    =004E  6    =0050  7    =0063  9    =0065  8    =00B0  99   =013B

FEATURES SUPPORTED
 IOCS

CALLED SUBPROGRAMS
 FADD    FSUB    FMPY    FDIV    FLD    FSTO    FSBR    FDVR    FAXI    FLOAT    TYPEZ    SRED    SWRT    SCOMP    SFIO
 SIOF    SIOI    PRNTZ

REAL CONSTANTS
 .120000E 02=0014    .100000E 03=0016    .100000E 01=0018

INTEGER CONSTANTS
     1=001A    6=001B    3=001C

CORE REQUIREMENTS FOR
 COMMON      0  VARIABLES    20  PROGRAM    304

END OF COMPILATION
```

FIGURE 2–5

I corrected these errors, entered the program again, and picked up one or two more errors. I will not show the intermediate program, for there is little to be learned from it. At last, about 15 minutes after entering the initial program, I had compiled a program which gave no error messages. Figure 2–5 shows the first part of the output on the line printer, partially due to the use of a *LIST ALL monitor control card before the program. The listing always tells where the variables and constants are stored in the program and how long the program is. Thus the program occupies 304 computer words with 20 words for variable storage. No nasty error messages were received. My program is now *grammatically* correct; the FORTRAN compiler does not complain.

However, it is very important to understand that even a grammatically correct FORTRAN program, with sentences following all of the FORTRAN rules, may not function correctly. This was made immediately obvious in this case when I tried to run the program. The rather surprising result of this apparently "correct" program is shown in Fig. 2–6.

This would indeed be a peculiar loan! The borrower does not expect the bank to end up owing him $469.75 after the period of the loan. This odd outcome demonstrates the advantage of having, within the program, some internal check of the validity of the calculation. Something is clearly wrong with our program; although grammatically correct, it is not producing the expected results.

Examining the results further, we discover another strange aspect: the interest is ridiculously low. We

```
INTEREST CALCULATION ON A LOAN
AMOUNT =    6000.00
INTEREST RATE PER YEAR =  5.00
NUMBER OF MONTHS =   36

   PAYMENT            INTEREST          BALANCE
$  179.83         $     0.25      $    5820.41
$  179.83         $     0.24      $    5640.82
$  179.83         $     0.23      $    5461.22
$  179.83         $     0.22      $    5281.61
$  179.83         $     0.22      $    5102.00
$  179.83         $     0.21      $    4922.38
$  179.83         $     0.20      $    4742.75
$  179.83         $     0.19      $    4563.11
$  179.83         $     0.19      $    4383.46
$  179.83         $     0.18      $    4203.81
$  179.83         $     0.17      $    4024.15
$  179.83         $     0.16      $    3844.49
$  179.83         $     0.16      $    3664.81
$  179.83         $     0.15      $    3485.13
$  179.83         $     0.14      $    3305.44
$  179.83         $     0.13      $    3125.74
$  179.83         $     0.13      $    2946.04
$  179.83         $     0.12      $    2766.33
$  179.83         $     0.11      $    2586.61
$  179.83         $     0.10      $    2406.88
$  179.83         $     0.10      $    2227.15
$  179.83         $     0.09      $    2047.41
$  179.83         $     0.08      $    1867.66
$  179.83         $     0.07      $    1687.90
$  179.83         $     0.07      $    1508.14
$  179.83         $     0.06      $    1328.36
$  179.83         $     0.05      $    1148.59
$  179.83         $     0.04      $     968.80
$  179.83         $     0.04      $     789.01
$  179.83         $     0.03      $     609.20
$  179.83         $     0.02      $     429.39
$  179.83         $     0.01      $     249.58
$  179.83         $     0.01      $      69.75
$  179.83         $     0.00      $    -110.07
$  179.83         $    -0.00      $    -289.91
$  179.83         $    -0.01      $    -469.75
```

FIGURE 2–6

```
   REAL I
   WRITE (1,2)
 2 FORMAT ( 'LOAN PROGRAM - ENTER AMOUNT IN FORM XXXXX.XX' )
   READ  (6, 3 )  A
 3 FORMAT (F8.2)
   WRITE ( 1,4)
 4 FORMAT ( 'ENTER INTEREST RATE PER YEAR IN FORM XX.XX'  )
   READ (6,5 )  RY
 5 FORMAT ( F5.2)
   WRITE (1,6)
 6 FORMAT ('ENTER NUMBER OF MONTHS IN FORM XXX' )
   READ (6,7) N
 7 FORMAT (I3)
   WRITE(3, 9) A, RY, N
 9 FORMAT ( ' INTEREST CALCULATION ON A LOAN' / ' AMOUNT = ' F10.2
  1/ ' INTEREST RATE PER YEAR = 'F5.2 / ' NUMBER OF MONTHS = ' I4 //
  2' PAYMENT' 13X 'INTEREST' 12X 'BALANCE'  )
   R = (RY/12.) / 100.
   P = (A * R * (1. + R ) ** N ) /  ( (1. + R) ** N - 1)
   DO 99 K = 1, N
   I = R * A / 100.
   A = A - P + I
   WRITE (3, 8)     P, I, A
 8 FORMAT  (' $'F8.2, 11X'$'F8.2, 11X '$' F9.2 )
99 CONTINUE
   CALL EXIT
   END
```

FIGURE 2–7

would expect the initial interest to be a sizable proportion of the monthly payment, but here it is trivial. This, coupled with the difficulties in the balance, suggests that we examine the program leading to these odd results (Fig. 2–7).

Since the monthly interest is too low, we naturally look at the statement which computes it, the statement beginning $I =$. We compute I by multiplying the monthly rate, R, by the current balance, A, and then dividing the result by 100. But this is wrong. You can see that I had already, in the statement calculating the rate, R, divided by 100 to convert from percent to decimal. Hence this additional 100 in the interest calculation is incorrect. The difficulty is not with the FORTRAN program, but with the programmer!

Correcting this card produces a program identical with the one discussed at the beginning of this chapter, the program introducing the DO loop (Fig. 2–1).

There is still another surprise for us. This difficulty is more subtle in some ways than any we have discussed so far; it forces us to consider the process of carrying out any numerical calculation. Figure 2–8 gives the initial result of running this program. The printout shows a small negative balance at the end of the loan period. We are much better off than with the large negative balance, but nevertheless, it does seem a little unreasonable that the bank should owe us even $.26 after the term of the loan. We get *almost* a zero balance at the end of the loan, so there is no major error in the calculation, and one would expect that the difficulty, if any, is some relatively minor factor. Note that the interest appears to be

```
INTEREST CALCULATION ON A LOAN
AMOUNT =     5000.00
INTEREST RATE PER YEAR =  5.00
NUMBER OF MONTHS =    30
```

PAYMENT	INTEREST	BALANCE
$ 177.65	$ 20.83	$ 4843.17
$ 177.65	$ 20.17	$ 4685.70
$ 177.65	$ 19.52	$ 4527.57
$ 177.65	$ 18.86	$ 4368.78
$ 177.65	$ 18.20	$ 4209.32
$ 177.65	$ 17.53	$ 4049.21
$ 177.65	$ 16.87	$ 3888.42
$ 177.65	$ 16.20	$ 3726.97
$ 177.65	$ 15.52	$ 3564.84
$ 177.65	$ 14.85	$ 3402.04
$ 177.65	$ 14.17	$ 3238.56
$ 177.65	$ 13.49	$ 3074.40
$ 177.65	$ 12.81	$ 2909.56
$ 177.65	$ 12.12	$ 2744.02
$ 177.65	$ 11.43	$ 2577.80
$ 177.65	$ 10.74	$ 2410.89
$ 177.65	$ 10.04	$ 2243.28
$ 177.65	$ 9.34	$ 2074.97
$ 177.65	$ 8.64	$ 1905.96
$ 177.65	$ 7.94	$ 1736.25
$ 177.65	$ 7.23	$ 1565.82
$ 177.65	$ 6.52	$ 1394.69
$ 177.65	$ 5.81	$ 1222.85
$ 177.65	$ 5.09	$ 1050.29
$ 177.65	$ 4.37	$ 877.01
$ 177.65	$ 3.65	$ 703.01
$ 177.65	$ 2.92	$ 528.28
$ 177.65	$ 2.20	$ 352.83
$ 177.65	$ 1.47	$ 176.65
$ 177.65	$ 0.73	$ -0.26

FIGURE 2–8

reasonable; you might calculate the initial interest yourself and see that it is correct. Hand calculations to check a computer program are often advisable.

We have noted that FORTRAN has two ways of storing numbers internally, integer and real; the payment, the interest, and the balance are real numbers. But the computer cannot keep an infinite number of significant figures for each number. Since the number must be stored as some *finite* collection of digits, many calculations must throw away the part of the result beyond the places being kept. Actually, the numbers are handled internally in the 1130 in binary, or base-two form, so the number of places stored reflects binary rather than decimal arithmetic. In FORTRAN calculation a real number is stored with the equivalent of seven significant decimal figures, or more accurately, between six and seven. Hence the amounts of the balance, with six significant figures, represent almost the limit of accuracy. Small round-off errors are introduced in each calculation, because the figures past the seventh place are being thrown away. Therefore it seems likely that the difficulty with the small negative final balance is due not to the program but to the number of places kept in each calculation. Fortunately, we are allowed an option in 1130 FORTRAN for correcting this error. By putting an *EXTENDED PRECISION card after the //bFOR card, we instruct the computer to store about ten significant figures for each real number, rather than the usual seven. When we run the program using the *EXTENDED PRECISION card, the balance is zero after the final payment, as in the results from our program in Chapter 1. Thus the small final balance when the program is run under standard precision occurs because we are pushing the the limits of accuracy.

This concludes our introduction to FORTRAN. We have examined some features of the FORTRAN language and some aspects of running a FORTRAN program on the 1130. We have by no means exhausted all the resources of FORTRAN but we have presented enough to allow you to begin writing your own programs. There is no better way to learn than to select a problem and then attempt to write a FORTRAN program to carry out its solution. The brief summary of grammatical rules in the next sections may be useful if you decide to follow this advice.

COMMENT SENTENCES

A C in column 1 identifies a *comment* included for the convenience and enlightenment of the program users. Comment statements are ignored by the computer during execution of the program; from the computer's point of view the program, with or without comments, is the same. They will, however, be listed if you request a program listing. Comment sentences are convenient for keeping track of what the program is doing.

NUMBERS AND VARIABLES

FORTRAN uses two forms of numbers and variables, integer and real. Integers contain no decimal point; they are "counting" numbers. An integer variable is so designated by the use of an INTEGER statement or by making the first letter an I, J, K, L, M, or N; its value at any time during the calculation is an integer.

Real numbers contain a decimal point. Two basic forms are employed in FORTRAN input, both of which are stored in the same way. The first form includes the explicit decimal point; the other is the FORTRAN equivalent of the scientific power-of-10 notation, with a structure such as $\alpha 10^{\beta}$. A special notation is used for "10 to the power of" in FORTRAN, the letter E. Thus the number 4.3×10^{17} may be written in FORTRAN as 4.3E17 or 0.43E18. Real variables can begin with any letter except those mentioned for integers (unless a REAL statement designates a variable with one of those letters as real).

Variable names must begin with a letter. In 1130 FORTRAN five letters or numbers are allowed in a name.

Examples

Integers: 4, −7, 84, 973
Reals: 3.14, −.073, 6.6E−27
Integer variables: I, KIM, KLOUT, LOUTZ, M3
Real variables: TIME, REED, A, C183D

ARITHMETIC STATEMENTS

The arithmetic statement represents a formula which defines a calculation. Many of the conventions of algebra are used. The left-hand side consists of a single variable, separated from the right-hand side by an equals sign. The right-hand side can be any algebraic expression involving the operations of addition (+), subtraction (−), multiplication (*), division (/) and exponentiation (**). Explicit functions such as SIN, COS, LOG, EXP, and SQRT in the subroutine library can occur within algebraic statements.

In 1130 FORTRAN the arithmetic statement can contain a mixture of real and integer variables. If both reals and integers occur on the right-hand side, numbers are converted to reals in the calculation when necessary. The result is converted to match the variable type on the left side, if necessary.

Parentheses can be freely used whenever any question may arise as to the precise meaning of the statement. (There is an assumed order to operations if parentheses are omitted.) Spaces can be used almost anywhere within a program if they are needed for clarity, since the 1130 compiler, like many other FORTRAN compilers, eliminates all spaces (except for those in FORMAT statements) before analyzing any statement.

Examples

```
A = (B*C) + D / SIN (E/F)
A = A - (REED**N)
I = J + K - (J*K)
VEL = VEL - (POS + A*VEL)*DELT
```

UNCONDITIONAL BRANCHING: GO TO

The unconditional branching statement, of the form

GO TO γ

where γ is the number of another statement in the program, transfers control to statement γ, breaking the linear sequence of commands. The statement immediately following a GO TO is not accessible unless it is numbered and referred to by some other transfer statement.

Example

GO TO 996

CONDITIONAL TRANSFER: ARITHMETIC IF

The arithmetic IF statement has the form

IF (A) α, β, γ

where A is an arithmetic expression, i.e., any numerical expression that could serve as the right-hand side of an arithmetic statement, and α, β and γ are statement numbers. First the computer evaluates this expression. There are three possible actions, depending on whether the calculated value of the expression is negative, zero, or positive. These cases correspond to the three statement numbers α, β, γ, which follow the parentheses. (Commas separate the statement numbers.) If the expression is negative, control is transferred to the first statement number, represented by α. If the value is zero, control is transferred to the statement having the second statement number (β). If the expression is positive, control is transferred to the statement with the third number (γ). These numbers need not all be different, but they must be statement numbers used in the program.

Examples

```
IF (Z) 78, 142, 96
IF ( B*B - 4.*A*C ) 1, 3, 5
IF ( I - J ) 4, 2, 4
IF ( A*COS ( HORSE/COW ) - FORD ) 9, 12, 12
```

LOOPS: DO

Form of statement:

DO α $\beta = \gamma, \delta, \epsilon$

where α is the number of the statement that ends the DO loop, β is an integer variable that is used within the program, and γ, δ, and ϵ, are integer variables or constants. During execution of the statement, γ must be 1 or greater. The ϵ specifies the amount that the integer variable β will be increased each time the group is executed. (The omission of this third number and its preceding comma leads to the assumption that it is 1.) The loop starting at the DO statement and ending at the statement numbered in the DO statement is executed until β exceeds δ, and then control is transferred to the statement following the DO loop.

Examples

```
DO 45    I = 1, 5
DO 999   KAP = 7, 35, 3
DO 2     JORSE = ICOW, 14
```

INPUT-OUTPUT STATEMENTS

Form of statement:

$$\left.\begin{array}{l} \text{READ} \\ \text{WRITE} \end{array}\right\} (\alpha,\beta) \text{ [variable list]}$$

Input-output statements instruct the computer to accept data for storage in memory (READ) or to reveal, i.e., print or punch, data from memory (WRITE). The possible devices in an installation are assigned numbers, and the input or output device to be used is indicated in the statement by the first number (α) in the parentheses. The second (β) is the statement number of a FORMAT statement. A list of the variables to be read or written, separated by commas, follows the parentheses in the statement.

Examples

```
WRITE ( 1,85 )
READ ( 2,6 ) HORSE, COW, FORD
WRITE ( 3,6 ) POS, VEL, TIME, MASS
```

The first statement writes the alphameric information in FORMAT statement 85.

Integer variables can be used for the device symbols. Thus if one wanted to choose the device to be used for output each time the program is run, one might use a statement like this:

```
WRITE (IOUT,7 ) A, B
```

Other statements could enter the value of IOUT before this statement is executed, or the program could compute a value.

FORMAT STATEMENTS

Form of statement:

FORMAT (Specifications, separated by commas)

A FORMAT statement has a statement number, referred to in an input or output statement. The material inside the parentheses following the word FORMAT describes the data. Different data descriptions are separated by a comma; the order of these specifications corresponds to the order of the list in the input-output statement referring to the FORMAT statement. Input-output (I/O) specifications may take the following forms:

1. *Integers.* The format specification for integers is $I\beta$, where β is an integer constant indicating the number of places needed.

2. *Reals, F-specification.* The standard real number specification is $F\alpha.\beta$, where α gives the entire physical length of a number, including spaces for decimal point and sign, and β specifies the number of places to the right of the decimal point. The number is assumed to be right-justified. If an input number contains a decimal point, the F-specification for decimal point location is overridden. (See Table 2–1.)

3. *Reals, E-specification.* Power-of-10 notation can be requested by a data specification of the form $E\alpha.\beta$, where α and β have meanings similar to their F-specification meanings.

4. *Alphameric information.* The letter H indicates alphameric input or output. H is preceded by a number indicating the number of characters to be considered and followed by the characters themselves. A comma after this specification is not required but is allowed. Single quotes can also be used to designate such data; then the compiler counts the number of characters between quotes.

5. *Blanks.* The specification αX, where α is an integer, requests α blank spaces. A comma is not required after this specification, but is allowed.

6. A slash generates a new line or starts a new card.

Examples

```
  3  FORMAT ( F6.3,E8.2,I5 )
 73  FORMAT ( 'VELOCITY IS NOW' F8.5 )
990  FORMAT ( 'A = 'F7.1,'B = 'F7.1,'HORSE = 'I8 )
  1  FORMAT ( 'TIME' 10X 'POSITION'/30X 'VELOCITY' )
```

TABLE 2–1
FORMAT INPUT WITH AND WITHOUT
A DECIMAL POINT IN THE DATA

For this FORMAT	These input data are equivalent
F6.3	+6.7, 6.7, 6700
E12.4	−7.821 E 19, −78210E 19

TABLE 2–2
FORMAT EXAMPLES—OUTPUT

b = blank (i.e., computer would print nothing)

These FORMATS	Might produce this output
F6.3	b7.341 −6.495 ****** [Number too large for this format]
F10.2	bbbbb79.82 bbbb973.62 bb−9874.00
I5	bbb72 b−841
4X I3	bbbb783 bbbbbb2 bbbbb−8
A4	FOUR bCOW bbAT
E10.2	bb0.47Eb19 bb0.67E−13 b−0.43Eb02

HALT COMMANDS AND EXITS

PAUSE makes the computer stop within the program and not execute the next instruction; pushing the PROGRAM START button on the console directs the computer to resume execution with the statement following the PAUSE statement. STOP also puts the computer in the manual mode, but when the operator then presses START on the console, control is transferred out of the program. CALL EXIT performs the same function as STOP, but it is not necessary to push START. So STOP is equivalent to first PAUSE, then CALL EXIT.

CARD FORMAT FOR FORTRAN

Column 1	Column reserved for a C, signifying a comment statement.
Columns 2–5	The statement number, if any. It does not need to be right- or left-justified.
Column 6	The continuation column. Usually it is blank, but if the statement is continued from a preceding card, column 6 is punched with any nonzero character.
Columns 7–72	The FORTRAN statement.
Columns 73–80	Columns reserved for optional identification or sequential numbering.

USING THE COMPUTER
AND THE MONITOR SYSTEM

CHAPTER 3

A BRIEF REVIEW OF THE 1130 SYSTEM

The computer can be viewed as a collection of physical components. Here we intend to look briefly at the large elements of the machine: the input-output units, the memory, and the central processor. As with our discussion of FORTRAN, we make no attempt to be comprehensive. Figure 3-1 shows the general structure and arrangement.

In Chapters 1 and 2 we discussed some of the input-output devices in the 1130 system. The console keyboard and the console printer or typewriter, built into the central processing unit of every 1130 system, are modifications of the IBM Selectric typewriter.

In addition, every system is likely to have either a *card read punch* or a *paper tape reader*. We shall assume that the system has a card read punch; the details are only slightly different for a tape reader. Devices of several speeds are available. The one we shall consider, the 1442 card read punch, has a single input hopper for loading cards, whether they are to be read or punched. Every card passes under both a reading station and a punching station. Although speed is affected by how much of a card is read or punched and by what is done between cards being processed, this machine can read 400 and punch 350 cards per minute. We can speak of the card read punch as either a reader or a punch, depending on the operation being considered.

The 1132 printer, another physically separate device we have already encountered, is optional, and may be lacking in some systems. It prints about 80 lines per minute, using 120 type wheels, each with 47 characters. A faster line printer, the 1403, is also available.

The two kinds of internal *memory* in the 1130 are a fast *core* memory and a slower but larger (and optional) *disk* memory. The basic core memory is a large collection of small donut-shaped magnetic cores, organized in *words* of fixed length, each identified by an *address*. In a minimum system the core has 4096 words (4K), with additional modules available to increase the core presently possible to 32,768 words (32K). Numbers are "written" by magnetizing the cores, with two possible pole orientations. Core memories are very fast; the standard 1130 memory has a *cycle time*, the time to obtain a number from the core, of about 3.6 microseconds, and a faster memory is also available. All the materials actively used in a program, i.e., the numbers calculated by the program and the full program itself, are in core memory.

The disk memory is optional with 1130 systems. The disk, with magnetic surfaces on the top and bottom, turns rapidly. A read-write arm can be in any one of 203

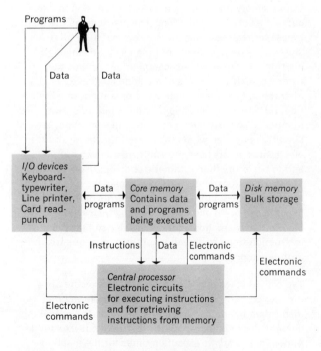

FIG. 3-1. Relation between the 1130 components.

places along the disk; it "writes," i.e., stores information, by making small magnetic "marks" on the disk. About 500,000 words can be written on one disk, and up to six disks can be in use at one time in presently announced 1130 systems. Since in any reading or writing operation, the arm moves and the disk turns, the disk is much slower than the core memory. The disk is used as a *backup* or *secondary* storage device. When material on disk is needed within the program, that material is brought in from disk to core memory. Likewise material not needed at the moment in core may be stored temporarily on disk.

There is considerable difference in operation, depending on whether or not a system has a disk. The FORTRAN compiler and the other parts of the monitor system may be kept on disk but a system without a disk must enter all this material from cards each time the material is used. In this book we assume that we are dealing with a system containing at least one disk; however, the language details, both for FORTRAN and for the *Assembler* language discussed later, are much the same with or without a disk.

The *central processor* is the computer part most directly concerned with the execution of the program. Its primary role is the execution of instructions. A special storage slot, the *Instruction Address Register* (IAR), contains the address in memory of the next instruction to be executed. (A register is a memory word in the central processor.) The central processor obtains this instruction from memory, increments the IAR by 1, and then executes the current instruction. The instructions the central processor receives from memory are *not* the FORTRAN statements we have seen, but the machine-language instructions the FORTRAN compiler has produced. Later we shall see details of machine language. Each instruction involves a single basic operation; one instruction, for example, might specify the addition of two numbers. To carry out an operation like addition, special circuitry is needed within the central processor; built-in electronic circuits have the ability to add two numbers and to perform other arithmetic or comparison operations. The basic transistor circuitry is complicated because so much is needed, but it is simple in terms of the basic logical design. In addition, branching instructions can modify the instruction address register so that the next instruction to be executed is not the next sequential one in the memory.

Typically it takes a few microseconds to execute an instruction on the 1130. The time differs from one instruction to another and may depend on the prevailing circumstances under which the instruction is executed. Appendix D-6 shows execution times for the machine-language instructions available in the 1130.

INTRODUCTION TO BUTTON PUSHING

The principal off-on switch for the 1130 system is on the central processor, above and to the right of the keyboard. The disk file has its own switch (inside the door on the right-hand side of the central processor) and the line printer also has a separate switch; both switches can be left on during normal operation, so that the one central processor switch serves to turn the whole system on or off.

The card reader and the line printer also have their own start and stop buttons. When the whole system is first turned on, the line printer must be started by pushing its start button, and the card reader must be set by pushing NPRO. START on the card reader brings a card into position so that card reading can commence if requested by the program in control.

The computer console contains two different buttons for stopping the machine; the full significance of these buttons will appear later. IMMEDIATE STOP halts the computer exactly where it is, stopping whatever is happening at that moment. Under some conditions using IMMEDIATE STOP will result in a loss of information, so it should not be used unless PROGRAM STOP has already been unsuccessful and the disk is not in use. The use of PROGRAM STOP transfers control to a special section of a program, eventually leading to a WAIT instruction. In the WAIT state the machine is not executing any instructions but simply waiting. The WAIT can be interrupted internally, when input-output operations have been completed, or the computer can be started again by PROGRAM START on the console. Note that the 1132 line printer (like other I/O devices) has its own STOP button and can even be turned off, if necessary.

The PROGRAM START button (to the right of the keyboard) starts the computer executing the instruction immediately following the instruction indicated in the instruction address register. Succeeding instructions are then carried out without pause if the mode switch (see below) is in the RUN position.

The RESET button clears certain internal registers in the central processor. It is used in restarting procedures. Most of the lights on the console go out when RESET is touched. These lights indicate what is in some of the registers.

The *mode switch* has already been mentioned. Usually it is in the RUN position. Two other positions are useful for the FORTRAN programmer. One is the LOAD position, which enables us, with the use of the console LOAD IAR button, to place an address into the instruction address register. The address is set in the *console switches*, the row of 16 switches above the keyboard. Another useful common position of the mode switch is SINGLE IN-

STRUCTION EXECUTE (SI); one instruction is executed each time PROGRAM START is pushed. The usefulness of executing one instruction at a time will come out when we consider debugging assembler programs.

The PROGRAM LOAD button instructs the computer to read a card in a special way, then to transfer control to the instruction just read in. Its normal use in the system is with a COLD START card, a card used in returning control to the monitor program when for some reason the skeleton supervisor is not in core.

The flow chart showing how to run a FORTRAN program through the system (see the inside front cover) gives more explicit details about how to use the buttons. The art of button pushing is simple on the 1130 and will soon be picked up by any user.

THE DISK MONITOR SYSTEM

We have referred several times to the *monitor*, a set of programs stored on the computer disk to handle the bookkeeping aspects of running jobs. The concept is relatively new; the first monitor systems were devised around 1960. *Executive* and *operating systems* are other common names.

Originally monitors were developed for large computers. Much of the time of such computers was devoted to putting programs into the machine; typically, after a program was finished, the operator loaded the cards for the next program. During this loading the computer was doing nothing. With a computer that can perform hundreds of thousands of operations per minute, the few minutes for loading cards represents that much wasted calculation time.

It was soon realized that it is not necessary to waste this time, and the first monitor systems were devised to enable the computer to proceed directly to the next job waiting in the card reader or on magnetic tape. This method of operation is called a *stacked job* mode. Later operating systems, more complex, assume responsibility for assignment of input/output devices, association of files in the program with named files in storage, record-keeping on usage, and traffic control of many terminals in time-sharing systems.

Increasing use of monitors also reflects increasing sophistication of computer *software*, i.e., the programs supplied. At first all programs were written in machine language; the manufacturer supplied few programs other than routines for jobs that were often needed. As new computer languages were developed, it came to be expected that the compilers for these languages would be part of the programming "package" provided by the manufacturer. Thus almost any computer purchased

today in the United States will have available a FORTRAN compiler, as well as an assembler for a symbolic language. Given several choices of programming language, the monitor must know the language used in the job it is about to receive.

Along with this increasing variety of software, including the monitor and compiler programs, has come the need for auxiliary storage in addition to core memory. In most computers the core memory is far too small to contain the FORTRAN compiler, the assembler, the monitor programs, necessary subroutines, and the users' programs; hence slower but more massive backup storage is essential. In some systems magnetic tapes or magnetic drums often provide such bulk storage. The monitor programs of the 1130 are on a disk (called the *master cartridge* in a multidisk system) and are brought into core, piece by piece, as needed.

In addition to the FORTRAN compiler and the 1130 assembler, the monitor system contains other programs. One group is for bookkeeping associated with using disks, particularly for the storage of system-supplied and user-written programs and data. Another group, the *supervisor*, is responsible for the reading and handling of the *monitor control records*, the cards which are punched with two slashes (//) followed by a blank in the first three columns.

A third section of the monitor is the *loader*, or *core load builder*, designed to prepare a disk program for loading into core. Since the program stored on disk is usually in a form different from that needed in core, there may be considerable work involved in this process. The system must be certain that all the necessary auxiliary programs are on disk, must prepare them for loading into core, and must load them.

One important program in the monitor system is the *skeleton supervisor*; its purpose is to make sure that there is always a return path to the supervisor program. The skeleton supervisor can be reached in a number of ways, usually through a CALL EXIT or STOP statement in a FORTRAN program or a similar statement in an assembler program. One can also go to the skeleton supervisor by loading its address (0038) in the instruction address register. (See Appendix G-3 for details on how to do this.) However, a misbehaving user program can alter the area of memory reserved for the skeleton supervisor, making it necessary to use a COLD START card to reestablish connection with the supervisor program. Figure 3–2 illustrates the components of the disk monitor system.

IBM has released two versions of the disk monitor system. The first version supports the system as originally announced, with 1132 line printer, 1442 card read punch, and one disk. Later options include other input/output devices, increased internal speed, up to six disks,

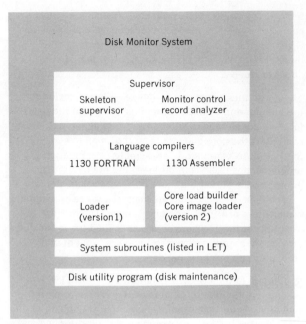

FIG. 3–2. Diagram of components of disk monitor system.

and additional core storage. The version 2 monitor supports these new options. The version 2 system is an extension of version 1, retaining most of the features of the initial system. Many of the new details concern problems that arise when there are several disks in a system, since some disk operations must specify which disk is to be used. It seems likely that both systems will be in use for some time. In the following discussion, references to the "monitor system" cover aspects common to both versions; either version is specified where appropriate.

USING THE MONITOR SYSTEM

The chart inside the front cover of this book shows the use of the monitor programs and the control buttons in running a typical FORTRAN program. Here we will briefly describe the process.

Usually the first monitor control card for a task to be performed is a //bJOB card, signaling the supervisor that it is about to receive a new job. (Where necessary for clarity, we indicate a blank column by b.) One result is the start of necessary bookkeeping activities. Stored both in core and on disk is a table of information about the system and some of the programs on disk; in core it is called COMMA, on disk, DCOM. Since it is possible to alter COMMA during a program, either intentionally or unintentionally, the monitor program assumes that it

must "restore" this area from the disk at the beginning of every job. Thus alterations from a previous program are "erased" by the JOB card.

This description of the JOB card applies to the version 1 monitor. The JOB card has additional functions in version 2. With multiple disks some information must be given as to which of the available disks are to be used for which purposes. A disk may play four different roles during the execution of a FORTRAN (or assembler) program. With a single-disk system, using the version 1 monitor, all the functions must use the one disk. However, if separate disks are available, additional speed is possible. The master cartridge always contains the disk monitor system itself. With version 2 a disk is assigned a four-position name. The master cartridge name is specified on the JOB card in columns 11–14. Disks are physically located on *drives*, and the drive which contains the master cartridge identified in these columns of the JOB card is referred to as *logical drive zero*. This logical drive can be any one of the physical disk drives in use.

During the compilation of FORTRAN and assembler programs, and during preparation for core loading, two additional disk areas are needed. These can be on separate disks in a multiple-disk system using the version 2 monitor, and indeed some speed is gained if separate disks are used. *Working storage* is used in compilation, and the identification for the disk to be used for working storage is in columns 41–44 on the JOB card. This *can* be the master cartridge named in columns 11–14. In preparing core loads, the system also uses an area on disk called the *Core Image Buffer* (CIB); the disk containing the CIB is specified on the JOB card in columns 36–39. Finally, disks may contain programs or data files. There are four possible logical drives that can be associated with disk areas in which programs or data are stored, and these have their identifications respectively in columns 16–19, 21–24, 26–29, and 31–34.

The next monitor control card used in a FORTRAN job, //bFOR, indicates to the compiler that the language to be used in the following program is FORTRAN; with more than one possible language, the computer needs to know which will be used. Since no other columns on this card are required for other purposes, //bFOR can also be punched as //bFORTRAN; any other identification, such as the programmer's name, can be printed on the card.

After the monitor control record announcing that the succeeding program is in FORTRAN, the program deck contains one or more FORTRAN control cards. They are not part of the FORTRAN program, but supply information to the compiler. Some control cards allow the user to make optional selections; we have seen an example of this in the use of an extended precision FORTRAN control card.

One control card is required for all (main line) FORTRAN programs, the IOCS card taking the following form:

```
*IOCS (CARD, TYPEWRITER, KEYBOARD,
            1132 PRINTER, PAPER TAPE, DISK)
```

Only the devices used in the program need to be listed, and we do not show all the possibilities. The necessity of the IOCS card may seem slightly questionable to you; the programs we have already seen specify the devices directly in the READ and WRITE statements, so the information here seems redundant. However, it is always required. Its use takes care of the possibility that a READ or WRITE statement may contain an integer variable instead of an assigned device code, in order that the device can be chosen when the program is run. In different runs you might want to obtain output sometimes on the line printer and sometimes on cards; 1130 FORTRAN allows this choice of input or output device at run time. If the choice is delayed until run time, then the program does not indicate the devices, and the IOCS card tells the compiler which ones may be used.

Other FORTRAN control cards will not be discussed here. They provide optional features, such as listing the program, listing the storage of variables within the program, listing the *subprograms* your program requires, and *tracing* facilities useful for debugging purposes. Details are given in Appendix A-4.

The chart inside the front cover shows (at "Order") that the program cards follow FORTRAN control cards. You already have learned something about punching FORTRAN programs, so no further discussion is necessary.

The FORTRAN compiler processes the FORTRAN statements, "translating" them from FORTRAN to 1130 machine language. This translation process is complex, and the FORTRAN compiler is a complicated program. It is a *string processing* activity: the FORTRAN program is stored in memory as a string of characters, the successive statements separated by a special character inserted into the string. The string is worked on successively by the phases (subprograms) of the FORTRAN compiler. Each phase is brought in from disk to perform some operation on the string. Gradually the string looks less and less like a FORTRAN program and more and more like a machine-language program. The details of the operation of the FORTRAN compiler are in the *1130 Program Logic Manual*, and Chapter 12 gives some information about it. After compilation, the translated program is on disk in the working storage area. The programmer can select which disk to use for working storage if his system has more than one disk in use at the same time.

In the early stages of working with a program, compilation may be as far as we want to go, since we are still correcting the program, guided by the error messages

generated during compilation. If it is a working program, however, we may want to execute it. Execution requires another monitor control card, //bXEQ.

The first task performed because of the XEQ card is to *call* a monitor program we have mentioned, the loader. (In version 2 the program called is the core load builder.) The loader converts our program into *core image format*, a form suitable for core memory, then finds on disk all the subprograms needed, converts them in similar fashion, establishes communications between our program and the needed subprograms, and places the converted programs in core memory.

You may be wondering what subprograms are "needed." The first part of the output from the loan program (Fig. 2–5) shows the subprograms called by that program. To run any FORTRAN program, many system-supplied programs are needed; these programs, stored on disk by name, provide for arithmetic and input/output functions, among other things. The loader looks up the name of a called subprogram in the *Location Equivalence Table* (LET) stored on disk. Effectively associated with each name in LET is its disk storage address, so the program can be located and converted to core image format. After the XEQ card is read, the disk arm makes a characteristic buzzing as it moves back and forth picking up the necessary materials.

This is by no means an exhaustive discussion of running programs under the disk monitor system, but it describes the steps for a simple FORTRAN program.

USING THE DISK UTILITY PROGRAMS

Monitor programs of one group are known as *Disk Utility Programs* (DUP). Let us consider some uses of this group with the loan program discussed in Chapters 1 and 2.

So far, the loan program exists for us only as a FORTRAN program, punched statement by statement on cards. Each time we wish to use this program the cards must be read, and the program must be translated into machine language and prepared for use in core by the loader or core load builder.

However, if the loan program is a production program, used over and over again, retranslating for each use would be wasteful. The translated program can be stored on a disk under a name, or it can be punched on cards in its translated form.

Let us identify the program as LOAN—a reasonably descriptive name. Names of disk-stored programs can be up to five characters long (with the first character always a letter), just as within FORTRAN. Suppose that the LOAN program is on disk in working storage; this would be the case if no program had been compiled since the last run of LOAN. Then the following two cards will store the program on disk under the name LOAN:

```
1     6     13  17   21
|     |     |   |    |
//bDUP
*STOREbbbbbbWSbbUAbbLOAN
```

The numbers above these lines indicate card columns. We are assuming the version 1 monitor and a single disk. (Appendix B-6 shows how disk utility programs are adapted when several disks and the version 2 monitor are in use.)

The first of these cards, //bDUP, notifies the supervisor that a disk utility program is to be used. The second is a STORE command. The LOAD program, now in working storage (WS) on disk, is to be stored in an area on disk known as the *User Area* (UA), under its name, LOAN. Columns 13 and 14 are called the "FROM" field, and columns 17 and 18 are called the "TO" field. This name, LOAN, is entered in LET, the location equivalence table.

To call LOAN from storage at any time after it is stored on disk, the only card needed is an execution card:

```
1      8
|      |
//bXEQbLOAN
```

First the location equivalence table is used to locate LOAN, and then the loader places it in core. Programs do not occupy a fixed location in the user area; as programs are taken out of it, the remaining storage is repacked for most efficient use and LET is corrected.

The program stored on disk in the manner just indicated (called *disk system format*) must be processed by the loader (version 2: core load builder) before it is ready for execution; after compilation the working storage program is not in final core form, as already indicated. The loading job is one of the most time-consuming within the monitor system; considerable time must go into picking up all the necessary subprograms and converting everything into a form suitable for core. If LOAN is to be used many times, it might be advantageous to store it in a form already suitable for core. This can be done with the following cards:

```
1            13   17   21
|            |    |    |
//bDUP
*STORECI     WS   UA   LOAN
```

Again we are assuming that the program has just been compiled and so is currently available in working storage on disk. The CI on the second card indicates that the program is to be stored in core image format. The information stored will include not only the main program, but all the necessary subprograms and linkages, with the addresses reflecting the final core form. In this procedure the loader or core load builder operates *before* the program is placed in the user area on disk, so it is no longer needed when the execution card (of the same form as above) is used, and the program can be brought immediately into core.

A noticeable reduction in time is effected by storing in core image format, but as you might suspect, this procedure also has a disadvantage. Since the subroutines usually require more room than the main program, a complete core load occupies much more storage space on disk than a disk system format program. Storage space is measured in several ways on disk; one method used by the disk monitor system is disk *blocks*, groups of 20 words. Stored in disk system format, LOAN occupies 22 disk blocks of space. On the other hand, if LOAN is stored in core image format, it occupies 127 disk blocks, a much greater number! Hence the gain in execution speed must be weighed against greater disk storage requirements. If the disks are not heavily used and therefore have a large amount of storage available, the greater amount of storage needed will not be important. But as the disks become filled with programs and there is less and less available space, it may not be reasonable to store a program in core image format. This might be more of a problem if there is only one disk in the system.

Another kind of intermediate storage is available in the form of punched cards. If the LOAN program is to be used only once a month in an installation where storage space is at a premium, keeping it in disk storage for the entire month would be wasteful. Instead we can *dump* the program onto cards. The following two cards, followed by a stack of blank cards to be punched, will give an output similar to that stored on disk by STORE, but now punched on cards in a concentrated form, 54 computer words to each card.

```
1            13   17   21
|            |    |    |
//bDUP
*DUMP        WS   CD   LOAN
```

The CD refers to cards. It is important, when using this option, to check that there are enough blank cards in the card hopper. It does not hurt to have too many blank cards, because the monitor will simply pass them all looking for another monitor control card (a card beginning with //) after the program is punched.

To execute this punched translated program, the following sequence can be used:

```
1            13   17   21
|            |    |    |
//bJOB
//bDUP
*STORE       CD   WS   LOAN
```

[loan deck punched as indicated above]

```
//bXEQ
```

Here we are transferring the program from cards to working storage and then executing the program in working storage.

Other sequences can be used. We might want to store the program temporarily in the user area on disk and then delete it when the job is finished. The following sequence of cards would treat the problem in that way, producing the same results as above.

```
1       8    13   17   21
|       |    |    |    |
//bJOBbT
//bDUP
*STORE      CD  UA  LOAN
[loan deck]
//bXEQbLOAN
```

This is the first use we have made of the T on the JOB card, indicating a temporary job. Its effect is that any programs stored on disk during this job will be deleted automatically when the next JOB card is encountered. Thus under this mode the LOAN program will not be permanently stored on disk, but it must be referred to by name in the XEQ card. (There are some limitations on the DUP operations possible during temporary jobs; they are given in Appendix B-7.)

We can also dump programs on cards in core image format. First we store the program on disk in core image format and then dump it onto cards from the user area. The card deck might be as follows:

```
1       8    13   17   21
|       |    |    |    |
//bJOBbT
//bFOR
[FORTRAN program cards]
    ⋮
//bDUP
*STORECI    WS  UA  LOAN
*DUMP       UA  CD  LOAN
```

We have spoken of disk storage vs. card storage as alternative ways of keeping the compiled program, but the two are not exclusive. The wise user may keep on cards the same program he has stored on disk; occasionally, either because of system failure or programming failure, accidents occur with disk, destroying programs stored there. Having the compiled program available on cards provides a convenient way of restoring it on disk without compiling again. Within a particular computer center a collection of important compiled programs on cards can be added to the monitor subroutine library, so that if it is necessary to reload the monitor system, these will be reloaded also. It is also wise to store the original FORTRAN program cards if there is a possibility of later use of the program.

We can see the translated program either in disk system format or in core image format by dumping it onto the line printer, PR. The output is in hexadecimal words; later we shall see how to "read" such output.

It is not hard to imagine other useful bookkeeping activities. One might make changes in the LOAN program after storing it on disk and therefore want to replace the earlier program with the revision. Or the LOAN program might have outlived its usefulness. In either case the desired result can be accomplished by a DELETE statement:

```
1                   21
|                   |
//bDUP
*DELETE             LOAN
```

When a program is deleted from disk storage, its entry is taken out of LET and the user area is repacked. Packing may take considerable time, and the user should be cautioned never to stop the computer during this operation.

It is useful to understand that, although we have been showing the DUP card in each sequence, a series of disk utility jobs requires only a single preceding DUP statement.

So far we have spoken of storing programs only in the user area. However, the monitor also allows the establishment of another area, the *fixed area*, in disk storage. The principal difference between the user area and the fixed area is that no repacking of programs goes on in the fixed area when a program is deleted; a fixed-area program stays at the disk location first assigned to it. Occasionally it is convenient (or essential) to know that a program is always at a given location. Another table, the *Fixed Location Equivalence Table* (FLET), identifies and locates the programs in the fixed area. It is necessary to *define* a fixed area; details on defining and extending the area can be found in the 1130 monitor manual and in Appendix B-4.

Finally, it is convenient to know which programs are currently stored on disk. They will include, in addition to the user-stored programs, many system subroutines needed during the execution of FORTRAN or assembler programs. One can obtain a list of these programs with the following cards:

```
1
|
//bDUP
*DUMPLET
```

This long list, produced on the line printer (or console typewriter if there is no printer), shows the name of each program, the number of disk blocks it occupies, and the current sector address of the program on disk. The sector addresses change as programs are deleted from the user area, but they remain the same for the fixed area.

The disk utility programs for a multidisk system must allow for the movement of information from one disk to another, and for the inclusion on each disk of its own LET and FLET tables for programs stored on each. Therefore, under the version 2 monitor, many DUP control records can specify, with a four-place hexadecimal identification in columns 31–34, the cartridge *from* which information is to come, and, in columns 37–40, the identification of the cartridge *to* which information is to go. Many of the disk utility program control records can contain both of these fields, but the DUMPLET card has only a FROM ID field, and the DEFINE FIXED AREA card and the DISK WRITE ADDRESS OPERATION card (DWADR) contain only TO ID fields.

The disk utility programs for version 2 also contain a few additional facilities not available in version 1. For example, it is possible to dump the FLET table alone and, as one might expect, it is possible to dump those parts of the LET or FLET table that are stored on one disk rather than the entire table. The version 2 monitor allows one to *reduce* the size of a fixed area by the use of a minus sign in column 31, while with the version 1 monitor a fixed area can be made smaller only by reloading the monitor system. Disk utility program control cards in version 2 also allow one to change the principal print device and the principal input device, as in these examples:

```
1                       21
|                       |
*DEFINE PRINC PRINT 1132
*DEFINE PRINC PRINT 1403
*DEFINE PRINC PRINT           [Console typewriter]
```

COMPUTER CENTER POLICY ON
DISK STORAGE OF USER PROGRAMS

Each computer center will have its own policies concerning disk storage to determine which users can store programs on which disks, how much can be stored, and how long. The user should inquire about local policies.

Usually a center owns more disks than may be in use at one time, and the user entering a program on disk needs to note which disk is to be used. Each disk may have an identifying label, or name, which can be used on the JOB card.

In the version 1 monitor this identification is a five-character name; a disk called REED might have the following JOB card:

```
1            11
|            |
//bJOB       REED
```

If a name is placed on the JOB card, the supervisor program checks to see whether that name was assigned to

the disk when the monitor system was initially loaded; if not, an error message is produced. One can, however, still proceed with the disk by pushing PROGRAM START on the console.

Because in a center serving many users huge numbers of programs will accumulate, eventually filling all the available disk storage, it is essential to keep an inventory of programs stored on disk, including information on when they may be erased. A notebook in the center is useful for this purpose. The notebook can show the name of the program, the date stored, the disk name, the program's length, the date or conditions for removal, and other relevant information. This procedure also makes the programs available to others, since the notebook can contain additional information necessary for using the program. The notebook can be checked periodically to ascertain which programs are due for removal.

MORE FORTRAN

CHAPTER 4

We now return to FORTRAN in order to consider some features that will provide us with increased flexibility in programming. Previously we studied a FORTRAN subset which might be called basic FORTRAN (although other sets also have this name). This subset is sufficient for simple programs, and the beginner may not see the need for more. However, FORTRAN has additional facilities that can be very useful for more complicated programs. As before, we proceed through examples.

INTERROGATING THE CONSOLE SWITCHES

We return for the last time to our LOAN program, again making a slight modification. Unlike previous changes affecting only the mode of calculation, this program modification will have a noticeable effect on the results.

As the LOAN program is presently written, it is a "one-shot" affair, a program that is run only once each time an XEQ card is used. However, when using this program, we might like to consider a *series* of loans rather than only one. To enable us to do this, our strategy is to make the program loop back on itself whenever another loan is to be computed. The modified LOAN program can be represented diagrammatically as in Fig. 4–1.

The question as to whether or not another loan is to be considered is to be decided by us rather than by the computer. Hence we want to add statements to our program that allow a decision by the computer operator. One way of doing this is to use the console entry switches, a set of 16 switches above the keyboard. They are two-position switches: down for off, up for on (Fig. 4–2). A FORTRAN program can check the position of any console switch and take differing action, depending on whether the switch is off or on; thus we can influence the calculation by setting the switches.

Figure 4–3 gives the new version of the LOAN program, under the control of switch 1. The differences between this and our previous loan programs are not great. The first WRITE statement now has a statement number, 1; if we are to return to the beginning of the program, there must be a numbered statement that identifies the beginning.

The two statements new to this program,

```
CALL DATSW (1,J)
GO TO (85,1),J
```

are types of statements not previously encountered in our

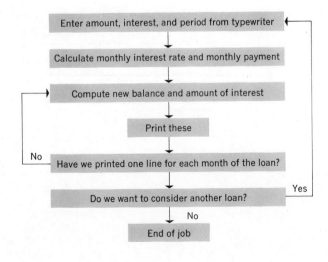

FIG. 4–1. Flow chart for the modified loan program.

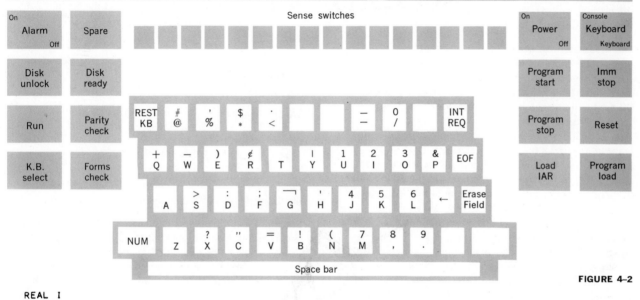

FIGURE 4–2

```
      REAL I
1 WRITE (1,2)
2 FORMAT ( 'LOAN PROGRAM - ENTER AMOUNT IN FORM XXXXX.XX' )
      READ  (6, 3 )   A
3 FORMAT (F8.2)
      WRITE ( 1,4)
4 FORMAT ( 'ENTER INTEREST RATE PER YEAR IN FORM XX.XX'   )
      READ (6,5 )  RY
5 FORMAT ( F5.2)
      WRITE (1,6)
6 FORMAT ('ENTER NUMBER OF MONTHS IN FORM XXX' )
      READ (6,7) N
7 FORMAT (I3)
      WRITE(3, 9) A, RY, N
9 FORMAT ( ' INTEREST CALCULATION ON A LOAN' / ' AMOUNT = ' F10.2
 1/ ' INTEREST RATE PER YEAR = 'F5.2 / ' NUMBER OF MONTHS = ' I4 //
 2' PAYMENT' 13X 'INTEREST' 12X 'BALANCE'   )
      R = (RY/12.) / 100.
      P = (A * R * (1. + R ) ** N ) /  ( (1. + R) ** N - 1)
      DO 99 K = 1, N
      I = R * A
      A = A - P + I
      WRITE (3, 8)     P, I, A
8 FORMAT   (' $'F8.2, 11X'$'F8.2, 11X '$' F9.2 )
99 CONTINUE
      CALL DATSW (1, J )
      GO TO (85, 1 ), J
85 CALL EXIT
      END
```

FIGURE 4–3

study of FORTRAN. The first is a simple example of a subroutine CALL, and the second is a computed GO TO statement.

First we shall consider the joint effect of these statements and then examine what each does individually. Considered together, the two statements constitute a check on console switch 1. If this switch is *on*, the computer is instructed to branch to statement number 85. If console switch 1 is *off*, program control transfers to statement number 1. Thus, turning on the switch causes an exit from the program when the loan calculation is finished. On the other hand, if the switch is off, we return to the beginning of the program and enter the information for a new loan. The switch is checked *only* when these two statements are executed; if the switch is turned on during the printing of the results, nothing will happen until the printing is finished.

The first statement is a call to the subroutine DATSW; the items in parentheses following the subroutine name supply needed information. The DATSW subroutine works as follows. Inside the parentheses there are two integers, the first either constant or variable, the second variable. The switch to be interrogated is identified by the first item in the parentheses, in this example switch 1. The subroutine checks the position of switch 1. If on, the integer variable J (the second item in the parentheses) is set equal to 1; if switch 1 is off, J is assigned the value 2. In other words, after the execution of the CALL statement, J has the value of either 1 or 2, depending on whether the switch is on or off. Note that J is used in this program only for this purpose, although such exclusive use is not essential. We have used an integer constant for the switch number, but an integer variable or integer expression is also allowed; the different switches might be checked in different executions of the same CALL DATSW statement. The console switches are numbered from 0 to 15.

The second new statement, the computed GO TO, is a common conditional branching statement in FORTRAN. Within the parentheses is a series of statement numbers separated by commas. These statement numbers must be used elsewhere in the program. The integer variable at the end, after the comma outside the parentheses, determines which branch occurs. The value of J, established by the subroutine call, picks out the statement number in that position in the series within the parentheses. Thus if $J = 1$, the branch is to the first statement number listed. If $J = 2$, the branch is to the second statement number listed, and so on. (More than two statement numbers can be listed in a computed GO TO, but only two are needed here.) If J has a value greater than the number of statement numbers in the list (possible in other circumstances though not here), the resulting action generated by the GO TO will be undefined, and troubles are likely.

THE STATEMENT FUNCTION

In the next sections we shall consider three ways for making FORTRAN a more versatile language by writing program material to be used at many places within the same program. Thus we can avoid repeating sections of the program which are used several times. These three procedures differ in flexibility and versatility. The first, the statement function, is limited to a single statement, while the other two types are groups of statements called subprograms.

The Pythagorean theorem can be employed to calculate the distance of a point from the origin, given the coordinates of the point. Suppose we have a point with coordinates (X,Y), as shown in Fig. 4–4. The distance we want is the length of the hypotenuse of the triangle, or

$$\sqrt{X^2 + Y^2}$$

We often find it useful to determine the distance of a point from the origin, knowing only its *X*- and *Y*-coordinates.

We can easily translate this method of calculating the distance into a FORTRAN expression:

SQRT(X*X + Y*Y)

SQRT is the *library* routine for taking a square root. (We shall discuss library functions in more detail later.)

We could write this expression wherever needed in the program, but it would be a bother to write it many times. FORTRAN has a facility, the *Statement Function*, which allows us early in the program to assign a name to an expression like this, and then use that name as often as desired during the program. We might call the distance from the origin DIST. Then the FORTRAN statement function could look like this:

DIST (X,Y) = SQRT (X*X + Y*Y)

The statement function must precede any executable statement in the FORTRAN program. (See Appendix A-1 for a list of executable statements.) Figure 4–5 shows the skeleton of a program which first defines this FORTRAN statement function and then uses it several times on different quantities.

It should be clear that we effect a considerable reduction in programming effort by not having to write the expression for calculating the distance whenever needed. In any calculation where such a subcalculation is to be done often, the statement function is valuable. However, it cannot exceed one statement, and it can define only a single function. The other types of remote programming which we shall consider next eliminate two of these restrictions, but in different ways.

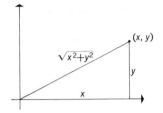

FIG. 4–4. Problem: How far is the point (x,y) from the origin?

```
DIST ( X, Y ) = SQRT ( X*X + Y*Y )
              •••
              •••
Z = DIST (P,Q)
              •••
              •••
Q = A * DIST(X1, 7.1) + C
              •••
              •••
R = SIN ( S** DIST(7.34E7, .69E8))/ C
              •••
              •••
IF(B*B - 4.*A*A - DIST(P,Q))  17, 85, 97
              •••
              •••
END
```

FIGURE 4–5

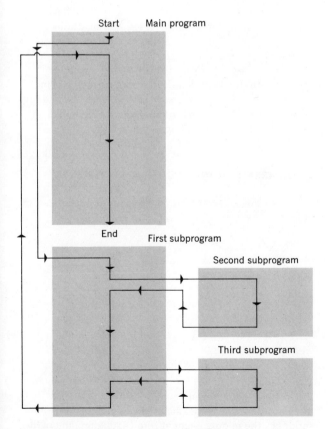

FIG. 4–6. A possible flow of control for a main program and three subprograms.

FORTRAN SUBPROGRAMS

Each sample FORTRAN program inspected up to now has been composed of one "piece," except for possible statement functions early in the program. However, one of the most useful programming tools is the ability to write "side" programs, called *subprograms*. These subprograms may be required by many system users or many times within a single program. They also can simplify the problems of finding errors in a program. When a sequence of steps is to be used many times, it is advantageous to code the sequence once for all uses. FORTRAN has two kinds of subprograms, *functions* and *subroutines*. Although written similarly, functions and subroutines are used differently within the main FORTRAN program.

Some sense of the various structural relationships possible between main programs and subprograms is very useful. Subprograms may be used within main programs, and subprograms may themselves use subprograms. One possible arrangement is illustrated by Fig. 4–6, in which the flow of control follows the arrowed line through a maze of program and subprograms. We usually begin and end in the main program, but this is not essential.

Besides giving a unique status to a frequently used set of instructions, subprograms can play another role. It is often easier to write complex programs as a series of pieces, each one of which can be tested individually. Either function or subroutine subprograms furnish a convenient way of structuring these pieces.

We shall learn about subprograms by inspecting a sample. One relatively simple task often needed in certain calculations is that of finding the maximum number in a set of numbers; we will use this calculation to illustrate the writing of a function subprogram, but first we need to make a detour.

FORTRAN ARRAYS

The first problem in writing the maximum number program is storing and specifying the collection of numbers whose maximum is required. We could give each number a FORTRAN variable name and use the names in the program to refer to these variables individually. However, FORTRAN, reflecting a common mathematical device, provides a convenient method for specifying and manipulating a collection of numbers, the *array*.

If a mathematician wants to designate a collection of related numbers, he may use the same symbol for all of them, adding changing subscripts to distinguish one number from another; for example,

A_1, A_2, A_3

might designate three numbers. A two-dimensional array

of numbers, a matrix, can be specified by two subscripts. Four numbers in a matrix might be written in linear arrangement as

$$A_{11}, A_{12}, A_{21}, A_{22}$$

or, in a two-dimensional matrix arrangement, as

$$A_{11}, A_{12}$$
$$A_{21}, A_{22}$$

Such notation could be extended to three subscripts, four subscripts, etc.

The FORTRAN array is similar, with notational changes imposed by the use of linear printing devices, and with limitations on the allowable number of subscripts. Thus one might designate a collection of five entities in FORTRAN by the following five variable names.

```
A(1), A(2), A(3), A(4), A(5)
```

One can sometimes refer to this collection or array by using the single letter A, both in connection with subprograms and with READ and WRITE statements. Similarly,

```
KIM(1,1), KIM(2,1), KIM(1,2), KIM(2,2)
```

are the ingredients of a 2×2 FORTRAN matrix, with integer values.

The program can specify a member of the array which will vary during the calculation. Thus at one point the quantity A(K) might appear in an arithmetical expression. Before this expression is encountered, K would have been assigned some value; for example, the first time the statement is to be executed, K might have the value 3, so the element used in the calculation would be A(3).

Only integers can be subscripts; limited subscript arithmetic is permitted, as in these examples which illustrate allowable subscript arithmetic:

```
KOP + 3
INDEX - 43
7*LOOP
16*LORSE - 83
```

FORTRAN also allows two-dimensional arrays,

```
C(J,K)
JOB(KOST, LOSS)
```

and three-dimensional arrays,

```
POS(IX,IY,I2)
K374L(I1,I2,I3)
```

The rules for naming real and integer arrays are the same as for other variables.

The FORTRAN compiler needs to know how much storage to allocate for an array. This amount may not be obvious from the program. Storage is specified by a special statement, the DIMENSION statement, which must precede any executable statement in the program. If the array A is a one-dimensional array of 42 numbers, and if the array ZQR is a two-dimensional array, with the first index running from 1 through 6 and the second from 1 through 10, the DIMENSION statement required would be

```
DIMENSION A(42), ZQR(6,10)
```

This same information can also be conveyed to the compiler in a REAL or INTEGER specification. If C3 is a linear array of 92 integers, and KUT is a three-dimensional real array with all indexes going from 1 through 10, the following statements, preceding any executable statement, would provide the compiler with the necessary information:

```
INTEGER C3(92)
REAL KUT(10,10,10)
```

These statements would precede a DIMENSION statement, if present to allocate storage for other variables. All allocation of storage for constants and variables is done by the compiler in advance, rather than during execution. The 1130 compiler stores the variables and constants in memory just before the program itself. Arrays are stored "backward," with higher subscript values nearer the beginning of the core memory. Some recent computer languages save storage space by allowing dynamic allocation during the running of programs, rather than during compilation.

USING ARRAYS IN INPUT/OUTPUT STATEMENTS

There are special FORTRAN facilities for input and output of arrays. Consider the following program fragment:

```
DIMENSION  MAT (5,5)
     ⋮
DO 1  I = 1,5
DO 1  J = 1,5
MAT(I,J) = I*100 + J
1 CONTINUE
     ⋮
END
```

Two DO loops set values for the 5×5 integer array named MAT. The value of any element in MAT is a three-digit integer, with the leftmost digit the value of the first subscript (I), the middle element zero (*100), and the rightmost digit the value of the second subscript (+J). Thus

MAT(I,J) = 203 when I = 2, J = 3; or 401 when I = 4, J = 1. We are identifying the array elements so that we can see the effects of different formats.

We can use array elements in WRITE statements using only facilities we know about, but now with subscripted variables. MAT(2,1) and MAT(4,3) represent definite numbers in storage. Thus they can occur in READ and WRITE statements just as we have seen previously with other variable names. If we wish to output only selected elements of an array, we can simply list them one by one in a WRITE statement. However, we can list an entire array as well. Consider these two statements:

```
   WRITE (1,10) MAT
10 FORMAT (//5(I4,I4,I4,I4,I4/))
```

By specifying only the array name MAT with no subscripts in the WRITE statement, we instruct the computer to type the entire array. If we study the output from these statements as shown in Table 4–1, we quickly see the order in which output is given from the machine. Remember that the first digit in each element comes from the first subscript, and the third from the second subscript. The 5 in the FORMAT specification indicates that the specification is to be used five times, each giving one line of five numbers.

The order of output (and input, similarly) is fixed by the FORTRAN programming system when one uses simply the array name in the WRITE statement. The first subscript changes most rapidly, as in the example. Unfortunately this ordering leads to a result opposite to that obtained from the usual mathematical convention of using the first subscript to label the rows and the second to label the columns. The two slashes early in the FORMAT statement give two blank lines before the table is printed, and the third slash signals each new line.

TABLE 4–1

101	201	301	401	501
102	202	302	402	502
103	203	303	403	503
104	204	304	404	504
105	205	305	405	505

The FORMAT statement here is a little clumsy. We can simplify it by introducing a new format feature. The format specifications we have used so far all had a one-to-one correspondence with the variables of an associated READ or WRITE statement; for every variable there was a format specification. However, this is not essential. The case of more specifications than needed is trivial—the unneeded formats are ignored. If, however, we exhaust the format specification list before we have finished outputting all the variables in the WRITE list, the rule is to

return to the beginning of the innermost parentheses still in use in the FORMAT statement, including any preceding number. A line is changed for each such return.

Thus the format

```
FORMAT (//(5(I4)))
```

will produce results identical with those obtained above, first skipping two lines and then typing five numbers per line, with no skips between lines. On the other hand, the statement

```
FORMAT (//5(I4))
```

will lead not only to two blanks before the table, but also to two blank lines before each new line of output. This repetition rule is *not* restricted to arrays, and is useful elsewhere.

We can get greater control over the output or input from an array with implied DO loops within the READ or WRITE statement. The following cards would give the same output as that shown in Table 4–1, with MAT defined as in our program fragment.

```
   WRITE (1,65) ((MAT(I,J), J = 1,5), I = 1,5)
65 FORMAT (//(5(I4)))
```

If we want to obtain the mathematician's standard arrangement for a matrix, we could use

```
   WRITE (1,65) ((MAT(I,J), I = 1,5), J = 1,5)
65 FORMAT (//(5(I4)))
```

The sequencing in the implied DO loop produces the results given in Table 4–2. Just as with other DO loops, subscripts do not have to range over all the allowable values; thus we could output a subset of a given matrix with this facility.

TABLE 4–2

101	102	103	104	105
201	202	203	204	205
301	302	303	304	305
401	402	403	404	405
501	502	503	504	505

FORTRAN FUNCTION SUBPROGRAMS: THE MAXIMUM FUNCTION

With FORTRAN arrays at our disposal we return to the problem of writing a function subprogram to find the maximum number in a collection. The obvious procedure for finding the maximum starts by considering the first number in the collection as a maximum, and proceeds by comparing it with the succeeding number, adopting the

```
// JOB
// FOR
*LIST ALL
      REAL FUNCTION MAX(A,N)
C A IS A ONE DIMENSIONAL ARRAY, N THE NUMBER OF PLACES IN THE ARRAY
C TO BE USED
      DIMENSION A(1)
      MAX = A(1)
      DO 2 I = 2, N
      IF (MAX-A(I)) 3,2,2
    3 MAX = A(I)
    2 CONTINUE
      RETURN
      END
```

FIGURE 4-7

new number as the maximum whenever it is larger than the previous maximum and continuing with the comparison to the end of the array. There are other ways, but this is a reasonable procedure.

The numbers, assumed to be real, are to be stored in a FORTRAN array in the main program, and we also specify how many of the numbers in the array are to be used. The program is shown in Fig. 4–7. The first statement identifies the program as a function subprogram. Usually the data type would be determined by the first letter, as with FORTRAN variables, so there would be no need for the REAL preceding the function. Here we are using a variable beginning with M, normally an integer, and we are specifying that it is real. The two *arguments* of the function, the given information, are A, the array, and N, the number of values to be used.

The DIMENSION statement is needed in the subprogram, but no storage is allocated in the subprogram, since the space for the array is provided in the main program. So the 1 is a "dummy" value not affecting the program; we could use any number, and the effect would be the same.

It should not be difficult to follow this program; it calculates the maximum by the procedure suggested, going through the set of numbers and keeping the largest. The RETURN is a FORTRAN statement we have not seen before. It indicates that control, along with the final value computed, is to be returned to the original program.

How can this program be used within another program? A function subprogram is *called* by using the function in the same way that we used the statement functions previously discussed. Thus if we wanted to let a variable B be the maximum value of the first 73 numbers stored in a one-dimensional array called WELL, the FORTRAN statement would be

```
B = MAX (WELL,73)
```

A FORTRAN statement using this function could be more complex:

```
A = B**MAX(CAB,4) + HORSE/MAX(DOG,I)
```

Here the MAX function would be used twice to carry out this one statement.

We will later write a similar program in the assembler language, a language closer to the one actually used by the computer.

FORTRAN SUBROUTINE SUBPROGRAMS

The next type of FORTRAN subprogram is the subroutine. The subroutine has a form much like the function subprogram, except that the word SUBROUTINE replaces the word FUNCTION in the initial statement. For reasons that we will soon see, no data type specification is needed. A typical subroutine heading statement might be the following:

```
SUBROUTINE NOISE (AMAX,AMIN,IRA,P,Q)
```

The list in parentheses after the subroutine name (NOISE) is a *parameter* list. The arguments in this list can be of any allowable data type, real or integer, variable or constant. In a subroutine they may play either of two roles. Some of the arguments transmit values from the calling program to be used in the subroutine calculations. However, other parameters may be variables assigned values within the subroutine, values to be made available to the calling program. A subroutine need not have any parameters at all. Subroutines use the RETURN statement, which returns control to the statement after the calling statement in the calling program.

The subroutine NOISE might be called by any of the following FORTRAN statements:

```
CALL NOISE (A(4,2), B(7,3), 17,Y,Z)
CALL NOISE (+B*B - 4.*A*C,-B*B + 4.*A*C,JOB,
   OUT1,OUT2)
CALL NOISE (AMAX,AMIN,IRA,P,Q)
```

We are assuming that the first three arguments in each subroutine list for NOISE are values coming from the main program, while the next two are variables that are assigned values within the subroutine. There is no need to insist on the same names in the main program and the subroutine, but the *order* of the parameters is important, since the association will be of corresponding parameters. Each parameter in the subroutine should be of the same type (real or integer) as its corresponding variable or constant in the calling program.

In addition to different methods of calling, an important difference between function and subroutine subprograms is that a function *always returns a single value*, the value of the function, while a subroutine subprogram may return any number of values.

Subroutines sometimes need data from the calling program. This information can be in the parameter list, as indicated, but another procedure is particularly useful if much information from the calling program is needed in the subroutine: the COMMON statement. COMMON identifies a fixed area of the core memory. Suppose the main program has the following COMMON statement:

```
COMMON PORT, ORE, LAP
```

Then the following COMMON statement in the subprogram,

```
COMMON ZZ, YY, JOB
```

would ensure that the real variable PORT occupies the same place in storage as the real variable ZZ, and similarly for the other quantities in the two lists. Thus the value of PORT is always available to the subroutine.

In the 1130 disk system, COMMON storage is allocated in high-address core (Fig. 4–8). We can place an array in COMMON by using only its name, with no subscripts:

```
DIMENSION GIRL (17)
COMMON DATE, GIRL
```

or, more briefly,

```
COMMON DATE, GIRL (17)
```

If both are used, the DIMENSION statement must precede the COMMON statement:

```
DIMENSION BOY (17)
COMMON DATE, GIRL (17)
```

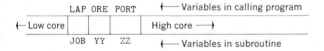

FIG. 4–8. Structure of COMMON for example in text.

USING SUBPROGRAMS

Although we have outlined the writing of subprograms and the calling of such programs in a FORTRAN program, we have not fully discussed the use of subprograms.

First, it should be clear that there is a main FORTRAN program being executed. The program might be read from cards or executed from disk or brought in by one of several other alternatives, but the function or subroutine subprograms needed in the main program *must* be stored on disk *before* execution of the main program, with the 1130.

Therefore the subprogram must be compiled and stored on disk before it can be called. We have already discussed the disk utility program facilities for storing a program on disk. When a subprogram is to be stored, the customary procedure is to start with JOB and FORTRAN cards, followed by the program cards for the subprogram, and then a DUP card and a STORE card:

```
1              13  17   21
|               |   |    |
//bDUP
*STORE         WS  UA   MAX
```

The name (here MAX) on the STORE card must agree with the name of the subprogram; if the names differ, an error message is typed and the STORE operation is terminated. Other error messages may also be encountered; for instance, if you attempt to load a program called MAX, not realizing that someone else had already loaded on the same disk a program with an identical name, the disk utility program will complain. DUP, when asked to store a program on disk, checks the location equivalence table (LET), which tells what programs are currently stored on disk. If the program name is already in LET, an error message is generated and the program is not stored. If, however, the subprogram is successfully stored, its name and length will be entered in LET.

The main program is prepared for running by the loader, the program called by an XEQ card. The loader searches the program for needed subprograms, looks up these subprograms in LET, finds the subprograms, and prepares the main program and the subprograms for loading in core. The subprograms may themselves call other subprograms, and for each one LET must be consulted and the programs loaded. If any program called for in your main program or in one of the subprograms is not stored on disk with the precise name used in the program, an error message stating that the subprogram is not in the location equivalence table will be generated; execution is then aborted.

Sometimes it is desirable to load a subprogram only for one job, erasing it immediately after the job is completed. This could be done with a DELETE card immediately after execution. Thus we could erase our MAX program by the following cards:

```
1                       21
|                       |
//bDUP
*DELETE                 MAX
```

A temporary JOB card (T in column 8) can be used to accomplish this, as explained in Chapter 3.

SYSTEM FUNCTIONS AND SUBROUTINES

We have suggested that the 1130 FORTRAN system contains functions and subroutines available to any user of the system, some intended for explicit use within programs. All the common mathematical functions are available, with names generally recognizable to users. Table 4–3 shows some of the functions in the 1130 monitor system.

Some examples of mathematical statements using some of these built-in functions are:

```
X = SIN(Y)
Z = 3*EXP(TAN(Y)) + COS(Y*Y - Z*3.1)
F = -X - A*V*ABS(V)
QUIRK = ALOG(A(4,I)**C) + D
```

Note that an arithmetic expression can be the argument of a function.

TABLE 4–3

NAME	FORTRAN NAME	TYPE
Sine	SIN	Sine of a *real* number is *real*
Cosine	COS	Cosine of a *real* number is *real*
Square root	SQRT	Square root of a *real* number is *real*
Exponential	EXP	Exponential of a *real* number is *real*
Natural logarithm	ALOG	Log of a *real* number is *real*
Arctangent	ATAN	Arctangent of a *real* number is *real*
Absolute value	ABS	Real to real
	IABS	Integer to integer

We have already seen that the output from the loan program included a list of subroutines necessary in the execution of that program. None of these subroutines appeared in CALL statements in the program; they were requested by the compiling program. Many of these were required because the 1130 does not directly perform real arithmetic operations, but relies on system subroutines for these tasks. We shall learn more about these subroutines later.

ALPHAMERIC INFORMATION IN FORTRAN

FORTRAN, initially developed as a scientific computation language, had no facilities for handling and manipulating character data such as the letters of the alphabet, the number symbols considered as symbols, and other special symbols. Demand for this ability quickly arose, and later versions of FORTRAN usually include facilities for reading, writing, and manipulating *alphameric* information. These facilities are often considered to be somewhat unnatural, almost a trick, reflecting the fact that alphameric information was not taken into account in the initial FORTRAN planning.

A character may be internally coded in several ways within the 1130 memory. FORTRAN makes use of one of these, the IBM *Extended Binary Coded Decimal Interchange Coding* (EBCDIC). For present purposes we can ignore the coding details, but it is important to know that in FORTRAN two characters of alphameric data may be stored in one computer memory word. We have had little to say about the computer words, but the user of the alphameric facilities in FORTRAN must have an elementary knowledge of the types of storage available. There are three methods for storing numerical data in FORTRAN, the storage of an integer in one word, a standard precision real number in two words, and an extended precision real number in three words. In accordance with the two-in-one feature, in place of one integer we can store two alphameric characters; in place of one standard precision real number, four characters; and finally, in place of one extended precision real number, six characters.

Assume that we wish to enter 20 alphameric characters, punched in the first 20 columns of a card. They can be considered as an array to which a name can be assigned. Examples of two FORTRAN procedures for reading 20 alphameric characters are:

1. Using integer variables:

```
      DIMENSION IMES (10)
      ⋮
      READ (2,1) IMES
1     FORMAT (10A 2)
```

2. Using real variables:

```
      DIMENSION CHAR (5)
         ⋮
      READ (2,1) CHAR
1     FORMAT (5A 4)
```

Similar instructions could be used to write alphameric information.

Both of these procedures function in the same way, reading and storing the input data, but unless the *one-word integer* option is used (see FORTRAN control cards), the first procedure uses twice as much internal space. In both, the strategy is to set up an array and use the variable name to refer to the whole character string. In the first program we dimension a ten-element integer array, since the storage space for an integer variable accommodates two alphameric characters. In the second program we need the space of only five variables, since the space for a standard precision real number can be used for storing four alphameric characters. In the READ statement, as with other READ and WRITE statements using dimensioned variables, the array name does not have any attached subscript. The two formats reflect the two types of storage.

When we read and write alphameric information in FORTRAN, the only "penalty" is that we have to use a dimension statement and another format type. However, if we need to manipulate alphameric information, the fact that FORTRAN was not originally written for using such information becomes more apparent. For manipulation, some knowledge of how the alphameric characters are stored is important.

Simple comparisons between alphameric information can be done with the IF statement, since different letters must be coded internally in different ways. Suppose, for example, that two character strings, IFILE and KFILE, are read in and stored with these names identifying them. We can determine whether the string stored in KFILE has the same first two letters as IFILE by using the following IF statement:

```
IF (IFILE(1) − KFILE(1))10,20,10
```

The middle statement number, 20, the branching statement if the result of the expression in the parentheses is zero, causes a branch to the part of the program that follows when KFILE(1) = IFILE(1), i.e., when the strings have the same first two letters. Even this simple use of the IF statement is a little strained, for our interest here is not in comparing two numbers as we have done in all previous uses of the IF statement.

With the version 2 monitor system it is possible to store alphameric data in variable names at the beginning of the program, by the use of the DATA statement. This is the only way to introduce alphameric data other than by a READ statement. The following example is taken from the preliminary version of the manual for the version 2 monitor. Assume an array A has at least seven elements and that the following DATA statement occurs at the beginning of a FORTRAN program.

```
DATA A/3*'ABCD', 2*'AB', 'A' 'BC', 'A.BC'/
```

Then the first three elements are assigned the value *ABCD*, the next two *AB*, the next *A′BC*, and the seventh *A.BC*.

USING DISK STORAGE IN 1130 FORTRAN

It is convenient to have access to a disk in at least two situations during execution of a FORTRAN program. There may be so much information to be stored that core storage is inadequate for the entire program at one time. Under these circumstances, some data can be temporarily stored on disk; access to the information is possible within the program. Such disk use will increase program execution time, because reading onto and writing from the disk are comparatively slow processes.

It is also useful in FORTRAN programs to be able to access data files permanently stored on disk, either to obtain information or to change in some way material stored there.

The FORTRAN resources for handling disk storage can be used in connection with the disk utility program, particularly the STOREDATA and DUMPDATA commands.

The requirements for enabling FORTRAN statements to write and to use information on disk are straightforward. First, one must allocate the necessary space for a disk file. Each file must be identified within the FORTRAN program by a number; if the file is to be stored permanently, it must be given a name. Facilities will be needed in FORTRAN, to move information from disk to core memory, and from core back to disk.

With this introduction let us consider a problem. Suppose that we want a class file on disk, initially with the names of the students in a class but eventually containing additional information concerning majors, grades, etc. Assume that the maximum enrollment is 50; then the file will contain 50 *records*. We must also decide how much information is to be stored in each record. A check on names in recent classes indicates that 26 characters can usually accommodate a full name. We need to specify the number of words in each file record. Rather arbitrarily we will require 40 words for each record, 13 for the name and the remainder for auxiliary information.

The names are to be punched, one to a card, starting in column 1, and arranged by hand or machine-sorted in the

```
// JOB
// FORTRAN
*IOCS(KEYBOARD,TYPEWRITER,1132 PRINTER,CARD,DISK)
*LIST ALL
      DEFINE FILE 1(50,40,U,NREC)
      DIMENSION NAME (13)
      DO 2 K = 1, 50
      READ (2, 3) NAME
      WRITE (1'K) NAME
    3 FORMAT ( 13A2 )
    2 CONTINUE
      CALL EXIT
      END

VARIABLE ALLOCATIONS
 NAME =0020  NREC =0022  I    =0024

STATEMENT ALLOCATIONS
   3   =0029  2    =0052

FEATURES SUPPORTED
 IOCS

CALLED SUBPROGRAMS
 FLD     FSTO    TYPEZ    SRED    SFIO    SIOAI   CARDZ   PRNTZ   SDFIO   SDWRT

INTEGER CONSTANTS
    1=0026     50=0027       2=0028

CORE REQUIREMENTS FOR
 COMMON     0 VARIABLES     38 PROGRAM      54

END OF COMPILATION
```

FIGURE 4–9

desired order. These cards are thus data cards rather than program cards. The cards are to be read and stored as part of a file on disk. Using the resources of FORTRAN and the monitor system, we want to establish a file with these properties. A program which will do this for us is shown in Fig. 4–9.

The DEFINE FILE statement gives the information necessary for the compiler to set up the file. The number 1 identifies the file within the FORTRAN program. (Several files with different numbers are allowed.) The WRITE statement in this program refers to this file, because the first number in the parentheses is 1. Any integer constant within the standard range of 1130 constants can be used as the file ID number. Note that WRITE specifies the disk as the output device by using an apostrophe rather than a comma; this is the identifying characteristic of disk I/O. A disk WRITE means "write on the disk." Disk READ and WRITE statements do not reference FORMAT statements; no format conversion is possible, so the entire record is handled as a whole.

The numbers 50 and 40 are respectively the number of records in file 1 and the number of words in each record. Thus 2000 words are needed. (The U is required for compatability with other more elaborate versions of FORTRAN.) The variable NREC will contain the number of the last record accessed; this information is sometimes convenient although this program does not use that variable.

The procedure is to read a card, storing the first 26 alphameric characters of the card in a variable called NAME. Then NAME is written on disk in record K, where K is the number of the card just read. The FORTRAN program establishes a 50-record file on the disk, with each record containing a 13-word (i.e., 26-character) name followed by blanks in the next 27 words if the data cards are blank except for the name. The first number in the disk WRITE statement identifies the file, the second the record within the file.

In our discussion of storing alphameric characters, we used the FORMAT statement with A (standing for alphameric) for character string information. NAME is a dimensioned variable, a collection of 13 integer variables, in which the 26 letters composing the student's name are to be stored, two per variable. The format specification associated with the READ (from card) statement, 13 A2, indicates that 26 alphameric characters are to be read.

After this FORTRAN program has been executed, our full objective will still not be achieved. The created file, containing the names of those in the class, is a temporary file in the working storage area on disk. However, we want a permanent file, identified by its name; to accomplish this we can use the facilities of the disk utility program. The two DUP operations for manipulating data files are STOREDATA and DUMPDATA.

If the next two cards follow the data cards, after the execution of the above program, a permanent file called

CLASS will be created on disk:

```
1          10  13  17  21        30
|          |   |   |   |         |
//bDUP
*STOREDATA  WS  UA  CLASS        7
```

We are moving the data file from working storage (WS) to the user area (UA). The number on the STOREDATA card, here 7, is the number of disk sectors (a sector contains 320 words) that we are storing. This number overrides the length of the file as originally defined in the FORTRAN program. We must use an integral number of sectors; seven sectors will give us more words (7×320) for our file than we need, but six sectors would not give us enough. As with other names, five characters are allowed for data file names, the first a letter.

The successful establishment of this file is indicated by the printing of two numbers. In one case the numbers obtained were 1910 and 0070. The first is a disk sector address; material that was already stored in the user area determined that the sector with address 1910 was the first available sector. This address is not permanent, because the contents of the user area are repacked as programs or files are removed. (If fixed storage is desired, the fixed area can be used.) The 0070 specifies the number of disk blocks, groups of 20 words, in the file. It is in hexadecimal notation; since $10_{16} = 16_{10}$, 70 blocks constitute seven sectors. Chapter 6 discusses hexadecimal numbers. The location equivalence table will now include CLASS.

With the version 2 monitor a third item, separated from the others by the usual comma, can occur inside each pair of parentheses in the DEFINE FILE statement, the disk identification. If no disk identification is given for a file in a multidisk system, that is, if the FILES card couples the name of the file only with a FORTRAN file number, the file named is assumed to be on the master cartridge, the one containing the disk monitor system.

It is desirable to see whether the file does contain the information it is presumed to contain. Hence it is useful to have a test program, similar to our file loading program, which prints the information from the file. DUMPDATA, dumping to the line printer, is not what is wanted here, since this instruction dumps the computer words in hexadecimal. We could decode these and get the names, but this approach would be inconvenient. Figure 4–10 shows the program which will list the file items in readable form. It also illustrates the process of associating a numbered file within a FORTRAN program with a named file on disk.

We have again called the FORTRAN file 1, although we could have used a different number. This file is to be identified with the CLASS file. This association is established through the XEQ statement and the FILES state-

```
// JOB
// FORTRAN
*LIST ALL
*IOCS(1132PRINTER,DISK,TYPEWRITER)
      DEFINE FILE 1(50,40,U,NREC)
      DIMENSION NAME (13)
      DO 2 K = 1, 50
      READ(1'K)NAME
      WRITE (3,3) NAME
   3  FORMAT(' '13A2)
   2  CONTINUE
      CALL EXIT
      END
// XEQ          01
*FILES(1,CLASS)
```

FIGURE 4–10

ment following it. First, the 01 in the XEQ statement indicates that one card with execution information is to follow. Here we use a FILES card, but there are several other possibilities for execution information cards within the FORTRAN system. The FILES card associates the file 1 with the file CLASS. No embedded blanks are allowed in a FILES card, but a number of different files can be associated by using a comma between the parentheses. Thus if file 1 in a program were to be associated with a file named CLASS and file 2 were to be associated with a file named GRADE, the FILES card would look like this:

```
*FILES(1,CLASS),(2,GRADE)
```

If more than one FILES card is needed, leave a comma at the end of all except the last one:

```
*FILES(1,CLASS),(2,GRADE),
*FILES(3,CREDT)
```

The XEQ card here would indicate two FILES cards. All the supervisor control records use a comma in this way for continuation.

This completes our discussion of disk files within FORTRAN. You can easily see that a bank might keep information on its loans in a disk file; each record could contain current information about one loan, and a loan program could update the whole file each month by incorporating the monthly payments into individual records.

FORTRAN TROUBLES—DEBUGGING

CHAPTER 5

FORTRAN PROGRAMS THAT ARE TOO LONG

The beginner's FORTRAN programs are usually short, but as he becomes more experienced and bolder, his programs become longer. Sooner or later almost anyone will write a program which will be too large for the 1130; this is more likely to happen with a 4K core than with a larger memory, but even in the second case it is common.

To speak of FORTRAN programs as long is imprecise, for a program can be too long in two ways. The first is recognized during compilation of the program, while the other is noted only when the loader prepares the full program for core execution.

During the compilation of a FORTRAN program the following error message may be typed out:

    C00 WORKING STORAGE EXCEEDED

In such a case the output will be suppressed. We know that after the program is compiled, it is stored on the disk in working storage. The amount of space available for working storage depends upon the number and size of user programs in the user area. If the disk has a large number of programs already in storage, there is relatively little space left for this temporary storage of the FORTRAN program being compiled, so it is possible to exceed the available space during compilation. Errors of this kind can often be remedied by deleting from the user area programs that are no longer active, particularly if only a small amount of additional space is needed. Or another disk with more working storage available can be used.

The other length error, perhaps more common, is discovered during the loading process. During compilation of a program, no record is kept of the length of the subprograms needed, so there is no way of knowing whether the program is too long to fit into core memory. However, this information is available to the loader, which checks whether sufficient storage is available. An error message is produced if the program will not fit into core:

    R40XXXX(HEX) = ADDITIONAL CORE REQUIRED

One variant of this message indicates a particular problem associated with the COMMON area:

    R41XXX(HEX) TOO MANY WDS IN COMMON

It is possible to estimate in advance whether a FORTRAN program will fit into the memory of the computer. The information necessary for making such an estimate can be found in the IBM manual, *Core Requirements for 1130 FORTRAN*. The average FORTRAN statement generates about 14 machine-language words; the manual lists the length of the FORTRAN library programs, and examples illustrate how to calculate the lengths of FORTRAN programs. However, it is usually not necessary to make such a preliminary calculation; one can let the system determine whether the program is too long, by running the program and watching for error messages.

The program is not necessarily terminated after an R40 error message, since there are some built-in resources that may solve the problem; the system itself tries to use the disk to save space.

CLEANING UP THE PROGRAM

The programmer confronted with an overlong program wants to know what to do. His first thought may be that it is necessary to abandon the program. However, there are procedures which may allow him to carry out the desired calculation.

The first question that should be asked is this: Is the program longer than it needs to be? Novice programmers often write sloppy programs, and a careful analysis of the program may show that much space can be saved, either in storage or in the program. One of their most common extravagances is their tendency to choose very large arrays, without considering how much storage will be required. Thus a program which contains at the beginning the statement

    DIMENSION X(200,200)

is asking the machine to set up storage for 40,000 real variables, occupying (with standard precision) 80,000 words of storage. This will be impossible on most 1130's, for no standard configuration has this much core memory. The novice programmer may find that little or none of this dimensioned storage is essential for the working of the program and that, by slight rewriting, he can make the program fit comfortably into core. Or it may be necessary to establish a disk file to hold it. There may be other aspects of the program that need to be cleaned up; almost no program is as efficient in the use of space as it might be.

An interesting and instructive example of how a FORTRAN program can be cleaned up so that it both occupies less space and works more efficiently is included in the IBM manual *1130 FORTRAN Programming Techniques*. This manual also discusses many of the tricks for running long programs mentioned here.

Sometimes minor differences in writing programs lead to considerable differences when the programs are executed, both in storage requirements and in time. This is particularly true in FORTRAN, where the compiler sees the program differently than the human programmer sees it.

For example, consider the two following statements:

A = 0.
A = 0

Most FORTRAN programmers would consider these statements to be functionally the same. The decimal point identifies the first zero as a real or floating-point zero, while the other zero is an integer. The A, unless specified otherwise in a data type statement, is a real variable. The second sentence assumes, usually correctly, that variable types are converted across the equals sign; this is true in 1130 FORTRAN, but this conversion process involves a subroutine not needed in the first statement.

Counting of 1130 instructions shows that the statement A = 0. requires the execution of 40 machine-language instructions, while the statement A = 0 requires the execution of 58. Although 18 machine-language instructions, each executed at microsecond speed, do not waste a great deal of time, if the sentence occurs in a loop executed many times in a program, a noticeable saving might be realized by the explicit presence of the decimal point. There is also likely to be a saving of space. Hence, the wise programmer, in spite of the available FORTRAN conversion, will include the decimal point on the right-hand side, to work toward optimizing his program.

FACILITIES FOR LONG FORTRAN PROGRAMS

A resource in the FORTRAN language which we have not yet discussed is particularly useful for long programs. It often happens that certain variables are needed in only part of the program calculation. Then the same space in core can be *shared* by several different variables. Suppose, for example, that two two-dimensional arrays, A and B, are specified by the following dimension statement:

DIMENSION A(50,50), B(50,50)

Suppose further that whenever one of these arrays is in use, the other is not needed. Then one can use them at separate times in the same core area, thus saving 5000 words. The following statements, which must precede any executable statements, and be in this order, accomplish this.

DIMENSION A(50,50), B(50,50)
EQUIVALENCE (A(1), B(1))

With these specifications the two matrices A and B could both be used, but only one core storage area would be reserved. Naturally the program would have to take this into account. One could not expect to find values of the first matrix in core just after the second matrix had been used unless the first matrix had then been reentered by the program, because the new values are written over the old values. EQUIVALENCE also has other uses in programming; for example, with alphameric data it is convenient to make integer and real arrays equivalent, so that the data can be referenced either way.

We can also save space within a program, particularly if much variable storage is needed, by storing data on the disk, using the DEFINE FILE statement; we have already seen how to do this. For programs requiring very large quantities of data the use of the disk is almost essential.

LINKED PROGRAMS

All these techniques save storage space in core memory. But even after we have saved all possible storage by careful rewriting of the program and elimination of unnecessary details, it is conceivable that the program is still too long. There are at least two procedures that permit us to run even a long program; both, however, also increase the running time.

The first technique is particularly useful if the program naturally falls into a series of separate pieces. The strategy is to write the program as a series of separate FORTRAN main programs and to *link* them together. Every program except the last will contain a FORTRAN statement whose purpose is to bring the next program into core. This statement takes the following form:

CALL LINK (name of the next program segment)

Suppose, for example, that the main program was named STEP1, the second program STEP2, and the third program STEP3. Then STEP1 would contain the following statement:

CALL LINK (STEP2)

and the STEP2 program would include this statement:

CALL LINK (STEP3)

The flow of control can be seen easily in Fig. 5–1 where we use the FORTRAN control card *NAME to show the name of each piece. All the pieces except possibly the first are stored by name on disk, and therefore they are listed in the location equivalence table. The first program is entered by one of the usual techniques, and it calls the next one by means of a LINK statement.

If programs are linked in this fashion, one precaution is necessary. When the new program is loaded, the old program, including most of its storage, is wiped out. But presumably some of the data calculated in the first program will be needed in the next stage. Only one part of the core memory, the COMMON area, is preserved during such transitions; thus any information to be used in the next link must be stored in COMMON in *both* links. Variables stored in the same position in COMMON in the two programs are effectively equivalent. As in subprograms, COMMON provides for communication between linked programs. (This precaution concerns only core memory. All data on disk, including any in working storage, are unaffected.)

There is no limit to the number of programs that can be linked. If many programs needing a carry-over of data are linked, the COMMON area will be heavily used, since it must bring the data from the last link and carry the data to the next. Remember that all the programs except the first must be stored on disk before the calculation begins. Each will be brought into core by the loader when needed, so execution is slower than with a single program. Storing the links in core image form will increase speed of execution but will also increase disk space requirements.

Although we have talked about the sequence of linked programs as if it were a strict linear sequence, linkage can occur within a program instead of at its end, with the timing of the actual link depending on calculations within that program; there might be several CALL LINK statements leading to different programs being called during different executions.

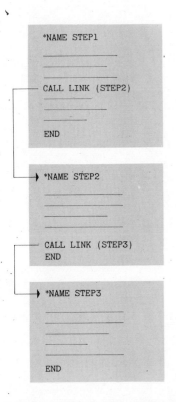

FIG. 5-1. Three "linked" programs.

LOCAL SUBPROGRAMS

Another important space-saving method is the use of the LOCAL specification. The strategy here is to group subprograms and allocate space in core memory only for the longest program in the group. Each subprogram is brought in from disk to the allocated space in core as needed. Although this procedure leads to a slower execution of the program, it may enable us to run programs not possible without this facility. It contrasts with the usual procedure, in which all the subprograms necessary for a given program are loaded into core before execution of the program starts. Here the loader or core load builder *prepares* all the subprograms, as usual, but those specified on LOCAL cards are held in working storage on disk, ready to be transferred to core as needed.

Suppose a given program needs two subprograms, BOY and GIRL, but that BOY is needed only in the early stage of the program and GIRL is needed only in a later stage. The program is too long, so the programmer must find a way to save core space. Since only one "swap" will be necessary under the circumstances, a LOCAL usage seems reasonable. The following cards after the program, replacing the usual XEQ card, would accomplish this.

```
1        8       17
|        |        |
//bXEQ           1
*LOCAL,BOY,GIRL                (no embedded blanks)
```

Columns 16 and 17 of the XEQ card indicate the card count (right-justified) of supervisor control records to follow, just as with the FILES records (see p. 39). BOY and GIRL would be prepared for core, but held in working storage on disk. Each would be loaded when called; a single area of core would accommodate both separately called subroutines.

The preceding example assumes that the main program to be executed has just been compiled and is in working storage on disk. If the program is stored in the user or fixed area on disk, this not only affects the XEQ card, as we already know, but also leads to a change in the LOCAL card. The following sequence could be used in these circumstances with a main program named CHILD.

```
1        8       17
|        |        |
//bXEQbCHILD     1
*LOCALCHILD,BOY,GIRL
```

Comparing these two cases, we find that the main program's name is listed just after the word LOCAL if the program is called from the user or fixed area on disk. A comma immediately following the word LOCAL and omission of the main program's name indicate that the program is in working storage. No embedded blanks are allowed in a LOCAL statement; the relative freedom in the way other FORTRAN statements can be written is not permitted in a LOCAL statement. CHILD, the main program, is always in core during execution, but only BOY or GIRL is there at one time.

If an XEQ card has an L in column 14, a core map showing the location of subprograms in core is produced. The local programs are indicated in this map by the word LOCAL following the core address. All the programs called by a LOCAL program are also treated as LOCALs.

There are restrictions on what programs can be used as LOCAL. Generally any user-written subroutine can be used. Functions, however, whether user-written or system-provided, are not allowed as LOCAL. Many of the system subroutines can be used as LOCALs to save space. For example, if two (or more) input/output routines are needed, one to run the typewriter and one to run the line printer, it is possible to use LOCAL. We can see that knowledge of the system beyond that mentioned so far becomes more and more necessary as one wants to use the LOCAL facilities. If a FORTRAN program is compiled with a LIST ALL or LIST SUBPROGRAM NAMES control card preceding it, we obtain a list of needed subprograms. This is useful in deciding which programs to use as LOCALs.

Another restriction on the use of LOCAL cards is dictated by the need to avoid logical tangles. Often a given subprogram calls other programs. LOCAL cards must take this into account. Thus if the program HORSE called the program COW it would not be reasonable to use HORSE and COW on one LOCAL card.

A comma at the end of a LOCAL card means that the next card is a continuation. The two records

*LOCAL,SUBP1,SUBP2,
*LOCALSUBP3

are equivalent to

*LOCAL,SUBP1,SUBP2,SUBP3

The CALL LINK and LOCAL facilities can be combined. Figure 5–2 gives an example of a short, trivial program which illustrates their joint use. We note that the two different LOCAL cards refer to two different main programs which are joined by a linking statement. Thus the first two subprograms, FSTO and WRTYZ, will be LOCAL in program P1, and the two subprograms mentioned on the second LOCAL card will be LOCAL in program P10. One can see this clearly by using an XEQ with an L in column 14. The core map produced before loading the first program contains the information about the location in core memory of all the subprograms of that program, including its LOCALs, while the core map for the second program is generated only when that program is called by the linking statement.

The monitor system also has built-in facilities for creating LOCAL programs. If the loader discovers that your FORTRAN program is too long for core, it creates system-generated locals, called SOCAL (system overlays). The monitor manual discusses which subprograms are used in system overlays, but a user who is not concerned with the details can allow the system to do the work for him. Messages identify the overlays created. If you specify in a LOCAL card a program that would have been involved in a system overlay, the LOCAL card takes precedence.

Both LOCAL and EQUIVALENCE facilities lead to sharing of space in core memory. However, with EQUIVALENCE several *data items* share the same locations, but with LOCAL several *subprograms* share storage space in core. Furthermore, EQUIVALENCE does not use the disk, whereas LOCALs are kept on disk until the particular subprogram is needed in core.

It should now be apparent that considerable resources are available to the programmer for running long FORTRAN programs.

```
// JOB  T
// FOR
*IOCS(TYPEWRITER)
*LIST SOURCE PROGRAM
      A = EXP(2.)
      B= ABS(2.)
      WRITE(1, 2) A, B
2     FORMAT(2F5.2)
      CALL EXIT
      END


// DUP

*STORE        WS  UA  P10


// FORTRAN
*IOCS(TYPEWRITER)
*LIST SOURCE PROGRAM
      A = SIN(2.)
      B = COS (2.)
      WRITE (1, 2) A,B
2     FORMAT(2F5.2)
      CALL LINK( P10)
      END


// DUP

*STORE        WS  UA  P1


// XEQ P1        2
*LOCALP1,FSTO,WRTYZ
*LOCALP10,FGETP,SCOMP
```

FIG. 5–2. LOCAL cards with linked programs.

DEBUGGING IN FORTRAN

We had an introduction to the process of *debugging*, or finding errors in programs, in our discussion of the loan program. That debugging is necessary often comes as a surprise to the beginning programmer; he feels that after he learns the details of the language he should be able to write programs without errors. But the experienced programmer knows that almost any program other than the simplest will not work when first written.

Much of the working programmer's time goes toward making programs work as they are supposed to work. Debugging is an art, partly dependent on the facilities available in the language being used. In this section we discuss the error-correction techniques for 1130 FORTRAN. Later we will consider debugging assembler-language programs; some of these techniques can also be used within FORTRAN by the experienced programmer.

With the loan program the first indication of trouble was the printing of error messages after compilation. The correction of such syntactical errors is the first order of business. As we have seen, these messages do not necessarily give a direct clue to the source of trouble; some errors will automatically lead to other errors. Even the more sophisticated compilers used with large computers cannot always indicate accurately the cause of the error, but they can always determine when the grammatical rules of the language have been violated and therefore where ambiguities exist. If nothing else, the error messages from the 1130 FORTRAN compiler identify at least some of the troublesome statements. Usually these errors are relatively easy to correct.

After the program has been successfully compiled, the next stage in which messages may indicate trouble comes after the machine reads the XEQ card, but before it enters the program. The most obvious difficulty, already discussed, is that the program may be too long to fit into core. The loader error list contains other possible error messages.

RECOGNIZING TROUBLES

Undoubtedly the most serious difficulties, the hardest to pin down, are those that occur during execution of the program. How do you know you are in trouble at all, if the program appears to "run"? Presumably your program is supposed to accomplish something, to produce some output. If you do not get this output, then you can rightfully conclude that the program is not behaving as intended. Here the presence of difficulties is obvious.

Sometimes asterisks will be printed or typed, instead of the numbers expected. This indicates that the numbers could not fit into the space allowed in the FORMAT specification. The problem may be only an improper FORMAT statement. However, if the printed results are far from the expected range, it may well be that the program does not accomplish the intended task. We have seen an example of this in the improper statement for interest calculation in the loan program.

There may be still other signs of trouble. First, the computer may come to a halt because it has encountered an instruction which cannot be executed. To recognize this you must consult the lights on the 1130 console. The row of five lights in the upper right-hand corner of the panel represent the *operation register*, showing the type of machine-language instruction being executed at a given moment. During a normal stop, lights 2 and 3 will be on, indicating a legitimate WAIT instruction. (You can tell when the computer stops because the console lights are then steady and bright instead of flickering, and the RUN light is off.) If the operation register does not show a WAIT, the pause is abnormal; it was not intended to occur and it indicates that something is wrong with your program. Since most of the possible combinations of operation register lights do correspond to instructions, stopping because of an illegal operation code is relatively rare except for the case of the instruction with code "zero" (all lights off).

Even legitimate WAITs are sometimes indications of trouble. Perhaps the most commonly encountered one arises from problems concerning input and output. In 1130 FORTRAN, if the input or output does not correspond in type to the format specifications, or if there are troubles with the IOCS card, the system goes to a WAIT. In addition to lights 2 and 3 in the operation register indicating a WAIT, the 16 lights on the left-hand side of the panel, which show the contents of the *accumulator register*, are also critical in detecting I/O errors. Whenever there is a FORTRAN I/O problem, the four lights on the left-hand end of the accumulator will all be on in a hexadecimal configuration representing the F in the table of FORTRAN I/O error halts, in Appendix A-7. The other accumulator lights, with each vertical group of four lights constituting one hexadecimal digit, indicate the precise I/O problem identified in the table. When PROGRAM START is pushed after a FORTRAN I/O error WAIT, the program is terminated, and control is returned to the monitor program.

Incidentally, we can also use this "error" to exit from a FORTRAN program. Suppose that the FORTRAN program calls for typewriter input. When the computer reaches this point in the program, the KEYBOARD SELECT light, near the keyboard, comes on. If we wish to leave the program when the KEYBOARD SELECT light is on, we type "nonsense," that is, anything not acceptable as data. For example, if the format specification calls for a number to be entered, in the E, F, or I format, then typing alphabetic characters will lead to a FORTRAN I/O error, and when START is pressed, control is returned to the monitor program.

Other WAITs may also indicate errors. For example, some subroutine failures, particularly with input/output subroutines, produce error exits. But these are relatively less common. Appendix A–7 gives further information concerning computer action after I/O errors.

Other types of unexpected and undesired behavior can also occur. A common problem, sometimes identifiable by a careful study of the console lights, is an uncontrolled loop. Often within normal computing processes the computer loops many, many times through one set of instructions. A conditional branching statement should eventually cause an exit from the loop. However, because of programming errors, the conditions for exiting from the loop may never be satisfied, and therefore the loop is performed over and over again without end.

A loop is visible as a steady flickering of the console lights, but some nonloops may also give this appearance. During a loop the lights may appear to be unchanging, but a comparison with the brightness of the lights when the computer is halted will show that there is a dimming during the loop. If one wants to be certain that a loop is in progress, one can put the mode switch on SI, single instruction execute. The lights will shift to a steady, strong pattern indicating a single instruction; then each time PROGRAM START is pushed, the computer will execute just one instruction. In the case of a *very* small loop, one might wish to see how many instructions it takes to get through the loop by observing the different numbers in the operation register until the pattern is repeated. To resume regular operation, one returns the mode switch to RUN and presses PROGRAM START.

However, the number of instructions in a loop is seldom important; what is important is to know whether or not the computer is in an unintended loop. Unfortunately there is no completely unambiguous way to determine this. Some knowledge of the program will help; if you know that you have used a DO statement which will execute a part of the program 500 times, you *expect* a long loop before the exit. On the other hand, if the lights indicate a long loop when no highly repetitive calculation is called for in your program, trouble with branching conditions is likely.

One type of error indication can be rather upsetting to the novice. Difficulties connected with input and output routines will sometimes lead to the feeding of paper, either on the console printer or on the line printer. Paper suddenly flows from one of these devices at a rapid rate! Usually, because of the interrupt system of the computer, PROGRAM STOP will be of no avail. The only button that is likely to help in this situation is IMMEDIATE STOP. In some situations the use of IMMEDIATE

STOP may result in loss of information, making it necessary to begin the program again. Particular care should be taken not to use this button during input-output operations, unless essential.

HIDDEN TROUBLES

So far our concern has been with recognizing the more obvious causes of trouble. The most insidious errors are not those we have described; they occur in situations where everything appears to be normal. The program compiles, loads, runs, produces output, and exits to the monitor program. Under these conditions the tendency is strong to believe that everything must be satisfactory. However, we must learn to be cautious in all situations. How can we be sure that the computer is actually doing the intended computation?

With the loan program there was a simple inherent way of determining whether the computer was doing what we intended it to do. The first time the program was run, the final loan balance was a large negative sum rather than zero, a sure indication that something was wrong in the program. Often, however, there will be no obvious way of determining whether the calculation is reasonable.

As a first step in checking the results, the programmer should give careful thought to what output he expects: the range of the numbers, the relative ordering of the data, etc. This consideration may be only a quick guess, or it may be based on rough hand calculations. It is always wise to have such an estimate in mind in any problem-solving activity, with or without the computer. In many situations it is possible to make a guess with relatively little work. Then the output can be inspected to see whether it corresponds reasonably to the rough guess. The importance of this procedure cannot be overstressed; it is all too easy to write grammatically correct programs which generate nothing but "garbage."

The programmer can also test whether his program is functioning properly by adding an internal check, even though there is no natural one in the program. It is impossible to give any general advice here, because such checks must depend on the nature of the problem, but one example may be helpful. Suppose that we are computing the motion of a satellite, with a program based on Newton's laws of motion. There are other physical principles which apply to such a motion; the total energy is always the same, for example. By writing into the program a computation of the total energy at occasional stages of the program and printing the results, we can obtain a basis for judging the accuracy of the calculation. This example pertains specifically to mechanics, but the ingenious programmer can often invent some method of internal testing.

However, it is often true that only hand calculations will show that the program is doing what is expected. Although the popular literature on computers tends to picture them as allowing us to escape from performing calculations, the serious user of a computer quickly discovers that the human calculator is still essential. In many instances the only guarantee that the program is performing properly comes from choosing some simple data and performing a few hand calculations. If these calculations are to check the program, obviously they must use calculational procedures that are the same as those in the program.

Fortunately, we do not need to carry out the complete calculation intended for the computer! This would indeed be silly, but if we compute directly a few cases and compare these with the computer output in the same situations, then we have greater faith in the efficacy of the program. The choice of data for the trial hand calculation is important. The tendency is to use very simple data, to make the computation easier. For instance, in the satellite problem we might calculate initial conditions for a perfectly circular orbit and use this case as a check. However, for a case that is too uncharacteristic, that is, too simple, the computer answers may agree with the hand calculation, whereas more complex data might not produce agreement. Again, as with many aspects of debugging, the "correct" choice of trial data is an art rather than a science, depending heavily on the experience of the programmer.

FINDING FORTRAN TROUBLES

Knowing that there are difficulties and finding the precise cause of them are two quite different operations. Sometimes the nature of the difficulty leads directly to the cause, as with the loan program. But for the vast majority of programs, debugging is more complicated.

Several conceptual tools are very useful in the error-finding process. Perhaps the most important was used in connection with the loan program. A program often has a complex branching structure, with many IF and computed GO TO statements which send the calculation off in various directions under various conditions. If one has only the written program to deal with, it is easy to be confused by the intricacies of the various loops involved. It is therefore advisable to produce a *flow chart* of the program.

The flow chart is a diagrammatic representation of the operation to be performed. Such a diagram can give complete detail, showing every instruction in the entire program, or it can be a skeleton-like specification of the general flow of the program. Particularly when a program has been modified many times, the flow chart helps to provide an overall view of the nature of the operation;

study of it will often indicate branching errors. In some systems it is possible to produce flow charts on the line printer or other output device directly from the program. However, at the moment such a procedure is not commonly available for the 1130, so we must rely on humans to make flow charts. There are standard symbols for flow charts, but so far as the present writer can see, there seems to be no vital significance in this standardization for most computer users, and the charts presented in Chapters 1 and 2 do not use standard symbols.

One simple device often useful in examining a FORTRAN program to find errors is the PAUSE command, bringing the computer to the WAIT state; pressing PROGRAM START resumes the execution of the program. If in an attempt to isolate the cause of error we want to determine whether a calculation ever reaches a particular place in the program, we can insert a PAUSE statement at that point when compiling the program. It is convenient to have PAUSE cards available to insert when needed.

One might legitimately wonder when the WAIT occurs whether it is due to that PAUSE or to an error condition. Again FORTRAN provides a resource for the user. If a four-digit number is written after the PAUSE on the FORTRAN card, this number is entered in the accumulator just before the WAIT. Each vertical group of four lights in the accumulator register on console corresponds to one digit in the number. Thus one can sprinkle a number of PAUSE commands in the program, each with a different identifying number, and thereby tell which PAUSE is which. The STOP statement can also have an identifying number to be displayed in the accumulator, but STOP causes an exit from the program when PROGRAM START is pushed.

TRACING 1130 FORTRAN

One of the most useful procedures for finding errors in computer programs is *tracing*. This takes several forms. Usually a FORTRAN program prints only the values of variables explicitly requested in WRITE statements. However, if there is trouble, it may be very helpful to obtain intermediate values to check that the calculation is proceeding as a hand calculation has shown that it should proceed. One might want to know the results calculated in all arithmetic statements, or in some selected subclass of particularly critical statements. We could do this with additional WRITE statements, but a built-in facility is available for this procedure.

The use of FORTRAN control record,

```
*ARITHMETIC TRACE
```

after the //bFOR card and before the beginning of the program causes the compiler to generate trace instructions for each arithmetic statement in the program. Tracing is controlled by switch 15 on the console. During execution, if console switch 15 is off, the program gives only the output requested within the program, performing as it would without the TRACE card. However, when switch 15 is turned on, the result of each arithmetic statement (the number that will be stored in the location indicated by the left-hand side of the statement) is printed. (If the IOCS card did not specify the printer, or if there is no printer in the system, the traced numbers are typed.) An arithmetic trace result is preceded by a single asterisk. If the output is used with a listing of the program, we can follow the action of the program and determine whether it is performing as expected.

Another extremely useful form of this facility, the *transfer trace*, concerns not the arithmetic statements but the conditional branching statements, the IF and computed GO TO statements. Since branching statements alter the flow of a program, complicated branching possibilities are a likely source of such programming errors as uncontrolled loops. Hence it is useful to know what decision is made each time a branching statement is encountered. To accomplish this, one uses the FORTRAN control card

```
*TRANSFER TRACE
```

to instruct the computer to generate transfer trace instructions. Just as before, the program will perform as usual, that is, with no trace output, if switch 15 is off during execution. But, if switch 15 is turned on at any time, the value of the expression in parentheses in any IF statement and the value of the integer variable in any computed GO TO will be printed, preceded by two and three asterisks respectively. Arithmetic and transfer trace can be used together, if desired.

The subroutine calls

```
CALL TSTOP
CALL TSTRT
```

are effective for both arithmetic trace and transfer trace, and they limit tracing to just part of the program. When CALL TSTOP appears in the program, the instructions following it are immune from tracing, even if switch 15 is on. On the other hand, an occurrence of CALL TSTRT returns tracing control to switch 15. Thus, if one wanted to trace only a small portion of the program, one could first use the appropriate TRACE card or cards before the program, then place a CALL TSTOP card at the beginning of the program, and CALL TSTRT and CALL TSTOP cards setting off the section to be traced. In this situation, if switch 15 is on, only the segment of the program between CALL TSTRT and CALL TSTOP will be traced. It should be remembered that the order of the program is

the order in which it is actually executed, rather than just the order of the statements. If switch 15 is off, the program runs as if no tracing were demanded. Thus it is possible, without activating switch 15 each time, to watch what is happening in a small group of statements. However, selective tracing can also be accomplished by the use of PAUSE statements and switch 15.

Tracing is most effective when combined with hand calculations following the flow of the program for a few selected cases. It enables the programmer to check whether or not the calculation is proceeding as he expects it to proceed. However, it is necessary to avoid too much tracing in a program; one can quickly obtain so much output with trace facilities that the sheer bulk of material is impractical.

Version 2 has a FORTRAN subroutine which is particularly useful in debugging procedures, the PDUMP subroutine. This allows another type of selective tracing. To illustrate its use, consider that at some stage in the program we should like to dump two one-dimensional arrays, a real array of 10 numbers called FAY, and an integer array of 15 numbers called KAY. The following statement in the FORTRAN program would lead to the dumping of these two arrays on the principal print device:

```
CALL PDUMP (FAY(1),FAY(10),5,KAY(1),KAY(15),4)
```

Here the 4 indicates integer format for the output, and 5 indicates real format. We could dump both arrays in a real (or integer) format, in spite of their different internal storage methods. Each sequence of three calling parameters corresponds to one group of data to be printed; the first two parameters specify two "ends" in storage, and the third parameter specifies the format. For hexadecimal format use zero for the third parameter.

BINARY ARITHMETIC PROBLEMS

Perhaps no problems are more bewildering to beginning programmers than those that come about because computer arithmetic differs from "human" arithmetic. Later we shall investigate the details of how the computer stores and manipulates numbers. For the moment we are concerned with some consequences of this difference that may seem strange.

Consider the following program:

```
    V = 0.
1   V = V + .1
    WRITE (1,2) V
2   FORMAT (F4.1)
    IF (V - .9) 1, 3, 3
3   CALL EXIT
    END
```

This seems to be a quite straightforward, if somewhat trivial, program. However, its output may well be surprising:

```
0.1
0.2
0.3
0.3
0.4
0.5
0.6
0.7
0.8
0.9
```

This looks most peculiar indeed. The first impression is that the computer failed to add during one of the steps in the program; our immediate suspicion is that there may have been a machine failure. However, if we run this program over and over, we find these results consistently. There is another related peculiarity. Our expectation might well be that with this IF statement, nine lines should be printed. But there are ten lines, with one line apparently printed twice.

Some insight can be obtained if we make one slight program alteration to print more decimal places. If we replace the FORMAT statement above by this statement,

2   FORMAT (F10.7)

then the output looks like this:

```
0.1000000
0.2000000
0.3000000
0.3999999
0.4999999
0.5999999
0.6999998
0.7999997
0.8999995
0.9999995
```

These values are closer to the values stored in the machine.

Now we can see more clearly what is happening. The number which the computer stores for the .1 in statement 1 is not an exact equivalent of .1 but rather the best approximation the computer is capable of, using its internal arrangement for storing numbers. (The problem here is similar to that of trying to express $\frac{1}{3}$ as a finite decimal fraction.) Internal storage is binary rather than decimal, and some numbers, even when they can be expressed exactly as decimal numbers, do not have an exact representation as binary numbers. Furthermore, routines used for real arithmetic can introduce inac-

curacies. Hence small errors may be introduced in each calculation, and these errors may eventually become significant.

With this new insight into what is happening, you can also see why the problem with the IF statement occurs. When statement 1 is executed for the ninth time, we expect that V will be .9 and that the IF statement will cause a branch to EXIT. But because of the approximations, V is then actually .8999995, or very slightly *less* than .9. Hence the desired branch does not occur, because the quantity in parentheses is still slightly less than zero, and an additional line is printed.

There is another aspect of the way the computer operates, and particularly of the way FORTRAN prints numbers, that is of great interest in connection with this little problem. Consider, for example, the fifth line. You can see that the decimal representation of the number is approximately 0.4999999. But in the first printout, the number actually printed was 0.4. It is clear that in the print operation, there is no rounding off. When you request one decimal place, all additional decimal places in the number are simply chopped off. If it is desirable to have numbers that are rounded in the usual fashion, the programmer must do this within the program.

Let us return to our trivial program and alter it to make it actually do what we want it to do. We will add a .05 to each quantity before printing, in order to perform any appropriate round off. The program doing this is shown in Fig. 5–3, and the output would now be what we probably expected the first time.

Just as in the case of our initial troubles with the loan program, we can sometimes overcome problems associated with binary arithmetic by using extended precision rather than standard precision. Then a greater number of significant binary places is retained, and there is less inaccuracy. We could also solve the problem by setting up an integer variable which is first incremented by 1, and then divided by 10 in each loop.

The reader may want to reread this section after the discussion of binary numbers in the next chapter.

```
// JOB
// FORTRAN
*LIST ALL
*IOCS (TYPEWRITER, 1132 PRINTER )
      V = 0.
    1 V = V + .1
      W = V + .05
      WRITE (1, 2) W
    2 FORMAT (F4.1)
      IF (W - .9) 1, 3, 3
    3 CALL EXIT
      END
```

FIGURE 5–3

OVERFLOW ERRORS

Because the computer can store information only in finite chunks, any number stored, integer or real, is limited in value. The limitations are different for integers and reals. For integers the maximum positive value that can be used in FORTRAN is 32,767 and the negative limit is −32,768. (After the next chapter you should be able to understand why these numbers are not the same.) For real numbers the absolute value can range between approximately 10^{38} and 10^{-38}.

Simple calculations can easily exceed these limits. The fact that the numbers are out of the allowable range may not be obvious, because an intermediate result in a computation may exceed 10^{38} even when the final result would be below the allowable limit. The value of the final output would be affected in such a case. In 1130 FORTRAN subroutines, when the computer generates a number larger than it is capable of storing, it sets the variable to the largest possible value. If the number is too small, the variable is set to zero. So the "true" value will be altered during the calculation, and the answer will not be correct.

An example may be useful. Consider the following simple FORTRAN program:

```
X = 1.E25
Y = 1.E30
Z = 1.E35
Q = ( X*Y + Z) / X
CALL EXIT
END
```

A hand calculation quickly shows that Q should be about 10^{30}, inside the allowable range. But running the program in trace mode produces a surprise! The value actually calculated for Q is

$$.1701412 \times 10^{14}$$

The difference arises because X*Y gives a number that is too large, so the result of this calculation is set to the maximum value.

The FORTRAN subroutines which carry out real arithmetic are written so that they set an indicator word in a special location in core when overflow problems occur. It is possible to interrogate this word within the program, by the use of the subroutine OVERFL. The CALL statement is

```
CALL OVERFL (J)
```

where J is a variable to be returned from the subroutine, with a value dependent on the overflow indicator. If

overflow has occurred in a calculation, J is set equal to 1 by OVERFL; if no overflow has occurred, J is set to 2. A computed GO TO following such a CALL statement, checking the current value of J, could send control to an error section of the program if overflow occurs. (The 1130 FORTRAN subroutines do not themselves generate an error message on overflow, but only set this indicator word.) This same subroutine also checks for an underflow, an arithmetic result smaller than about 10^{-38}. Then J is set equal to 3. The overflow indicator is reset after this subroutine has been executed, so another call to the subroutine may give different values for J unless an overflow has subsequently occurred.

We can write a skeleton program to make use of this internal facility:

```
       :
    CALL OVERFL (L)
    GO TO (10,20,30), L
10  WRITE (3,40)
40  FORMAT (' OVERFLOW')
    GO TO 20
30  WRITE (3,50)
50  FORMAT (' UNDERFLOW')
20  (Next program starts)
       :
```

We could also write this as a subroutine:

```
    SUBROUTINE OFLOW
    CALL OVERFL(L)
    GO TO (10,20,30), L
10  WRITE (3,40)
40  FORMAT (' OVERFLOW')
    RETURN
30  WRITE (3,50)
50  FORMAT (' UNDERFLOW')
20  RETURN
    END
```

Note the use of several RETURN statements for exits from the subroutine. Thus we would need only a

```
CALL OFLOW
```

card wherever we want to check for overflow or underflow. This simple subroutine would not indicate where the trouble occurred, but with only slightly more programming it would be possible to locate the trouble spot.

If you know that the numbers you will be getting in your program are well within the allowable range, such checking is superfluous. However, for calculations in which the values might become very large or very small, checking of this kind can be a useful debugging procedure. Tracing also can be used to check partially for overflow or underflow.

DIVISION BY ZERO

Another useful FORTRAN subroutine checks for attempts to divide by zero. The appropriate CALL statement is the following:

CALL DVCHK (J)

J is set to 1 if the division-by-zero indicator is on, to 2 if it is off. The indicator is turned off after the subroutine. Division by zero is a relatively minor problem, but it is sometimes useful to check. If an attempt is made in real arithmetic to divide by zero, no division occurs and the number is unaltered.

COMMON PROBLEMS IN FORTRAN PROGRAMS

It is impossible to foresee all the errors that a programmer may make in a FORTRAN program. We can, however, mention a few problems that will present difficulties to programmers. Some of these will plague the novice, others even the experienced person.

Perhaps the most common trouble encountered by a novice is due to his failure to use the asterisk for multiplication. Any programmer familiar with the algebraic convention of indicating the multiplication of two quantities by writing them next to each other easily slips into this error. Suppose, for example, a beginner wants to multiply *A* and *V*; he might write the FORTRAN statement

C = AV

A FORTRAN compiler, however, has a different view of this statement; it regards AV as a variable name and tries to set C equal to the value of the variable AV. Since the statement is grammatically correct, it would generate no compiler error message, but it will not do what the writer intends it to do, and the result when the program is run will be unsatisfactory.

This error is also common when one or both of the factors are enclosed by parentheses. Someone coming into FORTRAN with a background of algebra might be tempted to write the following statement:

F = (A + B) (C + D)

The compiler would now generate an error message, because this is not a grammatically proper FORTRAN statement.

Only the beginning programmer is likely to make the above mistake, and he is not likely to make it too many times in his career. But as his programs become more complex, other types of problems occur. He may, for example, forget what statement numbers he has used and attempt to use the same one on different statements. The compiler will catch an error of this kind.

Another frequent error (not found by the compiler, since it is not a syntax problem) is the unintentional use of one variable for two different purposes within a program. Occasionally the same variable name will be used to represent different values in different parts of one program, in order to save storage space. But this can be done only when the several values so named are not needed simultaneously in the program. What we are here concerned with is an unintentional use of the same variable in two different senses, with the result that the variable has values in part of the calculation that it is not intended to have. This mistake is relatively easy to avoid in the initial writing of a program, but troublesome when the program, particularly if complicated, is altered during the debugging process.

Still another common problem concerns dimensioned variables. When a variable is initially dimensioned, space in memory is set aside by the compiler. But the program does not check to see that we stay within this space! Thus if we have DIMENSION X(20), the computer will nonetheless accept a reference to X (22), retrieving the value from or storing it in a place reserved for other things. Thus the introduction of a variable too large for its dimensioned area will "eat up" material stored outside the intended range, and eventually troubles are almost bound to result. If one suspects this difficulty, statements can be inserted in the program to print the subscript for a subscripted variable each time the variable is encountered, or an IF statement can be added to see whether the subscript stays within range. Tracing might also be useful. It would be possible, as you probably realize, to design the FORTRAN program to make a range check whenever presented with a subscripted variable. However, since this would increase the time for running such a program, checking for range is usually done by the programmer rather than by machine. A FORTRAN program which suddenly ceases to run while executing a loop that involves dimensioned variables may be in this type of trouble.

Insufficient attention to switch settings is a human error often committed by beginners. It happens frequently enough to deserve explicit mention. Usually a switch setting is used to alter the flow of a program. For example, a switch may return control to the beginning of the program for new values to be entered for another run. But the careless user may forget to turn off the switch which initiated this return; thus he finds control thrown back again almost immediately to the beginning of the program—not his intent. A program that checks a switch setting should include some kind of halt after the switch is checked, to allow time for resetting. This halt might be a READ (from the keyboard) statement, or it might be a PAUSE.

We now discuss a programming difficulty experienced, although under somewhat different circumstances, by both the beginning and the experienced programmer. Before a variable can be used in a program it must be *initialized*, that is, it must be given some value. Otherwise the computer will accept for its value whatever garbage happens to be stored in that particular location at that particular time. There are only two ways to initialize variables: by input or by using the variable on the left-hand side of an arithmetic assignment statement. The first use of any variable within the FORTRAN program should be in a statement of one of these two types. (Version 2 monitor also allows the DATA statement for initialization.)

One might think that the compiler could check to see if the variable was initialized. Some checking is possible; the 1130 compiler lists unreferenced variables after compilation. But it is impossible to check for all possibilities during the compilation process, because the question of whether a variable has been initialized or not depends on the flow of the particular program. There is a difference in sequence between the FORTRAN statements on paper or cards and the *execution* of these statements, whenever branching statements are included. Consequently, the compiler is not always in a position to determine whether a variable has been initialized, especially when the program is complex. The FORTRAN program itself can be written so that such checking is done internally, and some FORTRAN systems have provided this facility, but the extra overhead for all programs is usually considered unwarranted. An 1130 compiled FORTRAN program does not check on initialization before a variable is used during a computation. Hence the burden of checking, if necessary, falls on the programmer.

A particularly catastrophic form of this initialization problem (in terms of unexpected results) can occur with subscripts. An uninitialized subscript may well lead to quite disastrous results; the array element may be referenced far outside the intended storage area, destroying everything in its path.

Tracing is often helpful in spotting the failure to initialize a variable, simply because it shows the variable as having a value quite different from that expected. Careful study of a logical flow chart will often aid the programmer to make sure that every variable is initialized before use.

DATA STORAGE

CHAPTER 6

COMPUTER STORAGE AND NUMBER SYSTEMS

We have discussed two kinds of storage used by the computer, the core memory for fast storage, and the disks for bulk storage, but we have not yet considered in detail how this storage takes place. We are not here concerned with the operation of the computer's circuitry, but rather with the manner in which mathematical and symbolic entities are directly represented in the computer's electronic hardware.

In the 1130, the memory, both core and disk, is divided into *words of fixed length*. Fixed-word-length memory is perhaps the most common, although many of the computers used for business purposes have a different organization, referred to as variable word length. Every word in the core memory has a unique address which the computer can use to find or store a unit of data. (The first word's address is 0, not 1.)

The disk addressing system is slightly more complicated. A disk is divided into 200 tracks (actually 203, but only 200 are usable); each track contains eight sectors, four on each side; and a sector contains 321 words.

What is a word, and what information is stored in these words? Every 1130 word, in core or on disk, contains 16 pieces of information, where "piece of information" means one or the other of only two possibilities. The terminology *bit* is often used for this "yes-no" choice, and it is a convention to say that a bit is either a one or a zero. Therefore the individual word in the 1130 can be said to contain some ordered collection of 16 zeros and ones. For convenience, the bits in an 1130 word are identified by the numbers 0 through 15, going from left to right, as indicated in Fig. 6–1.

The ability to represent all entities, whether they are numbers, letters, or other symbols, by combinations of zeros and ones is fundamental to the effectiveness of the computer. It is relatively easy to build high-speed electronic and magnetic devices which have only two possible states, and these two states can be called zero and one. For example, a typical electronic device involving transistors, the flip-flop, has only two possible states, which can be controlled by appropriate signals. In a similar manner, a magnetic core can be magnetized with the field pointing one way or the other. It would obviously be more difficult to represent decimal digits on physical devices requiring *ten* different and clearly distinguishable states.

Almost all computers are internally constructed on this *binary* (also called *base two*) *system*. Some, including the 1130, represent integer numbers directly in binary, whereas others represent numbers digit by digit in binary, using what is termed *Binary Coded Decimal* or BCD representation.

0 bit   15 bit

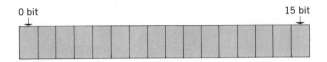

FIG. 6–1. The 1130 word.

TABLE 6–1

Decimal (base ten)	Binary (base two)
1	1
2	10
3	11
4	100
5	101
6	110
7	111
8	1000
9	1001
10	1010
16 ($= 2^4$)	10000
32 ($= 2^5$)	100000
64 ($= 2^6$)	1000000
128 ($= 2^7$)	10000000
256 ($= 2^8$)	100000000
512 ($= 2^9$)	1000000000

BINARY AND HEXADECIMAL NUMBERS

The binary, or base two, way of counting is one of the hallmarks of the "modern" mathematics in the elementary school. If the reader does not know how to count in binary, perhaps the third-grader in the family can offer some assistance! The process is simple. Positional notation, which motivates our decimal, or base ten, numbers, is also the basis of binary counting; the digit in any one position or place keeps increasing until it reaches its largest allowable value, and then to represent the next number in sequence, the position to the left is increased by one. Table 6–1 shows the correspondence between some binary and some decimal numbers.

The process of going from base two to base ten numbers or vice versa has often been described; we will give two examples, one in each direction, which will serve to illustrate the process. Note the use of subscripts to indicate the base.

Binary to decimal:

$$101101_2 = 1 \times 2^5 + 0 \times 2^4 + 1 \times 2^3 + 1 \times 2^2 + 0 \times 2^1 + 1 \times 2^0$$
$$= 32 \quad + 0 \quad + 8 \quad + 4 \quad + 0 \quad + 1 \quad = 45_{10}$$

Decimal to binary:

$$27_{10} = 1 \times 16 + 1 \times 8 + 0 \times 4 + 1 \times 2 + 1 \times 1$$
$$= 1 \times 2^4 + 1 \times 2^3 + 0 \times 2^2 + 1 \times 2^1 + 1 \times 1 = 11011_2$$

The addition of binary numbers proceeds as with decimal numbers, except that one must remember that $1 + 1 = 10_2$. Thus 1011 and 110 added give 10001.

Every 1130 word is a 16-place binary number. The writing of binary numbers is an annoying process, one that can easily lead to errors. Furthermore, a 16-bit word is small; large computers have words with more bits. For example, a word in the IBM System/360 is 32 bits long. Since long binary numbers are messy to use, shorter representations of such numbers were sought. The ease of "translation" from base two numbers to any other base that is a power of 2, such as 4, 8, 16, or 32, has led to the frequent use of one or another of these bases to represent binary material in computer output or input. (Remember, however, that as a FORTRAN user you needed only base ten numbers.)

Octal, or base eight, was once common. The 1130 monitor programming system uses hexadecimal, or base sixteen, for dumps and other output. Translating a number from binary to hexadecimal involves replacing each successive group of four binary digits by a single hexadecimal "digit"; thus four hexadecimal digits define an 1130 word. The relation between numbers in the three bases is shown in Table 6–2.

To write hexadecimal numbers we use the decimal digits 0 through 9 and then switch to the letters of the alphabet from A through F. It should be clearly understood that this use of hexadecimal notation is for the convenience of the machine users. Internal storage is basically binary, and one might consider hexadecimal words as being stored in binary form. That we find the computer typing hexadecimal information is due to programming, converting binary numbers to hexadecimal numbers before printing. Such conversion programs are part of the subroutine library. Incidentally, FORTRAN is not the best language for writing such translating programs. The assembler language we shall discuss in the next chapter is better suited for this as well as many other purposes.

The Appendix includes tables to assist in conversions between different bases.

TABLE 6–2

Decimal	Binary	Hexadecimal
1	1	1
7	111	7
9	1001	9
10	1010	A
11	1011	B
12	1100	C
13	1101	D
14	1110	E
15	1111	F
16	10000	10
151	10010111	97
3449	110101111001	D79
40743	1001111100100111	9F27

STORING NUMBERS

What are we storing in our 16-bit words? As you might expect, several types of information can be stored, although for the present we shall consider in detail only the storage of numbers.

First, there are the instructions which run the computer. We know from our discussion of the FORTRAN compiler that FORTRAN is not the form these instructions eventually take. We will later see the form of machine-language instructions.

Other kinds of information may be stored, such as variables and constants. Since the computer is often used for calculations, it is essential that we have uniform ways of storing numbers in the memory. Another type of coded storage is storage of alphameric information, characters, and we shall encounter that also. However, eventually everything must end up as 16-bit words if it is to be stored by the 1130.

We have already met two types of numbers in FORTRAN programs, integers (fixed point numbers) and reals (floating point numbers). Since these types are handled differently in FORTRAN, it should not be surprising that a similar dichotomy exists in methods of storing integers and reals in the 1130.

Fixed point numbers are handled directly by the instructions and circuitry of the machine, so their form is dictated by the electronic components, the *hardware* in the computer. The form for floating point numbers for the 1130, on the other hand, is determined by the programs written to manipulate them. We will consider first the storage of fixed point numbers.

FIXED POINT NUMBERS OR INTEGERS

The basic method of storing numbers in the 1130 is as integers, either in standard precision or extended precision. It is these numbers which are manipulated by the built-in arithmetic operations of addition, subtraction, multiplication, and division.

Standard precision numbers require one storage word. The leftmost or zero bit is the sign bit; a 0 in the sign bit denotes a positive number, and a 1 denotes a negative number. In extended precision integers, two words are used, an even-address word and the next higher odd-address word. (FORTRAN uses only standard precision integers). Here the leftmost bit of the first word is the sign bit.

Positive numbers are stored just as one would expect. That is, the binary equivalent of the number is stored in the word or words. The decimal number 5670 would be stored as indicated in Fig. 6–2.

This number, 1011000100110_2, represents the decimal number 5670 and can be converted as follows:

$$2^{12} + 2^{10} + 2^9 + 2^5 + 2^2 + 2^1 =$$
$$4096 + 1024 + 512 + 32 + 4 + 2 = 5670$$

The largest positive number which can be stored in a single word is one with all bits except the sign bit set equal to 1, or

$$0111111111111111_2 = 32,767_{10}$$

Negative numbers are stored differently; the method is not just a reversal of the sign bit of the positive number. Instead, what is known as the *2's complement* form is used to convert a positive to a negative integer. To obtain the 2's complement of any binary number, we interchange all the bits, replacing zeros by ones and ones by zeros, and then add 1 to the resulting binary number. To illustrate this, suppose we want the binary representation of -7_{10}. The following steps indicate the interchanging of zeros and ones and the adding of 1 to get -7.

$(+7)_{10} =$	0000 0000 0000 0111	positive number	of
Interchange:	1111 1111 1111 1000		same
$+1$:	1111 1111 1111 1001		absolute
	$= (-7)_{10}$	negative number	value

The use of 2's complement for representing negative numbers may not be familiar and may seem to be a strange procedure; one wonders why the negative number is not the same as the positive, except for a different sign bit. The advantage of the 2's complement form for negative numbers is that it permits ordinary addition to proceed without any attention to the sign of the number.

0 bit   15 bit

FIGURE 6–2

To illustrate this, it is convenient to work with shorter numbers. Suppose we employ an imaginary computer with four-bit words, one bit for the sign and three for the number. Then the number +3 would be represented as

0011

The number −3 would be represented in 2's complement form as

1101

Now add these numbers as though they were ordinary binary numbers.

```
    0011
 +  1101
   10000
```

The sum has five places but there is no fifth place in our four-bit-word machine, so the fifth digit is ignored. The sum is zero, as it should be.

We can easily see that adding a number to its 2's complement gives zero, but why do we need that strange step of adding 1 to get the complement? Assume for a moment that we keep the added 1 out of the picture. Wherever there was a 1 in the original number, we replace it by zero and vice versa. When the resulting two binary numbers are added, the sum will be a string of 1's, since we are adding a zero and a 1 in each place, one from each of two numbers. Now the added 1 will effect a carry through each successive place until there is one more place needed at the left end. Further play with the 2's complement form shows that it allows us to add positive and negative numbers with no special precaution.

We ignored the additional bit that occurs in the fifth position, but there is a related problem that cannot be ignored. The last bit to the left is the sign bit, which plays a different role from the others. Suppose again we had the following two positive numbers to be added in our imaginary four-bit-word machine:

```
  0 | 101
+ 0 | 110
```

We have drawn a vertical line to isolate the sign. If we add these numbers, the sum, 1011 *without* the sign bit, will no longer fit the three places allowed for a number, exclusive of its sign. This situation is known as overflow, and it is handled in a special way in the computer, as we shall see later. Without special handling of overflow, integers larger than +32767 in a 16-bit word would be effectively negative and those smaller than −32768, effectively positive. This "overflow" for integers is not the same as the real overflow we saw in the last chapter.

FLOATING POINT OR REAL NUMBERS

We shall next consider the method of storing standard precision real numbers used by the 1130 subroutines.

A standard precision real number requires two words of storage space in the computer. The address of the number in storage is the address (always *even*) of the first word, i.e., the lower address (Fig. 6–3). Floating point numbers consist of a mantissa and an exponent or characteristic, so any storage system must accommodate both of these "pieces" of the number. Thus a decimal number of the form $.347 \times 10^{17}$ must have in storage both the mantissa, .347, and the characteristic, 17, although these may not be stored in base ten form.

Since numbers are stored in binary in the 1130, both parts of a floating point number must be represented by binary numbers. In 1130 floating point storage, reading the two words from left to right, the first word and half of the second contain the mantissa; the second half of the second word has the characteristic (Fig. 6–4).

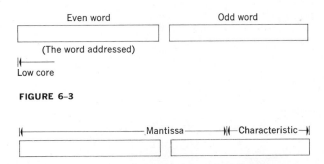

FIGURE 6–3

FIG. 6–4. Form of standard precision floating point storage.

Table 6–3 contains some examples of simple integers stored in the 1130 as floating point variables. In the following discussion we will refer to these examples.

For convenience, the examples are given in hexadecimal, rather than in binary as they will be stored by the machine. As we have seen, it is easy to translate each hexadecimal digit into its corresponding four binary digits to get the full binary representation. For example, we can translate the first two-word pair in the table as follows:

$$(4000\ 0081)_{16} = (0100\ 0000\ 0000\ 0000\ 0000\ 0000\ 1000\ 0001)_2$$

The leftmost bit of the left-hand word is the sign bit, containing in this case a zero for a positive number. If we translate into binary the leftmost hexadecimal digit of each number in the table, we see that for the positive numbers the leftmost bit is zero, while for the negative numbers it is one.

In the location reserved for the characteristic (the second half of the second word) we have in each case a two-digit number, 80 or higher. The *binary* characteristic it represents raises *two* to some power. Each hex characteristic in the table is said to be *excess 80*, meaning that 80_{16} is added to the true binary exponent. Such a characteristic shifts a binary point, just as the base ten characteristic shifts a decimal point. Thus in the first number, with a characteristic of 81, the binary point is to be shifted one place to the right. A characteristic of 87 would indicate that the binary point is to be shifted right 7 places; a characteristic of 8D shifts the point 13 places; and a characteristic of 90 shifts the point 16 places (90 is a *hex* number, and $10_{16} = 16_{10}$).

Similarly, less than 80 in the second half of the second word would indicate a negative characteristic, moving the point to the *left*. *No* sign bit is stored; the leftmost characteristic bit is 0 if the number is less than 80, and therefore the characteristic is negative, and is 1 if the characteristic is positive. The actual numbers stored for the characteristic will always be positive. This is why the excess 80 system is used. This may seem a peculiar way of storing the characteristic, but such a method is for the convenience of writing subroutines to manipulate (add, etc.) real numbers. With this method the subroutines need consider only positive characteristics.

Now consider the mantissa, stored in the first word and a half. We know that the leftmost bit of the first word is the sign bit. In 1130 floating point, the binary point is not actually present in the word but is assumed to be at the left end of the mantissa. Hence the mantissa of the first number in our table, with the point, is

.10000000000000000000000

TABLE 6–3

THE 1130 STANDARD PRECISION
FLOATING POINT REPRESENTATION

of this number (decimal)	is this pair of words (hex)
1.	4000 0081
2.	4000 0082
3.	6000 0082
4.	4000 0083
5.	5000 0083
6.	6000 0083
7.	7000 0083
8.	4000 0084
9.	4800 0084
10.	5000 0084
−1.	C000 0081
−2.	C000 0082
−3.	A000 0082
−4.	C000 0083
−5.	B000 0083
−6.	A000 0083
−7.	9000 0083
−8.	C000 0084
−9.	B800 0084
−10.	B000 0084

Since the hexadecimal characteristic of this number is 81, we shift the point one place to the right, obtaining the following binary number:

1.000000000000000000000000

Hence we come to the not too surprising conclusion that the 1 is stored as a 1! However, this example is deceptively simple. It may not be so easy to "translate" from binary into decimal form, as the example in the next section shows.

A negative mantissa is stored as the 2's complement of the corresponding positive number, just as with integers.

AN EXAMPLE OF 1130 REAL STORAGE

To illustrate the problems of converting a number from floating point storage within the 1130 to decimal form, consider the following floating point number in hexadecimal form:

6487ED82

This is stored in two words, the first containing the binary equivalent of hexadecimal 6487 and the second, of ED82. As before, 82, the characteristic of the number, determines the position of the binary point. Since 82_{16} is 2_{16} more than 80_{16}, the binary point is to be moved two places to the right.

The first word and a half contain the mantissa. Writing in binary we have the following string of numbers:

```
0110 0100 1000 0111 1110 1101    (binary)
  6    4    8    7    E    D      (hexadecimal)
```

The corresponding hexadecimal digits are placed underneath the binary groups. The leftmost bit is a zero, indicating that the number is positive. The implied binary point following the sign bit must be shifted two places to the right: after shifting, the resulting binary number is

11.0010 0100 0011 1111 0110 1

This *is* the number stored, but for convenience it is desirable to know its decimal equivalent. The integer part of this binary number gives no trouble, since 11_2 equals 3_{10}. If we had a more extensive integer part we could use the table in Appendix C-5, or we could expand in powers of 2:

$$11_2 = (1 \times 2^1 + 1 \times 2^0)_{10} = 3_{10}.$$

The fractional part gives more trouble. Grouping as in-

dicated above we can write the fraction as a hexadecimal fraction,

$.243F6_{16}$

dropping off the last bit. We could, with some labor, translate this number into the corresponding binary number, realizing that when the place value system based on 16 is used, the associated decimal number is

$$2 \times 16^{-1} + 4 \times 16^{-2} + 3 \times 16^{-3} + 15 \times 16^{-4} + 6 \times 16^{-5}.$$

To compute this expression by hand to the required number of decimal places would be a lengthy operation, but it could be done.

For conversions of this kind, it is desirable to have a table of the negative powers of 16 multiplied by the numbers from 1 to 15. A table of this kind can be produced on the computer; the one in Appendix C-3 was obtained by means of a FORTRAN program. Each line of the table represents values obtained by multiplying a number from 1 to 15 by the negative powers of 16, starting with 16^{-1}, 16^{-2}, etc. Thus the value of 2×16^{-1} obtained from this table is .125.

The following list shows the values for the number given above:

$$2 \times 16^{-1} = .12500000$$
$$4 \times 16^{-2} = .01562500$$
$$3 \times 16^{-3} = .00073242$$
$$15 \times 16^{-4} = .00022888$$
$$6 \times 16^{-5} = .00000572$$
$$\text{Total} = .14159202$$

We see, then, that the table facilitates translation, although it does demand some arithmetic. The decimal number represented is 3.14159202.

One can also resort to one of the conversion tables in the functional characteristics manual (included in the Appendix as Table C-6), giving functional parts of numbers. Using this table as directed, we can find quickly that $.243_{16} = .14135742_{10}$. This of course gives only three of the places in the original hexadecimal fraction. We could, however, take into account the last places by adding to $.243_{16}$ the last two terms in the expression above,

$$15 \times 16^{-4} + 6 \times 16^{-5}.$$

These are the last two terms on the list above, so we can find our number as follows:

$$.243_{16} = .14135742$$
$$15 \times 16^{-4} = .00022888$$
$$6 \times 16^{-5} = .00000572$$
$$\text{Total} = .14159202$$

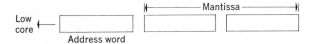

FIG. 6–5. Form of extended precision floating point storage.

EXTENDED PRECISION REAL STORAGE

Extended precision storage is slightly different from standard precision. Here three words are used for storage. The first word carries only the characteristic, in the same excess 80 form we have just seen. Thus half of the first word is wasted space in extended precision. The next two words carry the significant figures, so that one obtains eight more binary places than one obtains with standard precision (Fig. 6–5). Again the binary point is assumed to be in the leftmost place; its ultimate location is determined by the value of the characteristic just as before. The additional eight binary places correspond to about three more places of accuracy in the decimal number.

Because of this difference in storage, it is necessary to have different sets of subroutines to handle standard and extended precision numbers. In the subroutine library the subroutines intended for standard precision have a name beginning with "F" while those for extended precision begin with "E." The loader verifies that all the subroutines used in one program are of the same precision, and refuses to run programs calling for mixed precision.

STORING ALPHAMERIC DATA IN THE 1130

So far we have examined methods of storing several types of *numbers*, the ingredients of arithmetical operations. However, the computer is increasingly important for *symbol* manipulation as well, i.e., for the manipulation of letters, other symbols, words, and sentences of the English language. The ability to handle and manipulate character data is an important attribute of the modern computer.

The principal characters represented inside a digital computer are the letters of the alphabet (sometimes upper and lower case), the numbers, arithmetic symbols (such as those needed in FORTRAN), and sometimes other symbols. Each of the input-output devices has its own limitations as to available characters.

Some computers have one standard way of character coding, that is, representing each character internally in the machine, which is independent of the particular device used to get that character into or out of the computer. However, the 1130 was designed with multiple character codes; characters can be coded in different ways dependent on the input or output method and on the programs used. When a card is read, one type of character is stored for a punched A; but A can be coded in the machine in other ways.

The following discussion reviews quickly the character codings used by the 1130. Details about each are in the coding table in Appendix C-8.

IBM CARD CODE

The IBM card code is the standard code for key-punched cards. The IBM card has 80 columns, and each column can represent a letter or a number. Figure 6–6 illustrates the very simple coding involved. The letters are represented by two punches in a column, the numbers by a single punch. We can use the coding shown here to read bank statements, gasoline credit card bills, etc., provided we want to take the trouble of decoding the letters in each column.

When a card is read on the 1130, each card column, containing 12 positions from top to bottom, is transferred row by row to the first 12 bits (i.e., bits 0–11) of a computer word. Thus if there is a punch in the top position of the column (called a *twelve* punch), a 1 is stored in bit 0. If there is a *zero punch*, a 1 is put in bit 2, etc., down through the last (twelfth) line on a card. This coding is referred to as *card image*, because the word in core is the image of the word on the card, with 1 representing the punches, and 0 the nonpunches.

Card punching within FORTRAN always produces the standard IBM card code for the 1130. However, cards

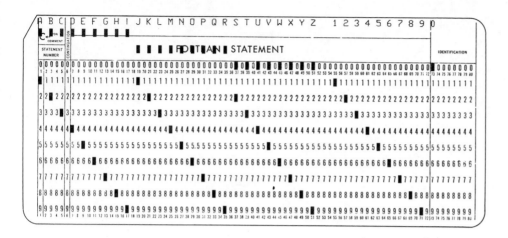

FIGURE 6–6

are not necessarily punched in the IBM card code; it is possible to "image" computer words on cards.

The coding used in the 1130 for characters entered from the console keyboard is similar to card coding, but it also allows for some additional information. A 1 in bit 12 of the word used for the character, means that the EOF (*End of Field*) button on the keyboard was depressed. A 1 in bit 13 indicates that the backspacer was depressed. A 1 in bit 14 indicates that the button labeled *Erase Field* was depressed. If these keys are to serve their functions, the program must examine these bits and take appropriate action.

CONSOLE PRINTER CODE

The console printer has a character code entirely its own. Since the listing of the general character codes in Appendix C–8 indicates this coding, it will not be described in detail here. Bit 6 contains a 1 if the letter is upper case. (The Selectric type ball of the console typewriter has *only* upper case, so lower case cannot be provided.) If bit 7 has a 1, the function is a control function.

EBCDIC CODING

Many of the monitor programs for the 1130 are designed for Extended Binary Coded Decimal Interchange Coding, or EBCDIC, which is not connected with any input or output device, and is widely used as a standard computer coding. The full EBCDIC code is eight bits long. Several versions are used in 1130 programs; in some programs the characters are stored one character per word, but EBCDIC coding can also be *packed*, two characters to a word, or even five characters in two words (in *name code*, where only the last six bits of the full eight-bit coding are used). This system allows a very large number of codings, for there are 2^8, or 256, different possible arrangements.

1130 ASSEMBLER VIA FORTRAN

CHAPTER 7

INTRODUCTION TO 1130 ASSEMBLER LANGUAGE

We have occasionally suggested that FORTRAN is not the only available programming language for the 1130. The second general programming language presently available for the 1130 is the *assembler* language.

Almost every digital computer has a symbolic language of the "assembler" type. Such languages are similar to machine-language coding, as we shall see. They were introduced to relieve the programmer of both the routine bookkeeping activities required by machine language and the need to manipulate long binary words, while allowing him to work closely with the detailed facilities available in the computer. Assembly languages use symbols or mnemonics for the computer operations and identify locations in the memory of the computer by names rather than by machine-language addresses.

Our approach to the 1130 assembler is through FORTRAN. When the FORTRAN compiler translates the FORTRAN program, it produces for every sentence in the FORTRAN program a series of machine-language instructions. From knowledge of the compiler or inspection of compiler output, it is possible to learn, for any FORTRAN sentence, the corresponding set of machine-language instructions. Since there is a one-to-one mapping between machine-language and assembler instructions, the former can also be expressed as assembler instructions. (But the reader should understand that the FORTRAN compiler produces machine-language rather than assembler instructions.)

Our strategy is to present the assembler coding that corresponds to simple FORTRAN statements, explaining each new assembler feature as it appears. In this manner, you will be introduced to the assembler language and at the same time see what is happening during execution of a FORTRAN program.

The basic information showing how the FORTRAN compiler operates is given in the *1130 Program Logic Manual*. The examples we shall use are given in an appendix in that manual. However, certain features in the discussion will not correspond exactly to features of assembly language. These pseudo-assembler features will be indicated by square brackets.

In this chapter we will use only integer variables. We begin with a FORTRAN statement so simple that you might not see any use for it. The FORTRAN statement is shown on the left, with the corresponding assembler language translation on the right.

```
         27    32 35
          |     |  |
I = J    LD    L  J
         STO   L  I
```

These two assembler statements are almost self-explanatory. The I and J are called the *operands* of the

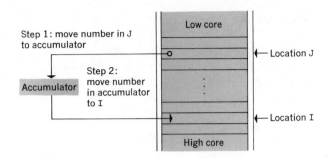

FIG. 7–1. Illustration of I = J.

instruction. Just as in FORTRAN, I and J are variable names; during the translation of the assembler program and its loading into core, these variables are assigned to addresses in the core memory. Again, variable names can have up to five letters and numbers in any combination, provided they begin with a letter. Unlike FORTRAN, assembler names do not attach any meaning to the first letter.

The first part of each assembler statement is the mnemonic for the computer operation requested by the instruction. LD stands, not too surprisingly, for "load," and STO for "store." Both instructions make use of an often used register (storage location) in the 1130, the *Accumulator*. Usually operations proceed to or from the accumulator; one of the two numbers in an arithmetic calculation is always in the accumulator, and the result is also stored there. The accumulator has the 16 bits characteristic of all 1130 storage. The load instruction causes the contents of the memory word identified by J to be loaded into the accumulator. The store instruction operates from the accumulator, telling the machine to store the contents of the accumulator in the location indicated by I. This procedure is illustrated in Fig. 7–1. To move an integer from one location to another in core, we first put it in the accumulator, then move it to its destination. This is typical of one-address machine languages; each instruction contains only a single address.

The L in these two instructions indicates that the instructions are *long form*; the corresponding machine-language instructions occupy two consecutive computer words, in contrast to a *short form* instruction (an assembler instruction without an L), which occupies a single computer word. Long instructions are sometimes indicated differently, as we will see. We shall not explain now why long instructions appear here. Often, as in the present case, the same instructions can be given either in long or in short form, and in some situations both forms accomplish the same purpose.

ADDITION AND SUBTRACTION

We now consider another FORTRAN integer arithmetic statement; this is slightly more complicated because it calls for some calculation.

```
              27  32 35
              |   |  |
I = K - M     LD  L  K
              S   L  M
              STO L  I
```

The load and store instructions are the same as before. The intervening instruction contains an S, standing for "subtract." The word stored at K is loaded in the accumulator, and then the word stored in M is subtracted from the number in the accumulator. The results of integer arithmetic operations remain in the accumulator. We store the difference in location I. Again, the subtract instruction is long. The small numbers 27, 32, and 35 indicate the card columns when the assembler statement is punched in a card.

The assembler language contains other arithmetic instructions similar to the subtract instruction. Remember that these instructions apply to single computer words. Hence an S instruction subtracts one 16-bit binary number, stored as indicated in the previous chapter, from another 16-bit binary number. If the FORTRAN statement had been I = K + M, then A, the mnemonic for "add," would replace the S. Similarly, the accumulator contains the sum when the addition is performed.

MULTIPLICATION AND DIVISION

One new feature comes in when we consider multiplication:

```
              27  32 35
              |   |  |
I = J * K     LD  L  J
              M   L  K
              SLT    16
              STO L  I
```

We easily identify the long form multiplication instruction indicated by M. But the presence of the short SLT instruction may be surprising. The problem here is that the multiplication of two 16-bit binary words *can* produce a 32-bit binary word, which the accumulator alone cannot accommodate. In order to accommodate the possible 32 bits, the computer must use an additional register, called the *Accumulator Extension*. If there is no overflow (i.e., if the product still fits in a single word) the product computed is in the accumulator extension. Thus some command is needed to move the product into the accumulator so that it can then be acted upon by the next instruction. The accumulator and the accumulator extension can be considered as one long register, so that if we "shift" both of them left by 16 places (physically moving the number to the left by 16 places) the number which was in the accumulator extension will now be in the accumulator. The shift operation SLT fills with zeros the vacated spaces at the right end.

To see how this works, assume that 2 and 3 (binary 10 and 11) are to be multiplied. After the multiplication instruction the contents of the accumulator and the accumulator extension are:

0000000000000000	0000000000000110
Accumulator	Accumulator extension

The result is in the accumulator extension; it is $110_2 = 6_{10}$. After the SLT instruction the accumulator and accumulator extension look this way:

0000000000000110	0000000000000000
Accumulator	Accumulator extension

If you think carefully about what has been said, you may see that overflow is also a possibility here.

Even if the integer variables in FORTRAN reserve two words, integers are stored in a single word. Thus a product of two integers which produces a binary integer requiring more than 16 bits cannot be stored in a single 1130 word—it is unacceptable to FORTRAN. Note that FORTRAN does not take any action concerning this. The machine does take an action, however, and you can test for it, if necessary. If the product is more than the allowable 15 significant figures, the overflow indicator bit is turned on. Subsequent programming can test this bit to see if it is turned on and then take the appropriate action.

FORTRAN integer division is like multiplication except that it is necessary to place the number to be divided in the accumulator extension *before* division occurs. This is accomplished in the following list of instructions by the shift instruction SRT, which shifts both registers right. The result of a division is in the accumulator.

```
              27  32 35
              |   |  |
I = J/K       LD  L  J
              SRT    16
              D   L  K
              STO L  I
```

Note that if a multiplication is followed immediately by a division, no shifting is necessary.

THE SHIFT INSTRUCTIONS

The FORTRAN compiler, in translating a program to machine language, uses shift instructions like those in our assembler language examples for moving words back and forth between the accumulator and the accumulator extension. The required shift is always 16 places in such a situation, but shift instructions can be used for any number of places. This ability to shift is particularly useful when one wishes to examine some of the internal bits in a word. For example, suppose we want to know what is in bit 7 in the accumulator. We could shift the number seven places to the left to bring bit 7 to the zero position. Then the "branch on negative" instruction, explained in the next section, could be used to check this bit, now in the sign bit position in the accumulator word.

There are three types of shift instructions. All are used only in the short form. Those of the first type shift the number either to the right or to the left, filling any vacated places with zeros. SLA and SRA shift the accumulator left or right respectively, while SLT shifts both the accumulator and accumulator extension to the left.

The second type of shift instruction, SRT, is a special shift-right instruction, which repeats in each of the vacated places whatever the zero bit was before the shift started. This is particularly useful for shifting a negative number, for it keeps a number in the negative (2's complement) form. To see this, suppose we wish to consider the last eight bits of an instruction as a number. (This happens with many machine-language instructions, since the last eight bits in a single-word instruction, as we will see, represent the displacement.) The procedure would be first to use SLA to shift the number to the left eight places, in order to get rid of whatever is currently in the first half of the word, and then to use SRT to shift the number back to its initial position, duplicating bit 9 in the vacated places. Because negative numbers are in 2's complement form, this procedure gives us the correct 16-bit expression for whatever number was stored in the second eight bits. An example of the SRT instruction follows.

Original number in accumulator   0101110110101011

```
      27        35
       |         |
First, SLA     8        gives   1010101100000000
Then,  SRT     8        gives   1111111110101011
```

The third class of shift instructions works on a somewhat different basis, in that the shift is not of a fixed number of places but of a number dependent upon the contents of the word being shifted. The two instructions of this type are SLCA, shifting only the accumulator, and SLC, shifting both the accumulator and its extension. These instructions, standing for "shift and count," always employ one of three special internal storage registers, the *index registers*, and the shift is always to the left. A number is first entered in an index register, to indicate the maximum extent of the shift. For each shift of one place, the number stored in the index register is decremented by 1. The shift can end in either of two ways: the value in the index register becomes 0, or a 1 has been shifted into the leftmost, or zero-bit position. This facility is particularly useful when we wish to examine the bits in a word in order to take action on each bit that contains a 1.

This concern with manipulating bits internally in a word is foreign to FORTRAN, although it is used in some of the FORTRAN subroutines.

The index registers are words in core memory, with addresses 1, 2, and 3, that the programmer can use in various special ways when he is programming in assembler and machine language. When an index register is indicated in an instruction, it is named in card column 33, just after the place where the L would be, if present. Thus a shift left and count instruction using index register 2 would be punched as in this illustration:

```
27      33
 |       |
SLC     2    [operand field not present]
```

SOME BRANCHING COMMANDS

We encounter several new assembler instructions corresponding to machine-language instructions when we consider how the FORTRAN compiler handles a DO statement, a statement setting up a DO loop within the program. Here is an example:

```
                        27   32 35
                         |    |  |
    DO 10 M = J,K       LD   L  J
                        STO  L  M
        :             α [First instruction in loop]
                                   :
10 CONTINUE             MDX  L  M,1
                        LD   L  M
                        S    L  K
                        BSC  L  [address of α],+Z
```

The DO statement translates into two groups of statements, the load and store statements at the beginning of the DO loop, and the incrementing and branching statements at the end. The load and store statements should be familiar; at the start of the DO loop, the instructions are to put J in the accumulator and then store it in M, i.e., setting M = J as the DO statement indicates. This initilization is done once each time we enter the DO loop. The CONTINUE itself does not lead to any computer coding.

The instructions at the end of the loop contain two new and important assembler statements. The first is the MDX instruction, meaning "modify index." The MDX is a versatile instruction within the 1130, with different forms to accomplish different things. The long MDX instruction such as this one, having two operands, M and 1, separated by a comma, adds 1 to the number stored in location M, leaving the result in M. Since M is the index for the DO loop, incrementing M by 1 prepares for the next pass through the loop. Then M is loaded into the accumulator, and K is subtracted from it.

The BSC is a branch mnemonic, standing for "branch (or skip) on condition," the first assembler branch instruction we have met. This is a long BSC, differing in behavior from a short BSC. Like the long MDX, it has two operands separated by a comma. The first operand gives the branching address, the address to which control will go if the branch is to occur. This would usually be an assembler variable, but here it is indicated by the square brackets. In this example "address of α," in brackets, could not be written in this fashion if this example were an assembler program; a name must begin with a letter.

The second operand in the BSC, after the comma, states the conditions under which the branch will *not* occur, always referring to the number currently in the accumulator. In this case the branch does not occur if the value in the accumulator is either positive or zero. Stated another way, the branch occurs *only* if the number in the accumulator is negative. So the conditions after the comma in a long BSC tell under what conditions the branch will *not* occur. The accumulator contains the result of the calculation M−K when the branching test is made. Thus, so long as M is equal to or less than K, the program will go back to the instruction here labeled α and execute the DO loop once more. However, as soon as M becomes greater than K, the program will continue with the next instruction after the long BSC instruction. In any assembler branch instruction the next sequential instruction is executed if the branch does not occur.

TABLE 7–1

Symbol	Meaning
O	Branch if overflow indicator is on.
C	Branch if carry indicator is on.
E	Branch if the number in the accumulator is *not* even; i.e., branch if bit 15 in the accumulator contains a 1.
+	Branch if the number in the accumulator is *not* positive; i.e., branch if bit zero contains a 1 or if all bits contain 0's.
−	Branch if the number in the accumulator is *not* negative; i.e., branch if bit zero contains a 0.
Z	Branch if the number in the accumulator is *not* 0; i.e., branch if any one of the accumulator bits contains a 1.

The long BSC statement can check for any of the six conditions (or for any combination of them) listed in Table 7–1. If the second operand is a combination of these, as in the example, all conditions must be satisfied for the branch to occur. A long BSC with no second operand, i.e., no conditions listed, is an unconditional branch.

The coding for a DO loop with variables incremented by some value other than 1 is not too different. However, the MDX instruction could be used only if the incrementing value is a constant. If it is a variable, the following sequence is used.

```
                              27  32  35
                              |   |   |
DO 10 I = J,K,M               LD  L   J
                              STO L   I
        α    [first instruction in the loop]
  ⋮                                ⋮
                              LD  L   I
                              A   L   M
10 CONTINUE                   STO L   I
                              S   L   K
                              BSC L   [address of α],+Z
```

The following example, a computed GO TO, shows coding with a symbolic address for a location in memory; again, an actual assembly program would have names.

```
                       21      27  32 35
                       |       |   |  |
GO TO (111,112,113),KOP        LDX I1 KOP
                  ADR1         BSC I1 ADR1+1
                               DC     [111]
                               DC     [112]
                               DC     [113]
```

There are several new features here.

In interpreting these commands we must remember that the 1130 makes special uses of three 16-bit words, the index registers, in core memory, with addresses 1, 2, and 3. Instructions can refer directly to the index registers. The LDX in this example is the first such instruction we have encountered. It can be read as "load index register," because it transfers a computer word to one of the index registers, rather than to the accumulator as in the LD instruction. The machine must know which index register to use, and the 1 following the I in the LDX instruction indicates that the first index register (the core word with address 1) is to be used. This index register is also mentioned in the BSC instruction that follows, with results that we shall see in a moment.

The first two assembler instructions corresponding to the computed GO TO have an I, for "indirect," in the place on the card previously used for the L indicating long form instructions. Indirect instructions, always long (the I implies an L), handle the operand differently than do direct instructions. If the LDX instruction were a direct instruction, without the I, then it would load in the index register the actual address KOP. An indirect instruction, however, loads not KOP but the computer word whose address is KOP. Not all instructions can be used in the indirect form, and the meaning of "indirect" differs slightly from one instruction to another.

The BSC instruction not only uses the index register and indirect addressing, but it brings in other aspects of the assembler language not yet encountered. No branching conditions are given; i.e., there is only one operand. The branch is therefore an unconditional branch, one that will always occur. But the branch is to different locations under different conditions.

The BSC instruction is named ADR1, the first assembler example we have of directly assigning a name, a label, or a symbolic address to a word in memory. The word identified by the label is the first word of the long (two-word) BSC instruction (indirect instructions are always long); the use of a symbolic address gives us a handle for referring to locations in memory.

In the operand of the BSC instruction, 1 is added to this symbolic address. ADR1+1 refers to the word following that labeled by ADR1. Address arithmetic is a useful aspect of the assembler. The symbolic address indicated in the operand of the BSC instruction is the second word in the BSC instruction. But the second word of a long instruction always contains the address associated with that instruction, so the second word of the BSC contains its own address! At first glance this seems rather strange. Why would one branch into the middle of an instruction, an operation that would almost always be unfortunate? But that is not the intent; both the index register and the indirect aspect are still to be considered.

The BSC instruction under consideration mentions index register 1. With most assembler instructions, when an instruction refers to an index register, that register is used in computing the effective address. The address indicated by the operand is not the full address for the instruction but only part of it. In this case (and in other similar instructions), the intent is to *add the content* of index register 1 to ADR1+1; this is the result of mentioning index register 1 in the instruction. Remember that the previous instruction loaded the number in KOP into index register 1. Hence if KOP contains 1, the effective address for the BSC instruction is ADR1+2, while if KOP is equal to 2, the effective address is ADR1+3. Such use of an index register allows an instruction to perform different functions each time it is used.

Thus if KOP is equal to 1, the effective address is the word in core immediately following the second word of the BSC. The assembler coding for this word is DC, standing for "defined constant." A DC is *not* an instruction; it sets up a word in memory for data storage. The three successive DC statements contain *the address* of the instructions

carrying out statement 111, *the address* of the beginning of statement 112, and *the address* of the beginning of statement 113, each address occupying one word.

Finally, we must take into account the fact that the BSC is an indirect instruction. This means that the effective address of the instruction is not the address to which the program branches but rather the address at which the branching address is stored. The effect of the BSC instruction in this coding is this: If KOP is equal to 1, a branch is generated to the address where the coding for statement 111 will be found; if KOP is equal to 2, a branch is generated to the coding for statement 112; and if KOP is equal to 3, a branch is generated to the location for statement 113. This is a tricky instruction, and the person unfamiliar with assembler languages would do well to read once more the discussion of the coding for the computed GO TO. Figure 7–2 may be useful in reviewing this sequence.

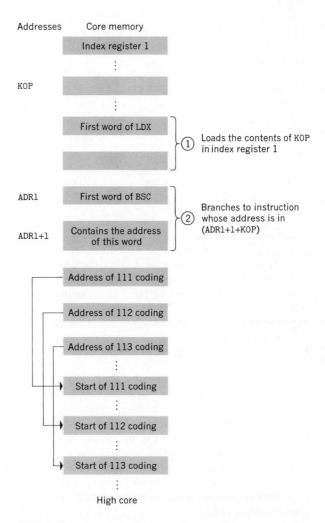

FIGURE 7–2

Some additional comment is called for in connection with the three DC statements in the program. In assembler language the programmer has full responsibility for setting up storage in memory; storage allocation is not done by the translating program as with the FORTRAN compiler. Here we are not storing variables but the three addresses that the BSC must branch to.

We can see from the coding why the FORTRAN program misbehaves if KOP takes on a value of 4 or greater. The value of KOP will be determined earlier in the program. Consider that in some case in this program KOP did take the value 4. Then the branching address is to the word just after the third DC. But this is not intended to be an address; it might well be an instruction word. So the results would be unpredictable. The FORTRAN compiler *could* have been set up to test that KOP was not too large, perhaps giving an error message if it were, but this would involve additional instructions and the translated program would probably run more slowly. Hence the 1130 FORTRAN compiler puts the burden of making the program work correctly on the programmer's shoulders, in an attempt to gain efficiency. (For example, a transfer trace could be used to check for this difficulty in a FORTRAN program.)

Finally we conclude this section with one of the forms of the FORTRAN IF statement, one with a fixed point argument.

```
                         27    32 35
                         |     |  |
IF (N) 111,112,113       LD    L  N
                         BSC   L  [111],+Z
                         BSC   L  [112],+-
                         BSC   L  [113],-Z
```

These assembler instructions involve aspects of the language you have already learned. All are long instructions. The N is loaded in the accumulator. Then there are three conditional branching instructions. The computer branches to the instructions for carrying out sentence 111 if the variable N is negative (i.e., *not* positive or zero). It branches to the instructions for 112 if the variable is zero (*not* positive or negative), and it branches to the instructions for 113 if the variable is positive (*not* negative or zero).

The compiler does not necessarily generate three branching statements for each IF statement; it takes advantage of cases in which two of the referenced statement numbers are the same, or where one of the branches is to a CONTINUE statement. So some attempt is made to "optimize" the program, avoiding the execution of unnecessary instructions. More sophisticated compilers have been constructed which go to great lengths to produce optimal programs.

LONG AND SHORT INSTRUCTIONS

Many of the instructions in our FORTRAN-related introduction to the assembler language have been in long form, occupying two consecutive computer words. We have suggested, however, that for many instructions there are short forms using only one word, in some cases performing different tasks than the long-form instructions.

To gain insight into this situation we will consider the "add" instruction in both long and short form; both accomplish the *same* task. We hope to explain why long-form instructions are often necessary, even though they use an additional computer word. Here are the two forms of the add instruction:

```
27    32 35
|     |  |
A        NUM
A     L  NUM
```

Both tell the computer to add the integer stored in memory location NUM to the word in the accumulator and leave the result in the accumulator. Since the effect is the same in both cases, one may question why the long instruction, taking twice as much space to store, would ever be used. To understand the reason, we must consider some aspects of machine language.

The basic problem, common to computers with "small" words, is that of representing the address NUM in the instruction. We know that an 1130 word contains 16 binary bits, a typical size for a small computer. Five bits at the beginning of every instruction are given over to representing in a binary code the particular operation to be performed. Thus "add," seen as an actual machine-language instruction in computer memory, starts with the following five bits: 10000. If auxiliary information is also needed in the instruction (e.g., long, index registers), they must occupy other bits. Even if the whole instruction can be crowded into a single word, half the bits, eight, are used for this basic information, leaving only the remaining eight for addressing.

This is the crux of the problem. Eight bits are just not enough to represent a full address. The typical 1130 is equipped with either 4000 or 8000 words of core memory. To represent any address in a (minimal) 4000-word core, 13 bits are required. In a long instruction the entire second word, 16 bits long, is given over to the address, so there is ample room. However, the eight bits available in the short-form instruction cannot store every address in the machine; some expedient must be used.

The trick in the machine-language short instruction is to use an address *relative* to the next instruction. This means that the last eight bits in the machine-language short instruction do not contain the actual address of a word in memory, but rather a number specifying how many words backward or forward one must go *from the* address of the next instruction to find the word being referred to. The address of the next instruction is contained in the instruction address register; this register is also displayed on the console.

Thus the "address" that appears in the short-form instruction is not an address at all, but a displacement, positive or negative, from the IAR address. The number of bits available sets a limit on how far one can go in either direction. In the 1130, with eight bits, the limitation is from -128 to $+127$. If the word referred to is stored within this "distance" in core from the next instruction, the short-form instruction can be used. On the other hand, if its storage location exceeds this distance, the long form is necessary. Usually the FORTRAN compiler uses the long forms.

The assembler programmer can ignore this distinction between a long and a short instruction when the address of his word is within the allowable displacement range. This means that he still uses in his operand the symbolic address that he requires, exactly as he would in the corresponding long instruction. It is the job of the assembler translating program to calculate the necessary displacement to insert in the instruction. It is possible, however, to specify that the operand in a short instruction is an address rather than a displacement, by using an X in the place in the instruction where we have previously seen L or I.

This displacement-address limitation poses a quandary to the writer of the program. The programmer has three alternatives open to him:

(1) He can carefully count backward or forward from every instruction to the word it refers to, to determine whether it is within the range. If he chooses to proceed in this way, he must remember to count in the same manner each time a change is made in the program when it is being debugged.

(2) He can use only long-form instructions when the program is first written. After he has developed a working program, he can go through the compiler listing and compute the displacements. He will be able to determine readily when he is within range, but to do this with an assembler-produced machine-language list, he needs proficiency in hexadecimal arithmetic, because the addresses on the list generated by the 1130 assembler compiler are hexadecimal. This procedure has the advantage of separating the job of deciding whether the instructions should be long or short from that of getting the program to run.

(3) He may choose an intermediate approach. Since the assembler program will report in the form of an error message if a short instruction demands too large a displacement, he can go ahead and guess whether a given instruction should be long or short, and then use the listing from the compiler to correct his wrong guesses. Sometimes he can change some instructions from long to

short by judicious rearrangement of the program, putting data words closer to the part of the program which uses them. Such rearrangement may be useful in shortening a program which is too long to fit in memory.

Different programmers may choose different alternatives.

EFFECTIVE ADDRESS COMPUTATION

In our examples the first operand in either a long or short instruction has been a name for a location in core memory. However, sometimes this location is modified by other aspects of the instruction such as the use of index registers. Here we review and extend our knowledge about the actual referenced address, the effective address.

We might start with several sample instructions. Here is an add instruction, in both long and short forms:

```
27    32 35
 |     |  |
A     L   NUM
A         NUM
```

The number stored in the location called NUM is to be added to the word in the accumulator; NUM identifies the effective address in both instructions.

We have already referred to address arithmetic. Suppose that we next need to add to the number in the accumulator a number which is stored three words past the word labeled NUM. We could give a unique name to this word in the program, but naming every word can become a messy operation. To provide a convenient way of handling such a case, assembler and other symbolic languages allow address arithmetic. Thus the following would be a valid assembler instruction:

```
27    32 35
 |     |  |
A     L   NUM+3
```

The effective address is that of the word that is stored three words past the one identified by NUM, so this word is used in the addition as desired.

This procedure is also called relative addressing, because one can specify positions relative to the labeled address of a computer word. No embedded blanks are allowed in the address operand, so we cannot use blanks freely for readability as we have done in FORTRAN. Any operand after a blank in an assembler statement is treated as a comment.

Multiplication can also be used in address arithmetic, although it is probably of less use than addition. We shall not give a detailed discussion of the possibilities with address arithmetic; many are useful only for advanced programmers. They are described in the assembler language manual for the 1130. Problems arise as to the

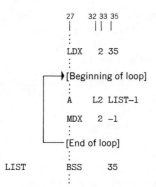

```
       27    32 33 35
        |     | | |
        :
       LDX   2 35
        :
    →[Beginning of loop]
        :
       A    L2 LIST-1
       MDX   2 -1
        :
    └─[End of loop]
        :
LIST   BSS    35
        :
```

FIGURE 7-3

"relocatability" of an address when address arithmetic is used in computing it. Most assembler programs are assembled as relocatable programs, to be stored in different places in core in different loadings, although there are also assembler facilities to ensure that the program always occupies a certain place in core.

Address arithmetic is only one method of modifying the address. Another procedure also familiar to us is the use of the index registers. This is particularly helpful because, with index registers, different uses of the *same* instruction in different executions of a loop can reference different words. In many instructions, if an index register is explicitly mentioned in the instruction, the number stored in the index register will be added to the address given in the instruction operand to yield the effective address. In a short instruction with a referenced index register, the operand is automatically treated as a displacement to be added to the value in the index register, except in such instructions as LDX and MDX, which directly concern the index registers.

Consider a skeleton of a program (Fig. 7-3). We want to manipulate in succession each of 35 numbers stored consecutively in memory. We will not describe the details except to say that something is to be added to each of the numbers.

The BSS instruction reserves a block of 35 words in storage, the first one of which is labeled LIST. The LDX instruction puts 35 in index register 2. In the add instruction, farther down in the program, we are adding to the number in the accumulator whatever number is in LIST-1 *plus* the value in index register 2. This will mean that the number we add first is in LIST+34, the last of the numbers in the BSS block of 35 words. The short MDX instruction (a new case for us) decreases by 1 the value in index register 2. Since these instructions are in a loop, the next time we come to the add instruction, the number in the index register will have been decreased by 1. So the effective address of the add instruction is decreased by 1 each time it is executed. In this way the index registers can be used to determine effective addresses. You can see that this device is particularly

useful when we have to access a number of elements, one after another, in a loop. We shall see later how to exit from loops.

There is another assembler device which we can use when dealing with addresses, although we do not see examples of it in our FORTRAN studies. Often it is of advantage in assembler to address *relative* to the location of the current instruction. An asterisk is used for such relative addressing in symbolic languages. The asterisk stands for the position in memory of the first word in the *next* instruction, the instruction following that containing the asterisk in its operand field.

The same thing could be accomplished by more labels and addressing relative to these labels. The asterisk can occur in two different senses within one operand, first to indicate the current address, then multiplication. Thus the expression **5 indicates that we multiply the address of the next instruction by 5 to get the effective address.

In considering effective addresses, we need to take account of indirect addressing. The general rule, which is easy to remember, is that all necessary computation for the effective address must be done *in advance* of going indirect. This means that any address arithmetic, and any adding of index registers, must be performed first, and the resulting effective address is interpreted as an indirect address.

In our examples the address operand has been represented by a name, a name with a constant added to it, or with an asterisk expression. It is also possible to use operands which are simply numbers. We have seen such instructions in the discussion of shifting. The number may be written as an ordinary decimal number, in the usual fashion. It will be translated into binary form before use. However, it may be desirable to indicate an address in hexadecimal as the operand of an instruction. A hexadecimal operand in the 1130 assembler language has a slash as the first symbol in the operand. Thus an instruction telling the machine to branch unconditionally to memory address 0038, the connection with the skeleton supervisor, could be written in either of the following forms:

```
27    32  35
 |     |   |
BSC   L   /0038
LDX   L   /0038
```

An LDX indicating no index register loads the quantity into the instruction address register, thus causing an unconditional branch.

An operand may also specify EBCDIC coding for a letter. This is indicated by placing a dot in front of the letter to be coded:

```
DC     .A
```

In the final program all labels will be assigned values, so an assembler instruction with a symbolic address and one with a hexadecimal address can be functionally equivalent.

DOUBLE PRECISION ASSEMBLER COMMANDS

All the assembler instructions presented so far concern the manipulation of single words. However, we have mentioned occasionally the need to group two or more words together. This need arises in double or extended precision integer arithmetic, and in standard precision real arithmetic. The assembler language contains instructions that enable us to handle such double words. For correct operation all these instructions assume that the effective address is even, and that the paired words are the one with that address and the word having the next higher address.

Double word

Even address referring to both words

Double-word instructions use the accumulator and the accumulator extension as a double-word register, in the same way that single-word instructions use the accumulator. The instructions are "load double," LDD, "store double," STD, "add double," AD, and "subtract double," SD.

ASSEMBLER FACILITIES WHICH ARE NOT INSTRUCTIONS

We have seen an instance of assembler facilities which did not correspond to any action on the part of the system, but instead specified storage, the DC used in FORTRAN-equivalent programming.

Except for the DC, all the assembler codes introduced correspond, one-to-one, to machine-language instructions. For example, the assembler instruction with mnemonic A becomes a machine-language add instruction when the assembler program is translated. However, the assembler has facilities that do something other than create machine-language instructions. Programming consists of more than writing a series of instructions, and the assembler must allow for other aspects, such as storage of information.

The programmer often is faced with the need to store data within a program. Such data may be numbers or character strings or both, on which the calculation may be based. Storage must also be provided for intermediate and final results. Furthermore, information of various types, numerical, symbolic, or logical, may be needed in connection with calculations, particularly in the execution of loops or in branching to particular addresses. Hence we should not be surprised to learn that there are several assembler methods of establishing storage.

A special assembler instruction exists for assigning floating point or real storage, with mnemonic DEC. Thus the instruction

```
27      35
|       |
DEC     3.
```

leads to the establishment in memory of the following two words, expressed in hexadecimal, at this point in the program:

C000   0082

From our discussion in Chapter 6 on the storage form for reals, we can determine that this is indeed the number we intended to store with the assembler command. Similarly, the assembler command XFLC stores extended precision real numbers. Once again our discussion is not complete; the DEC command can be used for a number of other types of storage, including double precision integers.

The mnemonic EBC indicates the storage of EBCDIC characters. In this case, the operand is a series of alphameric characters (letters, numbers, special symbols) preceded and followed by a period. The EBC statement causes storage in a packed form, two characters per word, at the location at which the EBC statement occurs. The version 2 monitor has additional assembler storage-assignment facilities.

These instructions can be used to reserve a word (or several words) in memory, for use in a calculation. Another facility is useful in making sure that a number of words will be available to the program. Two instructions can be used to define a block (a number of words, indicated by the operand), to be reserved for storage. BSS, meaning "block started by symbol," has its label (if any) attached to the first, or lowest, address for the group of words, while a label attached to a BES, "block ended by symbol," is the name assigned to the word immediately following the words reserved for the block.

There are other assembler mnemonics which also do not correspond to machine-language instructions. Some will be encountered in the discussion of the assembler-language subroutine for use in FORTRAN, and others in connection with the use of subroutines. A listing of examples of assembler instructions is given in Appendix D-8.

SUBROUTINES IN ASSEMBLER

CHAPTER 8

REAL ARITHMETIC

Although real arithmetic looks quite similar to integer arithmetic in FORTRAN, its programming for the 1130 is basically different. As we have noted, there are machine-language, and therefore assembler-language, commands for carrying out the operations of integer arithmetic. But most small computers have no hardware, i.e., electronic circuitry, for the direct execution of arithmetic operations with real or floating point numbers. Thus for the 1130 there is no single machine-language instruction, and consequently no single assembler-language instruction, enabling the machine to add two real numbers stored in its memory. (Larger computers, on the other hand, can usually execute real arithmetic operations directly, with a resultant gain in speed.)

In the 1130, floating point arithmetic must be done by subroutines, programs stored on disk (or in card decks in a system without disks) and placed into core if they are needed with a FORTRAN or assembler program. Such subroutines are supplied with the monitor system; they break down the operations of real arithmetic into the simpler kinds of arithmetic and logical manipulation which can be done by the machine-language instructions available. It is not too difficult to outline how to construct a subroutine for addition or multiplication of two real numbers, but we will not investigate this matter further.

Because real or floating point arithmetic is accomplished by subroutines, assembler statements corresponding to FORTRAN real arithmetic statements are a set of linkages to the necessary subroutines. We already know that real numbers are stored in two (or three) words in core, and that the first word must have an even address. (See Chapter 6 for further details.)

Again we examine some simple cases, giving the FOR-TRAN statement and the equivalent assembler coding. For our first example we choose the simple operation of storing a real variable in a new location in memory.

```
         27        35
         |         |
A = B    LIBF      FLD
         DC        B
         LIBF      FSTO
         DC        A
```

In these assembler instructions FLD and FSTO are names of system subroutines, stored on disk. The first is the floating load subroutine, and the second is "floating store," as you can quickly surmise from the names.

All floating subroutines make use of three words in core memory called the *Floating Point Accumulator*, or FAC. (The previously discussed accumulator is not part of core,

but is a central processor register.) FLD loads a real number stored in core into the floating point accumulator, and FSTO takes a number from the FAC and stores it in core. The location of the FAC in core varies from program to program; it can be located through a computation using index register 3, as we shall see.

The IBM Systems Reference Library includes a manual specifically dealing with the subroutines available in the 1130 disk monitor system. This manual describes 1130 system subroutines, including all the subroutines usually called within FORTRAN. A list of the 1130 subroutine library is included in Appendix E-1; some of these system subroutines will also be discussed later. In this example, as in the following ones, we are assuming that standard precision is used; the corresponding extended precision subroutines all begin with E rather than with F.

The 1130 assembler language has two different commands for calling a subroutine, CALL and LIBF; the two subroutines used here are called by LIBF commands. Each subroutine can be called only in one of these two ways; the subroutine list specifies how to call each one. The difference between CALL and LIBF concerns the calling mechanism, the machine-language statements which bring into play the necessary subroutine.

We have not yet explained all the statements associated with the FORTRAN operation of moving a real number from one storage location to another. Each of the LIBF commands is followed by a DC statement, setting up a word in storage. The operand in each of the DC statements indicates what is to be there. Remember that eventually A and B will correspond to locations, addresses in the computer memory, so

```
27        35
|         |
DC        A
```

indicates that the word immediately following the branch to the floating store subroutine will contain the address of A in the core memory (more carefully, the *even* address of the *first* word of A). In similar fashion, the word after the first subroutine call will contain the address of B in the core memory.

Typically a subroutine call, either a LIBF or a CALL, will be followed by a number of DC. The subroutine knows how many DC to expect, and it also knows where they are in memory. The addresses stored in these words give the necessary input information for the subroutine to do its job, information as to where the variables needed in the subroutine are stored. In this case they tell the floating load subroutine that the number to be loaded into the FAC is at address B, and they tell the floating store subroutine that the number in the FAC is to be stored at A.

Real arithmetic operations bring into play other subroutines:

```
            27       35
            |        |
A = B*C     LIBF     FLD
            DC       B
            LIBF     FMPY
            DC       C
            LIBF     FSTO
            DC       A
```

The floating multiply subroutine, FMPY, makes use of the floating point accumulator, as indicated. Thus after the value at B has been loaded in the FAC, it will be multiplied by the value at C, and the result will be in the FAC. Then the product is stored at A. Other real arithmetic operations are very similar to this example; they include FADD, FSBR, and FDVR.

New problems arise if the FORTRAN arithmetic expression involves both integer and real numbers or variables. Older versions of FORTRAN do not allow "mixed mode" expressions, but require, with certain exceptions, that all the quantities on the left-hand side of the equation have the same mode (real or integer). But 1130 FORTRAN does allow such expressions. We can see how it handles them by examining the following sequence:

```
            27   32  35
            |    |   |
A = B*I     LD   L   I
            LIBF     FLOAT
            LIBF     FMPY
            DC       B
            LIBF     FSTO
            DC       A
```

The FLOAT subroutine takes the integer in the accumulator and converts it into a foating point (real) number in the FAC. Thus the FORTRAN program does mixed-mode arithmetic by converting the integers into real numbers where necessary. (Parts of the calculation may be done using integer arithmetic.) Since the FLOAT subroutine involves many instructions, this conversion takes longer than the direct multiplication of two real numbers; hence the programmer should not use mixed mode carelessly, even though it is available. There are situations where it is the desirable thing to do, but in other cases it increases the operation time unduly. For example,

A = B + 1.

is preferable to

A = B + 1

because the second form involves additional instructions to convert the integer 1 to a real 1.

Just as with integer arithmetic, in the evaluation of complicated expressions it is sometimes necessary for the compiler to create temporary intermediate storage for results that are needed later in the computation.

THE FLOATING POINT ACCUMULATOR

We can gain insight into how FORTRAN employs the floating accumulator if we examine the execution of an IF statement which tests on a real variable rather than on an integer as previously seen. Here is the coding.

```
                          27   32  35
                          |    |   |
IF (A) 111,100,113        LIBF     FLD
                          DC       A
                          LD   3   +126
                          BSC  L   [111],+Z
100 CONTINUE              BSC  L   [113],-Z
```

First note that, as already suggested, the dummy CONTINUE is ignored; if neither branch is taken, the program proceeds with the instruction after the second BSC. The new aspect here is a test on the real variable, the determination of its sign. A is loaded into the floating accumulator. Branching statements, however, examine the number in the (ordinary) accumulator, so we must load the sign-bearing part of A in the accumulator. Knowledge of the location of the FAC is essential.

The FAC is a three-word block in the memory. Its location varies from program to program, depending on how many subroutines the program calls. Figure 8–1 shows the structure of the three words of the floating point accumulator. Thus it is the second word, the word addressed, that carries the sign bit. The location of the FAC is determined within a FORTRAN program by the address stored in index register 3; the word we want, the middle word in the FAC, is always 126 words higher than the address in index register 3. The FORTRAN-generated coding loads the index register. The load instruction in this coding, using index register 3, has the effective address needed to load this word into the accumulator. The branching then proceeds as before.

A corollary to these remarks is that index register 3 is essential to a FORTRAN program. Any user-written sub-

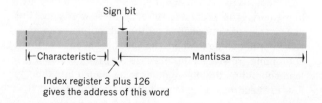

Sign bit

|←Characteristic→| |←————— Mantissa —————→|

Index register 3 plus 126
gives the address of this word

FIG. 8–1. The floating point accumulator.

routines must be careful to save index register 3 (if it uses this register) and restore it to its original value before returning from the subroutine.

USING SUBROUTINES—THE TRANSFER VECTOR

Knowing the assembler coding for subroutine calls is not equivalent to knowing how subroutines are called within a machine-language program. In this section we outline the process of using subroutines.

There is a special machine-language or assembler branching instruction for branching to subprograms. One problem in branching to a subprogram is that we must know how to get back to the calling program after the subprogram is completed, since we usually want to continue with the main program after completion of the subprogram. One way of establishing the return link is to *bring* into the subprogram the address of the next instruction in the calling program, the value currently stored in the instruction address register. This may be the address of the next instruction, or it may be the address of a DC. The branch and store IAR command, BSI, functions like the BSC command, but it causes the current value of the instruction address register to be stored in the effective address. The same branching conditions can be used in both instructions. Execution in the subroutine begins with the instruction just following the stored address, that is, at the *effective address plus one*. Since the subprogram knows how many DC statements follow the call, it can compute the return address, and so can get back to the calling program when necessary.

The details of the machine-language calling procedure are different for CALL and LIBF subroutines. Both make use of an area called the *transfer vector*, in high address core just below the COMMON area. We shall not discuss the building of the transfer vector, which is primarily the task of the loader or core load builder. Its structure is shown in Fig. 8–2, a modification of the diagram contained in the monitor manual.

We consider first the branching to a subroutine of the CALL type. There are two aspects, the CALL instruction itself and the CALL transfer vector. For each CALL subroutine in a program there is one word in the transfer vector which contains at execution time the core address of the entry point to the subroutine, the place at which the value in the instruction address register is to be stored. The final machine-language calling program contains an indexed indirect long BSI instruction, replacing the CALL instruction of the assembler program. The effective address of this indirect instruction is the CALL transfer vector word just mentioned.

The branching mechanism for a LIBF subroutine is more complex. The same two aspects, the branching instruction in the program and the transfer vector, must still be considered. Again, the program being executed contains a BSI using index register 3, although now the instruction is short; and the branch is not directly to the subroutine, but to a three-word instruction within the LIBF transfer vector. At execution time the three words in the LIBF transfer vector have the following structure. The first word is blank to accommodate the effective address of the BSI; when the BSI is executed, the value in the IAR is placed in this word. Thus the return address information is in the transfer vector, not in the subroutine. The final two words in the transfer vector are a long unconditional BSC instruction containing the entry address of the subroutine, the address of its first instruction, since no address is brought into the subroutine. The short BSI instruction in the calling program locates the transfer vector by use of index register 3 (as we have seen for subroutines needing the floating accumulator), adding a displacement to the value in index register 3 to obtain the branching address. Thus in executing a CALL subroutine, only one branching instruction is used, but in executing a LIBF, two branches are used.

There is one more trick involved with a LIBF. In order to have access to the return address, the subroutine must know which part of the transfer vector is used. Any subroutine using the LIBF transfer vector must reserve a special place, two words past its entry point, for storing the address of the first word in LIBF transfer vector associated with that subroutine. This address is placed into the subroutine by the loader.

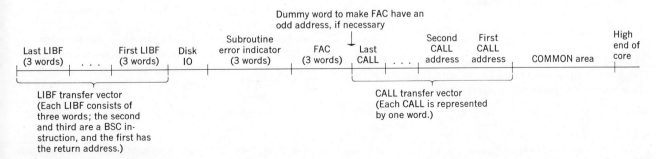

Dummy word to make FAC have an
odd address, if necessary

| Last LIBF (3 words) | . . . | First LIBF (3 words) | Disk IO | Subroutine error indicator (3 words) | FAC (3 words) | Last CALL | . . . | Second CALL address | First CALL address | COMMON area | High end of core |

LIBF transfer vector
(Each LIBF consists of three words; the second and third are a BSC instruction, and the first has the return address.)

CALL transfer vector
(Each CALL is represented by one word.)

FIGURE 8–2

TABLE 8–1

FORTRAN Real subroutines	Standard precision	Extended precision
SIN	FSIN	ESIN
COS	FCOS	ECOS
ALOG	FLN	ELN
EXP	FEXP	EEXP
SQRT	FSQR	ESQR
ATAN	FATN	EATN
ABS	FABS	EABS
SIGN	FSIGN	ESIGN
TANH	FTNH	ETNH

The DC corresponds in order and number to the parameters in the subroutine call. Each identifies the address of the corresponding memory entity referenced by the subroutine. Thus each DC allows the subroutine to have access to the data described in one of the parameters.

The system-supplied functions, such as the sine or cosine, are used somewhat differently. The FORTRAN names for these functions are not the same as the system names used in the location equivalence table, but are those familiar from algebra, e.g., SIN and COS. However, names in the subroutine library must include other information. Principally the subroutines must distinguish between standard precision and extended precision, since different procedures are needed to calculate the function. Names of standard subroutines, as we have already noted, begin with the letter F, and extended precision subroutines with the letter E. Table 8–1 lists the common FORTRAN functions and their names within the subroutine library for extended precision and standard precision use.

The entry addresses of both CALL and LIBF subroutines will be printed if we use an L in column 14 in the XEQ card.

The branching instruction is not generated by the assembler translating program, but is inserted by the loader or core load builder. The program as it goes to the loader contains the *names* of the subroutines (coded, as we shall see, in a form known as *name code*) plus indicators that show where these names are. The assembler manual gives a more detailed account of how the loader constructs the transfer vector.

USER AND SYSTEM SUBROUTINES

The compiler handles user-written subroutines as it does the system subroutines we have seen in the last few examples. Suppose we consider the MAX subroutine introduced earlier in connection with our discussion of FORTRAN. (See Chapter 4.) A typical FORTRAN call to this subroutine might look as follows:

```
CALL    MAX(X,I)
```

It will be recalled that X is an array name and I is the number of array elements to be plotted. The corresponding assembler statements will look like this:

```
27      35
|       |
CALL    MAX
DC      [address of X]
DC      [address of I]
```

THE SUBROUTINE LIBRARY—A SURVEY

A summary of the classes of subroutines in the library is in order, although many of these have already been mentioned. We list these in no particular order and with no attempt at completeness.

The first subroutines in this chapter dealt with real arithmetic. These subroutines are necessary because the 1130 does not have electronic facilities for arithmetic operations including real numbers. They will be heavily used within most FORTRAN programs.

We have already mentioned many times the arithmetic functions, such as SIN, that can be used within FORTRAN and also in assembler, and we have listed some of the corresponding subroutines. Subroutines of another class are intended for use in FORTRAN input/output operations. Later we will see more details of how the machine accomplishes these operations directly, but it is clear that there must be some bridge between the FORTRAN input/output instructions and the details for carrying them out. This bridge is partly furnished by a series of input and output programs for use within FORTRAN. Every READ statement, for example, calls upon a subroutine called SRED, and every WRITE statement upon a subroutine called SWRT. In addition each input or output device has a subroutine for running that particular device. The device subroutines for use within FORTRAN are identified by a name coding ending with the letter Z. For example, the FORTRAN subroutine to run the 1132 printer is called PRNTZ.

The FORTRAN input/output subroutines do not make full use of the machine facilities for input and output, because the FORTRAN language does not have full access to these facilities. Hence another set of subroutines has been written for the system for use within assembler programs. These bear names similar to those of related FORTRAN subroutines; only the last letter is different. Furthermore, this self-contained distinction has significance of its own; those subroutines whose names end in 1 allow more error control than do those whose names end in 0. These assembler-oriented I/O subroutines are called by LIBF, with up to three DC statements following the call. The first DC is the control word, specifying the function to be performed. The second DC is the address of the input or output area in core, if the function is read or write. This input/output area may have as its first word the number of characters that are to be input or output. The third DC, when present, is an error parameter, telling where to find a user-written error routine. Input/output also always involves another set of subroutines whose use will become clear only when we study the 1130 interrupt system; these subroutines are called the interrupt level subroutines.

Several system subroutines have been developed for debugging procedures. We have already seen trace facilities in FORTRAN, and later we shall learn to use these subroutines in assembler programs. Other subroutines are intended primarily for dumping all or part of the program material. Version 2 supplies additional dumping facilities not available in the version 1 monitor system.

We learned in Chapter 6 that character coding in the 1130 is device-dependent; an *A* may be represented internally in several different ways, with one coding when it is entered from an input device, and with another coding for an output device. Hence internal character conversion is necessary, and one collection of library subroutines is concerned with this procedure. These subroutines are often used by the I/O subroutines.

This survey is not exhaustive, but it shows some of the principle types of system subroutines.

Most of the aspects of the assembler language we have noted are those commonly used in connection with FOR-TRAN programs. However, this approach misses many features of the language. Furthermore, it is difficult to see what a full assembler program looks like from this fragmentary approach. Hence in the next chapter we will follow our earlier procedure of considering a complete example, this time of an assembler subroutine. Since this subroutine, like many assembler programs, is intended to be used either in a FORTRAN or assembler program, we shall need to be concerned with the problems of communication with a FORTRAN program.

A FORTRAN SUBROUTINE IN ASSEMBLER

CHAPTER 9

To continue our introduction to the 1130 assembler and to extend somewhat our knowledge of FORTRAN, we shall develop in this chapter an assembler-written subroutine to be used, after assembly, within a FORTRAN program. As with all subroutines, it could also be used in assembler programs.

THE PROBLEM

First, we must define the problem. Frequently we need information in graphic form, rather than as long tables of numbers. One can equip the 1130 with an on-line plotter which can be used to obtain graphic output directly; the system library includes a collection of subroutines that facilitate the process of programming for a plotter. However, even without a plotter it is possible to obtain a rough plot on the line printer or typewriter. We shall assume that the printer is to be used, because it is faster. The technique is to "plot" with one of the characters, perhaps an asterisk or a period; one or more can be printed on each line, one at each of the 120 print positions available on the printer. We cannot plot a point between positions or between lines, so some resultant curves may look crude, particularly if the values change slowly. Nevertheless, for many purposes such a plotting program can save the considerable drudgery involved in hand plotting. Once written, the routine can be stored in the system library and then used over and over in many programs. We shall assume that some calculations are performed within a FORTRAN program and that it is desirable to plot the computed (real) values. A statement within the FORTRAN program will call the subroutine to produce the plot.

Since the plotting subroutine should be usable in various programs with data differing in value, we will write it without any fixed limits of range of values for the numbers to be plotted. Instead, we will include within the subroutine a procedure that will *scale* the data just before the plotting is done. Use of a scaling procedure requires that we determine the maximum and minimum values of the data to be plotted, and then relate the range of these values to the maximum allowable space in the printed output. The minimum and maximum values will then be plotted at the two sides of the paper. The scaling part of the subroutine requires that all data be calculated and stored in the FORTRAN program *before* the subroutine is entered. (An alternative, not used here, would be to specify the maximum and minimum values in the calling parameters.)

As the calculation proceeds, the data for eventual plotting will be stored as a one-dimensional array. The plotting program must know where this array is, that is, where the points to be plotted are stored in the core memory, and it also needs to know how many values to plot. The limited capabilities of this program require that the

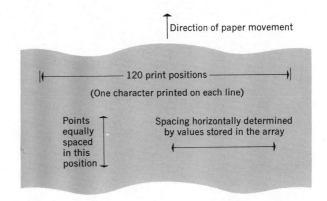

FIG. 9–1. Preliminary layout of PLOT.

points will all have the same horizontal separation, one line on the printer. Thus when the output is turned sideways, the usual format of vertical axis for the dependent variable is obtained. (One could, of course, write another program to plot arbitrary points stored in two arrays.) Figure 9–1 shows the preliminary layout of the output of our subroutine, which we will name PLOT, and Fig. 9–14 shows an actual output of the final program.

CALLING PLOT

A reasonable FORTRAN CALL statement for PLOT would be

CALL PLOT (X,N)

in which X is the name of the array containing the data, and N is the number of points to be plotted. As with all subroutines, N could be a constant, a variable, or an expression. If N is an expression, its value, i.e., the number of points to be plotted, would be the result of whatever calculation is called for by the expression.

In order to write our subroutine we must know how the FORTRAN compiler translates this CALL statement. From the discussion of subroutines in the last chapter we know that the CALL statement will become a branch and store statement, a BSI, followed by two DC statements, one containing the X address (we shall later learn in more detail just what this means) and the second containing the address of N. The machine-language statements are equivalent to the following assembler statements.

```
BSI  L  PLOT
DC      [address of the array X]
DC      [address of N]
```

BEGINNING THE PROGRAM

Since plotting requires the addresses of X and N, our subroutine will retrieve them from the calling program and store them. Our program begins with this task, after some identifying information. The initial sequence of instructions is shown in the left column.

Note that an assembler card with an asterisk in column 21 is treated as a comment and ignored. Further, anything after a space in the operand field is also a comment.

We explicitly specify an entry point, PLOT, in the subroutine; this must be the first "instruction." Note that PLOT is both a name of the subroutine and an entry point. Because we enter the subroutine via a BSI, the *word* in core labeled PLOT will contain the address in the instruction address register after the BSI is executed; thus the DC labeled PLOT will contain the address *of the address* of X, that is, to the address of the DC immediately following the BSI.

A subroutine can be entered at several entry points; each must have an ENT assembler instruction. The first actual instruction is at PLOT+1. This first sequence of instructions stores the address of X and the address of N in the subroutine, in locations labeled PARA1 and PARA2 respectively. The long MDX instruction is used after each STO to increment the address in PLOT by one each time. We use an indirect load instruction because PLOT is the address of an address. At the end of this sequence we increase PLOT by one, so that it has finally the address of the word after the second DC in the calling sequence, that is, the address of the next instruction to be executed after we return to the calling program. This enables us to get back to the main program.

So far we have not needed the data values, but since we will need them later for scaling purposes, we should now consider just how an array is stored in 1130 FORTRAN. Except for storage in COMMON, data storage in 1130 FORTRAN is located before the program. Figure 9–2 shows the storage organization of a one-dimensional array, X, with N real standard precision elements.

We are assuming that the FORTRAN program uses standard precision real numbers; each value in the array is stored in two words. The storage is "backward" in memory, the last value of the array being stored at the lowest address and X(1) at the highest. The address placed by the compiler in the first DC after the BSI branching to PLOT will be the address of X(1). (This will be the address of the low-address word of the pair, and it must be an even address.) Knowing where X(1) is stored and how many values are to be plotted, that is, the value of N when the subroutine is entered, we can access the data.

```
21   27   32  35
 |    |    |   |
     ENT      PLOT
PLOT DC       0
     LD   I   PLOT
     STO  L   PARA1
*                      ADDRESS OF X IS IN PARA1
     MDX  L   PLOT,1   PLOT   PLOT + 1
     LD   I   PLOT
     STO      PARA2    PARA2 CONTAINS ADDRESS OF N
     MDX  L   PLOT,1   PLOT HAS THE RETURN ADDRESS
```

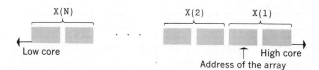

FIG. 9–2. Storage of one-dimensional arrays in core.

DETERMINING THE LARGEST AND SMALLEST VALUES

To make full use of the space available, we want the computer to plot the smallest value in the array at the left side of the paper and the largest value at the right side, with the other values at intermediate points; this is the process known as scaling the data.

We must first determine what the maximum and minimum values are. The procedure is simple. AMAX and AMIN are established somewhere in core as real storage locations by using two labeled DEC statements in our program. We load X(1) into both AMAX and AMIN. Then we successively compare each value stored in the array X with AMAX and AMIN. If we find a larger or smaller value, that becomes the "new" AMAX or AMIN respectively; the interchange is performed by two small sequences of coding, CHAN1 and CHAN2. Figure 9–3 gives a flow chart of this procedure, which stops when X(N), the last value of the array to be plotted, has been examined. Figure 9–4 shows the coding for the interchange subroutines.

CHAN1 is executed when the value being examined is larger than the value in AMAX at that point; it loads the current AI into AMAX, using the floating-load and floating-store subprograms. CHAN2 is used in a similar way to store the minimum value in the array. In both cases the short MDX is an unconditional branch to BACK, just before the end of the loop in the coding for testing for maximum and minimum.

The mainline sequence for determining the maximum and minimum values is given in Fig. 9–5.

Note the use of index register 3 to locate the floating point accumulator, as outlined in the last chapter. To test for maximum and minimum we load the next AI, the next element in the array, and then subtract the current maximum or minimum. The result is in the FAC. Then the word 126 places past the value in index register 3 is loaded in the accumulator; this is the sign-bearing part of the floating point accumulator, so the BSC instruction can check for the necessity of using CHAN1 or CHAN2.

The flow chart (Fig. 9–3) does not show all the programming details. Particularly it does not reflect the looping process, during which all the N–1 data values are examined. Since this process of examining all the elements in the array will be required again, with only a slight variation, we should consider it in detail. The general procedure, often useful in 1130 assembler for creating programming loops, is to use an index register plus the MDX commands to access the data values; this looping process is a common use of index registers. Since each X-value occupies two words, the effective address in the LDD instruction, NEXT, must change by 2 each time it is used. (See Fig. 9–5 to follow this.)

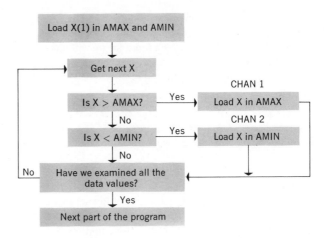

FIG. 9–3. Finding the maximum and minimum values in the array.

```
*BRANCHES FOR FINDING MAXIMUM AND MININUM
CHAN1 LIBF    FLD
      DC      AI
      LIBF    FSTO
      DC      AMAX
      MDX     BACK
CHAN2 LIBF    FLD
      DC      AI
      LIBF    FSTO
      DC      AMIN
      MDX     BACK
*THE FORTRAN CALL IS OF THE FORM CALL PLOT X,I
*WHERE X IS THE ARRAY WITH DATA TO BE PLOTTED AND I
*THE NUMBER OF POINTS.
```

FIG. 9–4. Coding for the interchange.

```
      LDD   I  PARA1
      STD      AMAX
      STD      AMIN      X1  IN AMAX AND AMIN
      LD    I  PARA2     N IN ACCUMULATOR
      SLA      1         2N IN ACCUMULATOR
      S        TWO       2N-2 IN ACCUMULATOR
      STO   L  1         2N-2 IN INDEX REGISTER 1
      A        TWO
      M        NONE
      SLT      16        -2N IN ACCUMULATOR
      A        PARA1
      STO      *&1       PARA1-2N IN 2ND WORD OF LDD
NEXT  LDD   L1 0         LOAD CURRENT A I
      STD      AI
      LIBF     FLD       LOAD CURRENT A I  IN
*                        FLOATING ACCUMULATOR
      DC       AI
      LIBF     FSUB      SUBTRACT AMAX
      DC       AMAX
      LD    3  &126      PUT SIGN-BEARING PART INACC
      BSC   L  CHAN1,-Z  BRANCH TO CHAN1 IF POSITIVE
      LIBF     FLD       NOW CHECK FOR MINIMUM
      DC       AI
      LIBF     FSUB
      DC       AMIN
      LD    3  &126
      BSC   L  CHAN2,&Z  TO CHAN2 IF AI LESS THAN
*                        AMIN
BACK  MDX   1  -2
      MDX      NEXT
```

FIGURE 9–5

First index register 1 is loaded with $2(N-1)$. PARA 2 is placed in the accumulator, and shifting it left by 1 multiplies it by 2. Elsewhere in the program we will have a DC labeled TWO which contains a 2, and this is subtracted. Then the result is placed in index register 1.

The LDD, ''load double,'' instruction retrieves the successive X-values; it always adds the contents of index register 1 to 2N less than the address of $X(1)$ to determine the effective address. Note that

```
STO   *+1
```

places, during execution, the address of the second word before the last element of the array in the operand of this LDD. Figure 9–6 may help to clarify the situation.

The first MDX instruction, labeled BACK in Fig. 9–5, decreases the number in the index register by 2 during each pass through the loop, finally skipping over the short-form unconditional branching MDX at the end of this section of coding when the index register contains a zero. The MDX instructions always skip one word when the index register (or word) they reference becomes zero or changes sign, so they should be followed by a short-form instruction unless such a change is impossible. Thus the effective address in the LDD is two less each time it is executed, and the successive elements in the array are accessed, one by one. The final skip, after index register 1 becomes zero, takes us to the next section of the program.

PRINTING

The next problem is to print the maximum and minimum values in order to identify the range of the plotted output. For this procedure, and for the later printing of the data values, it is useful to know how to use the FORTRAN input/output subroutines, particularly the one for the line printer. In order to gain speed in calculation, it would be possible, though tedious, to work directly with the input-output command XIO. (Details on using XIO are given in Chapter 11.) But we intend to use our PLOT subroutine primarily with FORTRAN programs, so it is certainly reasonable to use the I/O FORTRAN subroutines, since these will probably be needed elsewhere in the FORTRAN program. PRNTZ is the FORTRAN subroutine for the 1132 printer.

All the FORTRAN input/output subroutines work in the same way. The material to be inputted or outputted is stored in a fixed 121-word buffer in memory, extending from core address $003C_{16}$ to $00B5_{16}$. Data must be in EBCDIC coding, one character per word (the leftmost eight bits should be zeros). Thus an ''A'' is represented by ''00C1'' in the FORTRAN print buffer. The number of characters to be used is loaded into index register 2.

(Some of the I/O subroutines require that register 1 must also be loaded in this manner.) In an assembler program or subprogram it is the programmer's responsibility to load the buffer and the index registers each time a line is to be printed.

For PRNTZ the first word in the buffer area serves a special purpose; it does not store input or output, but rather a ''carriage control'' symbol, providing for single spacing, double spacing, or page skipping (with the aid of the punched carriage tape in the 1132 printer). These functions and the words (in hexadecimal) stored to provide for them are listed below:

No space before printing	004E
Single space before printing	Any other character
Double space before printing	00F0
Page skip before printing	00F1

Since there may already be some material in the buffer area, it is necessary to clear the area before use. The character coding chart in Appendix (C–8) shows that the EBCDIC coding for a blank (a blank *is* a character) is 0040_{16}. We shall want to put blanks in each place several times, so an internal subroutine CLEAR is advisable.

The CLEAR routine can be partially combined with another similar task, that of establishing top and bottom edges for the graph. Here we want to load the EBCDIC code for a dash in each word of the print area; the procedure is not too different from loading blanks. We can combine these two requirements into a single internal subroutine with two entry points, CLEAR and EDGE. The coding is shown in Fig. 9–7. The DC with the EBCDIC coding for zero and dash, presumably elsewhere in the program, are labeled ZERO and DASH. Note again the use of index registers for repetitive processes. The calling instruction for this subroutine can be either of the following:

```
27   32  35
 |    |   |
BSI   L   CLEAR
BSI       EDGE
```

Both CLEAR and EDGE use the same index register. If this register is used for some other purpose in the main sequence, it will be necessary to store the number in the register before executing the BSI and to reload it after return from the subprogram.

We want to print the words MAXIMUM and MINIMUM to identify those values to be printed at appropriate places. The EBCDIC-coded letters must first be loaded in the print buffer. In this program they are entered with two EBC commands. Since this command normally packs two characters in a word, each character is preceded by a space to generate the material for the print buffer. (PRNTZ ignores the fact that the left half of each word is

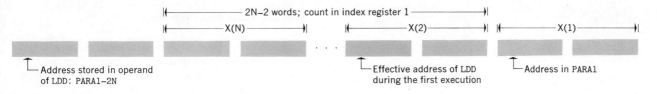

FIGURE 9-6

```
*CLEAR PRINT AREA FOR FORTRAN
CLEAR DC       0
      LD       CLEAR
      STO      *&3
      LD       ZERO
      LDX    2 120
      MDX      GO
EDGE  DC       0
      LD       DASH
      LDX    2 120
GO    STO   L2 /003B
      MDX    2 -1
      MDX      GO
      BSC    I EDGE
```

FIGURE 9-7

```
      BSI    L CLEAR
      LDX    1 7
M     LD    L1 MAX-1
      STO   L1 /00A3
      LD    L1 MIN-1
      STO    1 /003F
      MDX    1 -1
      MDX      M
      LDX    2 120
      LIBF     PRNTZ        PRINT HEADING
```

FIGURE 9-8

```
      BSI    L CLEAR       CLEAR FORTRAN PRINT AREA
      LIBF     FLD         CONVERT AMAX AND AMIN TO
*                          FLOATING POINT FORMAT
      DC       AMIN
      CALL     FBTD
      DC       /003F       POSITION FOR AMIN IN PRINT
*                          BUFFER
      LIBF     FLD
      DC       AMAX
      CALL     FBTD
      DC       /00A3       POSITION FOR AMAX
      LDX    2 120         NUMBER OF CHARACTERS TO BE
*                          PRINTED
      LIBF     PRNTZ       PRINT AMIN & AMAX
      BSI    L EDGE        LOAD DASH IN BUFFER
      LDX    2 120
      LIBF     PRNTZ       PRINT A LINE OF DASHES
```

FIGURE 9-9

40 rather than 00.) Again, the loop that will put material in the buffer is generated by the use of an index register plus MDX commands, as shown in Fig. 9–8.

The print buffer is cleared of symbols that may have been stored there from some previous usage. Index register 1 is loaded with a 7, and the coding for MAXIMUM and MINIMUM is loaded in the loop terminating with the unconditional MDX branch. The 120 in index register 2 indicates that a full line of 120 characters is to be printed (slightly more than we need). We use EBC statements elsewhere for the character coding.

```
MAX   EBC     .MAXIMUM.
MIN   EBC     .MINIMUM.
```

Under the identifying words we want to print the maximum and minimum values. The procedure is shown in Fig. 9–9.

It is necessary to convert the maximum and minimum values from the standard precision real form in memory to the appropriate external form. Again, there is a system subroutine, FBTD, for this commonly performed task. The subroutine calling procedure is

```
27        35
|         |
CALL      FBTD
DC        [address of first word of area for storage]
```

where the DC is the address of the leftmost character after conversion. It is assumed by FBTD that the word to be converted has been loaded into the floating point accumulator. This subroutine stores one EBCDIC character per word, as required. The number is in the form

$$\pm d.dddddddd \ E \pm dd$$

Since all these places are usually not needed, a refinement of the program might clean this up. Note also that it will not be necessary to clear the entire print buffer; we could clear merely the places where we have loaded symbols, since we *know* where we have placed them. This would save some execution time, but would be a little more bother in writing the program.

SCALING EACH GRAPHED VALUE

The main body of the graph is to be produced one line at a time. First the value to be printed must be scaled. The process, similar to conversion from one temperature scale to another, is illustrated in the diagram in Fig. 9–10. We are allowing a margin on the plot by not using the 10 positions at either end of the print area. From the diagram, by simple proportionality, we have

$$\frac{\text{Maximum A} - \text{Minimum A}}{100} = \frac{\text{AI} - \text{Minimum A}}{\text{A-scale} - 10}$$

or

$$\frac{\text{AMAX} - \text{AMIN}}{100} = \frac{\text{AI} - \text{AMIN}}{\text{A-scale} - 10}$$

Solving this for the A-scale, we obtain

$$\text{A-scale} = 100 \, \frac{\text{AI} - \text{AMIN}}{\text{AMAX} - \text{AMIN}} + 10$$

We calculate this expression by using the subroutines for floating point arithmetic (subroutines already discussed). The sequence is shown in Fig. 9–11.

After calculation, A-scale will be in floating point form and we round it to the nearest integer, by adding .5, combined in storage with the TEN we also need to add (Fig. 9–12). Another system subroutine, IFIX, converts this number to an integer. Again, storage is needed, and Fig. 9–12 shows what is necessary.

The number just calculated is the print-buffer location at which we put the asterisk to be printed; to find the address to store the EBCDIC coding for the asterisk, we add $003C_{16}$, (address of first word of buffer) to this location.

We also will put the coding for I in the print buffer at the maximum and minimum locations in each line, ten places in from each edge, both to improve the visual appearance and to identify these locations accurately. Further, if zero falls between maximum and minimum, it is indicated by a period at the proper position.

With this introduction we can examine the full program given in Fig. 9–13. You should be able to find the parts we have discussed, and thus follow the full calculation.

The listing here is that generated by the assembler program, with instructions in the form given in this chapter. The four characters on the left give the hexadecimal address of the first word of each instruction, relative to the beginning of the program. The one or two numbers immediately following to the right of the relative addresses are relocation and subroutine indicators. Then come the machine-language instructions, in a form called Disk System Format.

Minimum A ——— ——— ——— Maximum A

| AMIN | | AI | AMAX | ← Actual values |

← Relative print-buffer positions (decimal)

| 10 | | A scale | 110 |

FIGURE 9–10

```
LIBF    FLD
DC      AMIN
LIBF    FSUB
DC      AMAX
LIBF    FSTO
DC      RAN        RAN    AMIN-AMAX
LIBF    FLD
DC      AMIN       AMIN IN FAC
LIBF    FSUB
DC      AI         AMIN-AI IN FAC
LIBF    FDIV
DC      RAN
LIBF    FMPY
DC      HUN        100 AMIN-AI /RAN IN FAC
LIBF    FADD
DC      TEN
LIBF    IFIX
A       BEG
STO     ASLOC      ADDRESS OF ASTERICK IN
                   BUFFER
```

FIGURE 9–11

```
RAN     DEC     0
AMAX    DEC     0
AMIN    DEC     0
AI      DEC     0
TEN     DEC     10.5
HUN     DEC     100.
```

FIGURE 9–12

```
// JOB
// ASM
*LIST ALL
000A     174D68C0              ENT     PLOT
                     *BRANCHES FOR FINDING MAXIMUM AND MININUM
0000 20  064C4000    CHAN1 LIBF        FLD
0001 1   009A              DC      AI
0002 20  068A3580          LIBF    FSTO
0003 1   0096              DC      AMAX
0004 0   7031              MDX     BACK
0005 20  064C4000    CHAN2 LIBF        FLD
0006 1   009A              DC      AI
0007 20  068A3580          LIBF    FSTO
0008 1   0098              DC      AMIN
0009 0   702C              MDX     BACK
                     *THE FORTRAN CALL IS OF THE FORM CALL PLOT X,I
                     *WHERE X IS THE ARRAY WITH DATA TO BE PLOTTED AND I
                     *THE NUMBER OF POINTS.
000A 0   0000        PLOT  DC      0
000B 01  C480000A          LD    I PLOT
000D 01  D40000A0          STO   L PARA1
         *                               ADDRESS OF X IS IN PARA1
000F 01  7401000A          MDX   L PLOT,1   PLOT    PLOT & 1
0011 01  C480000A          LD    I PLOT
0013 0   D06F              STO     PARA2     PARA2 CONTAINS ADDRESS OF I
0014 01  7401000A          MDX   L PLOT,1   PLOT HAS THE RETURN ADDRESS
0016 01  CC8000A0          LDD   I PARA1
0018 0   D87D              STD     AMAX
0019 0   D87E              STD     AMIN      1  IN AMAX AND AMIN
001A 01  C4800083          LD    I PARA2    I IN ACCUMULATOR
001C 0   1001              SLA     1         2I IN ACCUMULATOR
001D 0   9066              S       TWO       2I-2 IN ACCUMALTOR
001E 00  D4000001          STO   L 1         2I-2 IN INDEX REGISTER 1
0020 0   8063              A       TWO
0021 0   A07F              M       NONE
0022 0   1090              SLT     16        -2I IN ACCUMULATOR
0023 0   807C              A       PARA1
0024 0   D001              STO     *&1       PARA1-2I IN 2ND WORD OF LDD
0025 00  CD000000    NEXT  LDD   L1 0        LOAD CURRENT A I
0027 0   D872              STD     AI
0028 20  064C4000          LIBF    FLD       LOAD CURRENT A I  IN
         *                               FLOATING ACCUMULATOR
0029 1   009A              DC      AI
002A 20  068A4080          LIBF    FSUB      SUBTRACT AMAX
002B 1   0096              DC      AMAX
002C 0   C37E              LD    3 &126      PUT SIGN-BEARING PART INACC
002D 01  4C300000          BSC   L CHAN1,-Z  BRANCH TO CHAN1 IF POSITIVE
002F 20  064C4000          LIBF    FLD       NOW CHECK FOR MINIMUM
0030 1   009A              DC      AI
0031 20  068A4080          LIBF    FSUB
0032 1   0098              DC      AMIN
0033 0   C37E              LD    3 &126
0034 01  4C280005          BSC   L CHAN2,&Z  TO CHAN2 IF AI LESS THAN
         *                               AMIN
0036 0   71FE        BACK  MDX   1 -2
0037 0   70ED              MDX     NEXT
0038 20  064C4000          LIBF    FLD       COMPUTE LOCATION OF ZERO
0039 1   0098              DC      AMIN
003A 20  068A4080          LIBF    FSUB
003B 1   0096              DC      AMAX
003C 20  068A3580          LIBF    FSTO
003D 1   0094              DC      RAN       RAN   AMIN-AMAX
                     *MAXIMUM AND MINIMUM HAVE BEEN DETERMINED
003E 01  440000E7          BSI   L CLEAR
0040 0   6107              LDX   1 7
0041 01  C5000084    M     LD    L1 MAX-1
0043 00  D50000A3          STO   L1 /00A3
0045 01  C500008B          LD    L1 MIN-1
0047 0   D13F              STO   1 /003F
0048 0   71FF              MDX   1 -1
0049 0   70F7              MDX     M
004A 0   6278              LDX   2 120
004B 20  176558E9          LIBF    PRNTZ     PRINT HEADING
004C 01  440000E7          BSI   L CLEAR     CLEAR FORTRAN PRINT AREA
004E 20  064C4000          LIBF    FLD       CONVERT AMAX AND AMIN TO
         *                               FLOATING POINT FORMAT
```

FIGURE 9-13 (see also pp. 86-87)

```
004F 1  0098              DC     AMIN
0050 30 060A3100          CALL   FBTD
0052 0  003F              DC     /003F        POSITION FOR AMIN IN PRINT
                   *    ,                      BUFFER
0053 20 064C4000          LIBF   FLD
0054 1  0096              DC     AMAX
0055 30 060A3100          CALL   FBTD
0057 0  00A3              DC     /00A3        POSITION FOR AMAX
0058 0  6278              LDX  2 120          NUMBER OF CHARACTERS TO BE
                   *                          PRINTED
0059 20 176558E9          LIBF   PRNTZ        PRINT AMIN & AMAX
005A 01 440000ED          BSI  L EDGE         LOAD DASH IN BUFFER
005C 0  6278              LDX  2 120
005D 20 176558E9          LIBF   PRNTZ        PRINT A LINE OF DASHES
005E 01 440000E7          BSI  L CLEAR        CLEAR PRINT AREA
                   *DETERMINE IF ZERO LINE IS TO BE PRINTED
0060 20 064C4000          LIBF   FLD
0061 1  0096              DC     AMAX
0062 0  C37E              LD   3 &126
0063 01 4C30007F          BSC  L AX,-Z        BRANCH IF AMAX IS PLUS
0065 0  1011              SLA    17
0066 0  D03C              STO    TEST         0 IN TEST IF AMAX LESS THAN
                   *                          ZERO
0067 01 4C0000AF          BSC  L CON3         GO TO CON3
0069 20 064C4000      CON LIBF   FLD
006A 1  0098              DC     AMIN
006B 0  C37E              LD   3 &126
006C 01 4C3000AC          BSC  L BX,-Z        BX PUTS 1 IN ACC IF AMIN IS
                   *                          PLUS
006E 0  1011              SLA    17           ZERO IN ACCUMULATOR
006F 0  F033         CON2 EOR    TEST
0070 0  D032              STO    TEST
                   *0 IN TEST IF BOTH HAVE SAME SIGN, 1 OTHERWISE
0071 01 4C1800AF          BSC  L CON3,&-
0073 20 064C4000          LIBF   FLD
0074 1  009E              DC     HUN
0075 20 06517A00          LIBF   FMPY
0076 1  0098              DC     AMIN
0077 20 06109940          LIBF   FDIV
0078 1  0094              DC     RAN
0079 20 06044100          LIBF   FADD
007A 1  009C              DC     TEN
007B 20 091899C0          LIBF   IFIX         LOCATION OF PERIOD ON PAPER
                   *                          IN ACC
007C 0  8029              A      BEG
007D 0  D026              STO    PELOC        ADDRESS OF    IN PRINT
                   *                          BUFFER
007E 0  7030              MDX    CON3
007F 01 C40000A2      AX  LD   L ONE
0081 0  D021              STO    TEST         1 IN TEST IF AMAX GREATER
                   *                          THAN ZERO
0082 0  70E6              MDX    CON
                   *                          CONSTANT S
0083 0  0000        PARA2 DC     0
0084 0  0002          TWO DC     2
0085    000E          MAX EBC    . M A X I M U M.
008C    000E          MIN EBC    . M I N I M U M.
0094 00 00000000      RAN DEC    0
0096 00 00000000     AMAX DEC    0
0098 00 00000000     AMIN DEC    0
009A 00 00000000       AI DEC    0
009C 00 54000084      TEN DEC    10.5
009E 00 64000087      HUN DEC    100.
00A0 0  0000        PARA1 DC     0
00A1 0  FFFF         NONE DC     -1
00A2 0  0001          ONE DC     1
00A3 0  0000         TEST DC     0
00A4 0  0000        PELOC DC     0
00A5 0  0000        ASLOC DC
00A6 0  003B          BEG DC     /003B
00A7 0  0040         ZERO DC     /0040
00A8 0  00C9          EYE DC     /00C9
00A9 0  004B          PER DC     /004B
00AA 0  005C          AST DC     /005C
00AB 0  0060         DASH DC     /0060
00AC 01 C40000A2       BX LD   L ONE
00AE 0  70C0              MDX    CON2
```

FIGURE 9–13 (cont.)

```
00AF 01 C4800083   CON3   LD    I    PARA2
00B1 0  1001              SLA        1              2I IN ACC
00B2 00 D4000001          STO   L    1              2I IN IR1
00B4 0  A0EC              M          NONE
00B5 0  1090              SLT        16
00B6 01 840000A0          A     L    PARA1          PARA1-2I IN ACC
00B8 0  D001              STO        *&1
00B9 00 CD000000   PLO    LDD   L1   0
00BB 0  D8DE              STD        AI             STORE CURRENT  I
00BC 20 064C4000          LIBF       FLD
00BD 1  0098              DC         AMIN           AMIN IN FAC
00BE 20 068A4080          LIBF       FSUB
00BF 1  009A              DC         AI             AMIN-AI IN FAC
00C0 20 06109940          LIBF       FDIV
00C1 1  0094              DC         RAN
00C2 20 06517A00          LIBF       FMPY
00C3 1  009E              DC         HUN            100 AMIN-AI /RAN IN FAC
00C4 20 06044100          LIBF       FADD
00C5 1  009C              DC         TEN
00C6 20 091899C0          LIBF       IFIX
00C7 0  80DE              A          BEG
00C8 0  D0DC              STO        ASLOC          ADDRESS OF ASTERICK IN
                     *                              BUFFER
00C9 0  C0DE              LD         EYE
00CA 00 D4000045          STO   L    /0045
00CC 00 D40000A9          STO   L    /00A9          EDGE IN BUFFER
00CE 0  C0D4              LD         TEST
00CF 01 4C1800D4          BSC   L    CON4,&-        BRANCH IF TEST   0
00D1 0  C0D7              LD         PER
00D2 01 D48000A4          STO   I    PELOC          PERIOD IN BUFFER
00D4 0  C0D5       CON4   LD         AST
00D5 01 D48000A5          STO   I    ASLOC          * IN BUFFER
00D7 0  6278              LDX   2    120
00D8 0  6902              STX   1    *&2
00D9 20 176558E9          LIBF       PRNTZ          PRINT THE LINE
00DA 00 65000000          LDX   L1   0
00DC 0  C0CA              LD         ZERO
00DD 01 D48000A5          STO   I    ASLOC          REMOVE THE ASTERICK
00DF 0  71FE              MDX   1    -2
00E0 0  70D8              MDX        PLO
00E1 01 440000ED          BSI   L    EDGE           DASHES IN PRINT AREA
00E3 0  6278              LDX   2    120
00E4 20 176558E9          LIBF       PRNTZ
00E5 01 4C80000A          BSC   I    PLOT           RETURN TO MAIN PROGRAM
                   *CLEAR PRINT AREA FOR FORTRAN
00E7 0  0000       CLEAR  DC         0
00E8 0  C0FE              LD         CLEAR
00E9 0  D003              STO        *&3
00EA 0  C0BC              LD         ZERO
00EB 0  6278              LDX   2    120
00EC 0  7003              MDX        GO
00ED 0  0000       EDGE   DC         0
00EE 0  C0BC              LD         DASH
00EF 0  6278              LDX   2    120
00F0 00 D600003B   GO     STO   L2   /003B
00F2 0  72FF              MDX   2    -1
00F3 0  70FC              MDX        GO
00F4 01 4C8000ED          BSC   I    EDGE
00F6                      END
```

NO ERRORS IN ABOVE ASSEMBLY.

FIGURE 9-13 (concluded)

TESTING PLOT

After writing a subroutine that compiles successfully, a main program is needed to test the subroutine. This testing program should be nontrivial, and the results should be known to the programmer in advance. A simple FORTRAN program for plotting a sine function furnishes a convenient check here. The program and the resultant output are shown in Figs. 9–14 and 9–15, respectively. The output is as expected, because the PLOT program has previously been debugged. Just as with FORTRAN, a complex program seldom works when it is first written. The next chapter considers assembler debugging.

```
// JOB
// FOR
*LIST ALL
*IOCS(KEYBOARD, 1132 PRINTER)
*LIST ALL
      DIMENSION X(50)
      DO 2 I = 1,50
      X(I) = SIN( I * .15 )
2     CONTINUE
      CALL PLOT ( X, 50  )
      CALL EXIT
      END
// XEQ
```

FIGURE 9–14

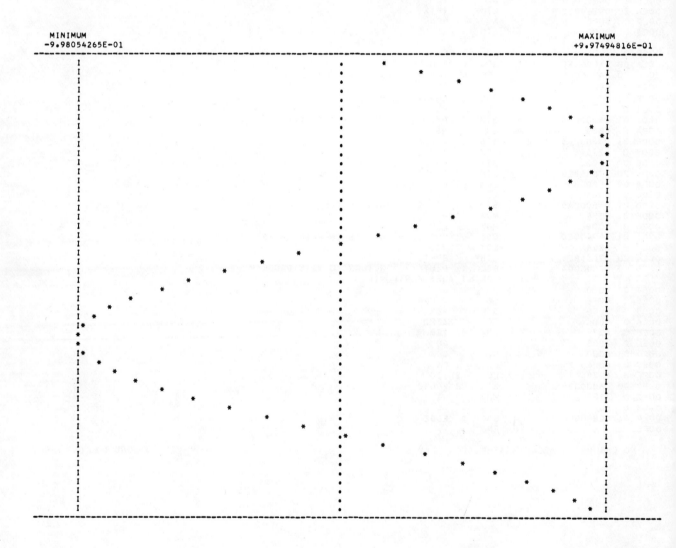

FIGURE 9–15

DEBUGGING IN ASSEMBLER

CHAPTER 10

The process of finding errors within an assembler program is more a matter of personal choice than it is with FORTRAN, because the variety of available techniques is considerably greater. Different programmers will go about the assembler debugging process differently, so the methods suggested here should be viewed as only one person's choice of some of the possibilities. Many of the techniques for debugging FORTRAN programs are appropriate here, so the reader may wish to review Chapter 5.

The first task is to develop a program that will assemble without error messages. There are far fewer types of errors which can be made in an assembler program, so there are fewer possible error messages. These messages are listed in the monitor manual, and in Appendixes D-2 and D-3. With the 1130 assembler you can get specific error messages only by using a LIST control card; without it the assembler will tell you the number of errors, but not where or what they are! Hence in the early stages of program writing it is essential to include a LIST card when assembling the program. The version 2 monitor allows selective listings, using the LIST ON and LIST OFF mnemonics; with these only a reworked part of a program need be listed.

The listing of the program shows your statements as punched and, to the left of each, the machine-language instructions into which your assembler instructions have been translated and their corresponding relative addresses. The error message letters appear between these two lists, no more than two for each instruction. By this method, errors are more exactly located than are FORTRAN errors, so there is usually little problem in determining the source of trouble. An error message can reflect an error in another statement, possibly one that was not completely analyzed because of an error, so several assembly passes may be necessary to find all the grammatical errors.

TESTING A PROGRAM

In our discussion of FORTRAN debugging we stressed that it may not be easy to tell when a successfully compiled program is not functioning properly. There may be obvious clues that a program is "sick." A program may produce an unending loop; it may stop with no valid instruction in the operation register. In either case the program is clearly in trouble. Another clue may be printed or punched output that is different from what was expected, or the total absence of expected output. Such apparent troubles must always be dealt with first.

After obvious difficulties of this type are removed and the program seems to be working well, the programmer must still establish that the program is doing what it is intended to do. The earlier discussion of testing measures

for FORTRAN is applicable here. However, simply inventing data and comparing program output with hand calculations, as suggested for FORTRAN, may be insufficient for a complex assembler program. Since a very complicated program almost inevitably has bugs, the method chosen for testing it becomes a critical issue. Sometimes running the program under many different circumstances, hoping to catch most of the possible errors, may be the only possible choice.

No amount of testing will catch *all* the problems in very complex programs. The history of the FORTRAN compiler for any particular machine shows that odd quirks are still being discovered and corrected, even years after the initial compiler was written. Perhaps one example in connection with the 1130 may be of interest. In the original version of the disk monitor system for the 1130, the FORTRAN compiler did not compile properly if a file was assigned the number 84 within a FORTRAN program. Any other number worked without difficulty. In the testing of the program it was not thought to try this particular file number so it was some time before this difficulty could be clearly identified. It was not until the third modification of the version 1 monitor that the error was corrected.

One intriguing possibility is to write programs which themselves generate programs to be used for testing purposes. In this way one takes advantage of the speed of the computer in producing test programs. But it does not seem likely that any infallible method for testing complex programs will be devised.

FINDING WHERE THE DIFFICULTY OCCURS

When difficulties are known to be present, the first step may be to determine the precise section of the program where a difficulty is occurring. One way to do this is to isolate a part of a program by inserting an assembler WAIT at an appropriate spot within the program. A WAIT is identifiable when lights 2 and 3 in the operation register are on. As with the FORTRAN PAUSE, any given WAIT can be assigned some identifying number to be loaded into the accumulator, and then, when the WAIT occurs, it can be recognized by examining the console lights. However, this takes additional instructions that will lengthen the program. (See the discussion of PAUSE later in this section.)

Using a number of WAIT commands without identifying numbers may make it difficult to tell where any particular WAIT occurs. However, it is possible to identify a WAIT if you have an assembler list showing addresses of instructions relative to the beginning of the program; if you have requested a core map (L in column 14 of the XEQ card), you can establish where you are in memory, and therefore where you are in the program, when the WAIT occurs.

If no subroutines are in use, all that is needed is the execution address, the address of the first instruction to be executed. The memory location is shown in the instruction address register.

An example might serve to make this clear. Let us suppose the following three things: the execution address of the program is known because we used an L on the XEQ card; this entry point has a relative address on the assembler list of 10_{16}; and at a WAIT in the program the IAR contains the hexadecimal address 200. Table 10–1 indicates this situation.

TABLE 10–1

Relative address	Program	Core address
(from assembler listing)		
0	Beginning	
10	Entry point	1D2
Desired	WAIT	200

What we need to find, in order to determine where we are, is the relative address of the WAIT, the address associated with that WAIT in your assembler list. We first subtract from the value in the IAR the execution address of the program, obtaining the number of words the WAIT is past the entry point. Then we add to this the relative location of the entry point:

$$\begin{array}{r} 200_{16} \\ -1D2_{16} \\ \hline 2E_{16} \\ +10_{16} \\ \hline 3E_{16} \end{array}$$

The final number we obtain is the relative address of the WAIT within the program, the address on the assembler listing that identifies the WAIT.

Another method for locating a WAIT is the use of the single instruction mode. After a WAIT the mode switch can be put on SI, single instruction execute. Then as each instruction is executed (one each time you press PROGRAM START) you can check your assembler listing to see whether the instruction, as indicated by the op-code lights, corresponds to a sequence of instructions after a WAIT. Usually one needs to watch the operation register for only a few instructions to see which instructions are being executed. This will necessitate either knowing the binary operation codes or having a card specifying them mounted at a handy place on the console. Such mounting is recommended if much console debugging of assembler programs is to take place. Appendix F-3 has a list of mnemonics arranged in operation-code order. Note that assembler debugging brings us into closer contact with machine language than does assembler programming.

The PAUSE can be used in assembler as well as in FORTRAN, since it is based on a system subroutine. The calling procedure is

```
27        35
|         |
LIBF      PAUSE
DC        [Address of a constant]
```

Thus if the DC address is that of a word containing 5555_{16}, this number will be in the accumulator lights on the console when the PAUSE is executed, with the binary pattern of five (0101) in each of the four groups of four lights. Often it is convenient to use constants already present in the program for other purposes.

USING FORTRAN DEBUGGING FACILITIES

Since the assembler language has full command of all the facilities of the system, it is not too surprising that it is possible to use FORTRAN trace routines within an assembler program. FORTRAN trace uses several special subroutines. These subroutines either replace other statements when translated by the FORTRAN compiler or they are called in as additional pieces of the program. These same subroutines can be used in an assembler program, both for arithmetic tracing and transfer tracing.

Arithmetic trace subroutines replace store operations. For example, in a standard precision floating point store operation if the coding

```
27        35
|         |
LIBF      FSTO
DC        A
```

is replaced by the coding

```
27        35
|         |
LIBF      SFAR
DC        A
```

then the program, in addition to storing the floating point variable A, will check switch 15. If the switch is on, the value of A will be typed or printed. Storage is accomplished by either coding. Therefore, the FSTO card can be replaced during debugging by the SFAR card. If the SFAR card is marked so that it can be easily located and removed from the deck, the FSTO card can be reinserted when the program is ready for execution. Table 10–2 shows alternative coding which can be used for tracing purposes, again using switch 15 for control.

These subroutines can be used more selectively in assembler than in FORTRAN, since they can be inserted specifically into those sections of the program card deck

TABLE 10–2

	Ordinary coding		Trace coding	
Extended precision storage	LIBF DC	ESTO A	LIBF DC	SEAR A
Integer storage	STO	I	LIBF DC	SIAR I
Branch on number in the accumulator			Insert LIBF SIIF before branching statements	
Branch on standard precision number in floating point accumulator	LD 3 +126 (branch statements)		LIBF SFIF (branch statements)	
Branch on extended precision number in floating point accumulator	LD 3 +126 (branch statements)		LIBF SEIF (branch statements)	

being worked on. One can also use in combination

```
27        35
|         |
CALL      TSTRT
CALL      TSTOP
```

to limit tracing just as one uses them within FORTRAN programs.

FLOW CHARTS

One general procedure recommended in connection with FORTRAN, flow charting, is also useful in writing and debugging assembler programs. Flow charting is, if anything, even more useful in assembler than in FORTRAN programs. Since each assembler statement is relatively more limited than a FORTRAN statement, an assembler program may have to use several statements to set up small loops for procedures which could be handled by a single FORTRAN instruction. A flow diagram provides a convenient way to "see" what is happening in a program for which the logic requires a complicated structure.

As indicated earlier, there are programs for producing flow charts on some computers, but at present the 1130 user, who is not likely to have such a program available, must flow chart his own. Reliance on flow charting varies considerably with individual programmers. Some prefer to draw a carefully detailed flow chart before beginning to write the actual program, then to annotate and update it to reflect each change as the program develops. Others, however, may omit flow charting entirely or make only skeleton charts, resorting to detailed charts only when they get into difficult situations.

DUMPS

One of the principal causes of trouble in assembler programs lies in the use of index registers. If you are writing a subprogram, you must be careful to save material in the index registers or the accumulator unless you know that these values are not needed in the main program. Looping processes within your program may use the index registers, so any difficulties there, such as neglecting them in this way, may set up unending loops.

Of particular concern to the programmer is index register 3, which is the link to the transfer vector. Since all LIBF subroutines employ the transfer vector, subroutines of this type will be inaccessible to the program unless register 3 is stored in core when you come into your program and restored to its original value immediately before entering any LIBF subroutines, assuming that you wish to use this index register. Index register 3 is also needed to locate the floating point accumulator.

If there are index register difficulties, dumping routines can check on the quantities in these registers at selected places during the program. One convenient way is with the "dump 80" subroutine, which dumps the first 80 words in core memory. The calling command is

```
27        35
|         |
CALL      DMP80
```

Since the index registers are in words 1, 2, and 3 in core, they can be found easily in such a dump, and other status indicators are also available.

There are other dump routines for printing parts of the program or data storage areas. Suppose that it is desirable to dump the entire program in hexadecimal form. If the first command in the program has a label BEGIN and the last command has a label END, then the following sequence would dump the program on the line printer.

```
27      35
|       |
CALL    DMTXO
DC      BEGIN
DC      END
```

DMTX1 gives the same result on the console printer. These routines also give, as the first line of the dump, the status indicators (overflow, carry, accumulator, accumulator extension, the three index registers).

A dump in decimal form is useful if the material to be dumped consists of decimal numbers; the two subroutine entry points are DMTD0 and DMTD1, for printing and typing, respectively.

IBM also supplies several dump subroutines on cards, and these will probably be available in your computer center. They work independently of the monitor or program and are entered as needed from the card reader in combination with the PROGRAM LOAD button on the console. The one-card console printer dump begins dumping at the core address in the console entry switches and stops only when PROGRAM STOP is pushed. The four-card printer dump begins at AO_{16}. Programs are also available for dumping sectors of the disk.

Programs in working storage on disk can be dumped using the DUMP control record of the disk utility program. These will usually be in disk system format. The list in Appendix E-3 giving the name code form for the system subroutines is useful in reading disk system format programs.

THE INTERRUPT-RUN FACILITY AND TRACING

We have emphasized that assembler debugging can be a matter of personal choice, depending in technique and procedure on the programmer. This is particularly true with programs written especially for use in debugging, i.e., programs not intended for performing calculations but for assisting in the discovery of errors in other programs. In this section we describe briefly one such program, using it also as an introduction to an 1130 facility which can help in debugging programs.

This facility is the INTERRUPT-RUN position of the mode switch, a position that we have not yet discussed. When the mode switch is in this position, a special action involving the interrupt facility of the computer (to be studied in Chapter 11) is taken. After each instruction is executed, if the mode switch is in the INTERRUPT-RUN position, a program break, called an *interrupt*, is generated by the system. The interrupt allows some

special action to be taken before the next instruction is executed, because it is accompanied by a computer-produced branch to a special part of the program. The ability to interrupt after every instruction can be very useful in a variety of debugging activities. Our sample program illustrates one use of this technique.

The program to be described was developed by the author and several others at the Reed College Computing Center; it is called HELP. Several versions of the program exist, although only one will be described. After the execution of each instruction has been completed, an interrupt produces a computer-created branch; in this case the branch is to HELP. The function of HELP is to locate the next machine-language instruction, translate it into an assembler instruction, type out the resulting instruction and its address in core, and then return control to the original program, which then executes the instruction just translated.

Thus with the use of HELP we can obtain a running account at the console typewriter of each instruction as it is being executed, and so follow in detail the flow of the program. Naturally the amount of output obtained in this way is limited. It is clearly impractical to ask the computer to type out hundreds of thousands of instructions in assembler form. But if this facility is used selectively to work through portions of a program giving particular trouble, HELP can be a very useful debugging aid.

A variant might be to print the contents of the index registers, whenever any instruction references them. As mentioned, index registers are a frequent source of trouble in assembler programming, particularly programming involving many different subroutines. It is all too easy to forget to save the contents of a particular register under some circumstances. Hence the ability to determine that a value in an index register is not behaving as expected—for example, increasing when it should be decreasing toward zero—may be very useful. Such a program could be combined with HELP, or it could be a separate program also using the interrupt-run facility.

The interrupt-run facility can be used selectively in certain parts of a program. One could have a WAIT beginning and ending the section to be affected. In this case the program would be started with the mode switch in the normal RUN position. When the first WAIT occurred the switch would be put in the INTERRUPT-RUN position; pressing PROGRAM START would then bring the HELP program into use. At the second WAIT the operator would return the mode switch to RUN.

Some special cautions are necessary when using the interrupt-run mode for debugging. Since an interrupt causes a branch after *each* instruction in the main program, it will interrupt a WAIT instruction just as it interrupts any other type of instruction, perform the branch, then return to the next statement in the program. In other words, a WAIT instruction in the main program will be ignored as a WAIT unless the debugging subprogram includes instructions to check for a WAIT and to wait if it finds one. A second problem concerns the fact that a level-5 interrupt can be caused by another device in the system, the PROGRAM STOP button on the console. Consequently it is important, when using the level-5 interrupt facility, to distinguish between these two devices. The details for doing this depend on knowledge of the interrupt system, which will be discussed in Chapter 11.

DEBUGGING AT THE COMPUTER CONSOLE

Console debugging has already been suggested in discussing the use of the WAIT facility. Using the computer console for finding programming troubles is often a last resort when other methods have failed.

For console debugging it is advisable to have a machine-language listing of your assembler program (perhaps compiled in Absolute mode) and a transfer vector storage map showing the location of the program and subroutines in memory. By including a WAIT in an appropriate place early in a program, preceding a section thought to be a source of trouble, we can put the mode switch on single instruction. Then we can follow the progress of the program, step by step, as it executes one instruction each time you push PROGRAM START. The console lights give the necessary information: the operation register shows the type of command being carried out; the instruction address register contains the address of the next instruction to be executed; the index register lights show which index register is being used, if any; and the accumulator contains the value currently being manipulated.

The configuration of each instruction in these lights can be inspected and checked against what was expected. Sometimes it will also be necessary to examine the contents of words in the memory other than those in the area in which you are proceeding one instruction at a time. For example, you might wish to know the contents of an index register. The procedure for displaying words in memory is listed in Appendix G-4. The IAR can be used to return to program execution after the display process.

Just as with FORTRAN, the process of debugging a complex assembler program is easier if the program is written in a modular fashion, as a series of pieces. Each piece can be tested separately. Usually it is easier to find an error in a small program than in a large one, so writing programs in separately testable parts may facilitate the debugging process.

MACHINE LANGUAGE
AND THE INTERRUPT SYSTEM

CHAPTER 11

INTRODUCTION TO MACHINE LANGUAGE

This section introduces the last language we shall consider, the actual language of the machine. It may not be clear why we should concern ourselves with machine language at all, except for the fact that it is, of course, another possible programming language, along with FORTRAN and assembler. However, few 1130 programs are likely to be written in machine language, since assembler has almost all its advantages and few of its disadvantages. Writing programs which consist of 16-bit binary words means handling (and punching) long lists of zeros and ones, and this task is not only inconvenient, but difficult to do without errors. The designers of the 1130 monitor system, taking into account the unlikelihood that machine language would be used in writing programs, considered it unnecessary to provide a convenient way of entering machine-language programs. (Such programs can be entered, independently of the monitor, through the use of console entry switches. This procedure is followed occasionally for short machine-language programs. Or one can write self-loading programs.)

There is another reason for learning machine language rather than its use as an active programming language. Knowledge of machine language can help the programmer to understand assembler details and it can be an especially valuable tool in debugging either assembler or FORTRAN programs. You will recall that although the programmer has a choice of languages in which to write, his program, no matter what its language, must be translated into machine language for execution. Consequently, any dumps called for during execution are in machine language, in hex, unless translation of some kind is specified. (An example of dumping in another form was given in the HELP program, which specified translation into assembler language. See Chapter 10.) If these dumps are to be interpreted to determine what the program is doing, an understanding of machine language is essential to the 1130 programmer.

We shall also consider in this chapter another machine feature, the interrupt system, and its use in input and output operations.

Many of the characteristic details of machine language will be familiar from our discussion of the assembler language, because there is a close correspondence between the two. For example, we know that some instructions occupy one 1130 word, others two words. The internal structure of the 16-bit machine-language word has not yet been discussed fully, but we have already learned some of the word's "ingredients" since they are the same as those used in assembler.

We shall begin by discussing the short- and long-form instructions.

THE SHORT INSTRUCTION

Figure 11–1 shows the layout for a short, or one-word, instruction. The five leftmost positions in the word, bits 0–4, contain the operation code (op-code). In our assembler examples, mnemonics were used to specify the operations to be performed. Each mnemonic corresponds to a binary five-bit number in machine language. The table in Appendix D-6 shows binary op-codes of and mnemonics associated with the operations which can be performed in the 1130 system. For example, the code for simple addition is 10000; that for loading a single word is 11000. The code combinations that do not correspond to instructions (and so do not appear in the table) function as wait codes, but all system-generated waits have code 00110.

When bit 5 contains a zero, the instruction is short. A long instruction will have a one in this bit, indicating that the word immediately following is the second half of the long instruction. Bit 5 is called the F-bit. Not all instructions can be both long and short, but many can be written both ways.

Bits 6 and 7 are the tag bits (T-bits). They indicate the index register, if any, that is being used. The tag bits contain the binary number for each index register. If the tag bits are zero, no index register is referenced.

The second half of the word, bits 8–15, usually contains the address displacement. The problem of addressing in short instructions was explained in our assembler discussion. You will recall that in a one-word short instruction there is not enough room for the full representation of any possible address in core. Therefore, a short instruction does not specify an actual address, but indicates the distance forward or backward, the displacement, of that address from the address currently in the instruction address register, the address of the next instruction. If both tag bits contain zeros, the displacement in the last eight bits is added to the value in the instruction address register to determine the effective address. If the tag bits specify an index register, that is, if they contain any value except two zeros, the displacement is added to the contents of the specified index register to determine the effective address. Negative displacements, like all negative values, are in the 2's complement form, and bit 8 is the sign bit.

Some short instructions use the last eight bits to specify information other than displacement. For example, every shift instruction has either one of only two operation codes: 00010 for shift left and 00011 for shift right. They are distinguished from each other by different coding in the 8 and 9 bits, as shown in Table 11-1. When used in this way, bits 8 and 9 are called modifier (mod) bits. Except for the two shift left and count instructions, the number of places to be shifted is determined by the

TABLE 11-1

	Op-code	Mod bits 8 and 9	Mnemonic	Name
Shift left	00010	00	SLA	Shift left accumulator
	00010	01	SLCA	Shift left and count accumulator
	00010	10	SLT	Shift left accumulator and extension
	00010	11	SLC	Shift left and count accumulator and extension
Shift right	00011	00 or 01	SRA	Shift right accumulator
	00011	10	SRT	Shift right accumulator and extension
	00011	11	RTE	Rotate right accumulator and extension

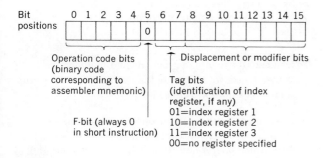

Bit positions 0 1 2 3 4 5 6 7 8 9 10 11 12 13 14 15

Operation code bits (binary code corresponding to assembler mnemonic)

Displacement or modifier bits

Tag bits (identification of index register, if any)
01=index register 1
10=index register 2
11=index register 3
00=no register specified

F-bit (always 0 in short instruction)

FIGURE 11-1

TABLE 11-2

Bit	Test condition
15	Overflow indicator *off*
14	Carry indicator *off*
13	Accumulator contents *even* (zero in rightmost bit)
12	Accumulator positive nonzero (zero in leftmost bit, not all zeros)
11	Accumulator negative (one in leftmost bit)
10	Accumulator zero (zero in all bits)

tag bits, the index register, and the rightmost six bits. If the tag bits are zero, then the shift is controlled by the rightmost six bits; the binary number stored there specifies the number of places to be shifted. On the other hand, if the tag bits specify an index register, that index register contains the number of places to be shifted. The shift and count instructions also use an index register rather than the last six bits, but for these instructions the register contains the limit of the shift instead of the specification. All shift instructions exist only in the short form.

The short form of the Branch (or Skip) on Condition instruction, BSC, uses the last six bits of the word to indicate the conditions under which the computer will skip the next word in memory and execute the instruction *after* this word. Table 11-2 identifies the conditions that can be tested and the bits used.

For each condition to be tested, a one is entered in the bit corresponding to the condition. If the computer, upon execution of a short BSC instruction, finds that any one of the specified conditions is true, it *skips the next word*. The next word must contain a *short* instruction, because a skip into the middle of a long instruction would produce undefined and probably undesirable results. If none of the specified conditions is satisfied, control goes to the next sequential instruction; there is no skipping.

The last eight bits of some short instructions are used for data values. In the load index register instruction, LDX, the last eight bits contain an actual value that is to be loaded into the index register specified by the instruction. The short MDX adds the value in these eight bits to the index register specified; if no register is specified, the MDX modifier bits are added to the IAR, causing an unconditional branch, as the IAR always has the address of the next instruction to be executed.

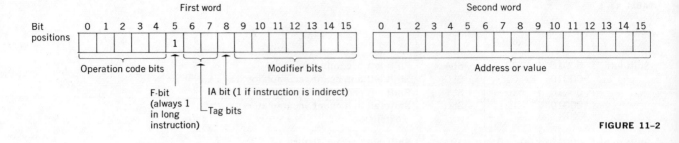

FIGURE 11–2

LONG-FORM INSTRUCTIONS

The two-word layout of a long instruction is shown in Fig. 11–2. Since the first word through bit 7 matches the word of the short instruction, we need to note only that bit 5 will always contain a 1 to indicate that the instruction is long.

Bit 8 is the IA (indirect address) bit, which indicates whether the address is indirect or direct. If the IA bit contains a 1, the effective address is interpreted as an indirect address; the actual address is at the effective address for indirect instructions. There is no need for this bit in the short form, since an indirect instruction must be long.

In long-form branch instructions the modifier bits, 9–15, are used as in the short-form instructions, but the condition for branching is different: when *none* of the specified conditions is true then the program *branches to the effective address*. If any of the conditions is true the next sequential instruction is executed. In a long MDX when the tag bits are zero, the modifier bits contain the second operand; this operand is added to the word whose address is in the second word of the instruction, but the modifier bits are not used when an index register is used.

The second word of a long instruction usually contains a full address rather than a displacement. Nonetheless, this full address may not be the effective address of the instruction, for when the tag bits are nonzero, the contents of the specified index register will be added to the contents of the second word to get the effective address. In the direct long LDX, the second word is the number that is to be placed in the index register.

INTERPRETING MACHINE LANGUAGE

Let us put some of our previous knowledge to use in interpreting machine-language instructions. Here are five words from an 1130 program as obtained, in hexadecimal, from a standard dump routine of the disk utility program:

D003 80F5 D00E 7580 01CB

TABLE 11–3

Hex	Binary			
	0	5		15
D003	1101	0000	0000	0011
80F5	1000	0000	1111	0101
D00E	1101	0000	0000	1110
7580	0111	0101	1000	0000
01CB	0000	0001	1100	1011

To translate these into instructions and to understand what they mean, we first write the five hexadecimal words in binary, as shown in Table 11–3.

Bits 0–4 in each word give the operation code, as we know; by referring to the table in Appendix F–3, we can find out which operations are specified. Note that bit 5 of the fourth word contains a 1. This tells us that the fourth and fifth words constitute a long instruction. Bit 5 in each of the first three words tells us that they are all short instructions. The following is a reasonable translation into assembler:

```
27   32  35
STO      *+3
A        *-11
STO      *+14
MDX  I1  /01CB
```

The *, as usual in the operand field, represents the value in the instruction address register when the instruction is executed. This coding is certainly not unique; other translations are possible, particularly if symbolic names for storage locations are introduced. Here is another possibility:

```
21     27   32  35
START  STO      START+4
       A        START-9
       STO      START+17
       MDX  I1  /01CB
```

Note that the slash is used to indicate a hexadecimal constant in the operand.

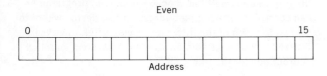

Even

Address

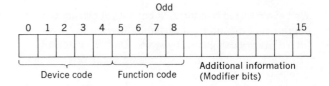

Odd

Device code   Function code   Additional information
(Modifier bits)

FIGURE 11–3

INPUT AND OUTPUT ON THE 1130

The astute observer will be aware that we have never dealt directly with questions of input or output. In FORTRAN we used the READ and WRITE statements, and in assembler-language discussions, we called in system-supplied subroutines to take care of input/output operations.

However, if there were no machine-language facilities for handling input and output, these subroutines could not even have been written! In early computer systems a series of machine-language instructions carried out all the possible input and output operations, usually one instruction for each type of operation. Early symbolic languages, one type of which is the assembler, included corresponding instructions. In modern computers, however, input and output are no longer the simple operations they once were. In a simplified way, because it is a small computer, the 1130 exemplifies current strategy for coping with input/output problems. We will here review only the situation; details are given in the *1130 Functional Characteristics* manual.

The approach to an input/output operation usually follows a general pattern. A machine-language instruction *starts*, let us say, an input operation. While this operation proceeds, the central processor continues executing the program. When the input operation has been completed, a signal is produced by the device performing the operation; this signal causes the computer to interrupt the flow of program execution and respond to the completion of the input operation. This mode of input/output operation is possible because of a facility known as an *interrupt* system, under which the computer can interrupt itself when some specified condition exists, in this case when the input/output operation has been completed. Thus the machine-language command simply initiates the operation.

The assembler instruction to initiate an input or an output operation, the only one for this purpose, is Execute I/O:

```
27      35
|       |
XIO     ADR
```

TABLE 11–4

Program fragment			Comments
	:		
	XIO	ADR	Begins the I/O operation ADR is the location of the IOCC (must be an even address)
	:		
ADR	DC	OUT	First word of IOCC OUT is the output area
	DC	/0900	Second word of IOCC (indicates "write" on console printer)
	:		
OUT	DC	/3C00	Contains console printer code for the letter A
	:		

The effective address of the instruction (ADR in this case) is the address of a pair of words which contain the description of the input or output operation. The description specifies the device to be used and the function that device is to perform. The XIO command can be long or short, direct or indirect, and index registers can be employed in the usual fashion for effective address computation.

The pair of words addressed by the XIO command is called the *Input/Output Control Command*, or IOCC. The first word, always at an *even* location, is often an address, usually the address from which reading or writing is to take place; with some functions this word serves no purpose, but it must always be present. The second word identifies the device and the particular function to be performed by that device. An illustration of the structure of these two words is given in Fig. 11–3. Details may differ for different devices.

Appendix F-10, I/O Function Codes and Modifiers, gives the information needed for writing the second IOCC word. For example, to cause an A to be written on the console printer a programmer could use the sequence given in Table 11–4. Often the first word of the output area contains the number of characters to be used.

THE INTERRUPT SYSTEM

We have referred to interrupts but not yet considered the operation of the interrupt system. Different types of interrupts are designated by *levels*. On the 1130 these levels are zero through five. Thus we speak of a "level-three" interrupt.

For each interrupt level there is an *address* stored in a fixed location in the core memory, the interrupt *branching address* for that level. For example, word 9 in core is the location for an address associated with a level-zero interrupt, word 10 with a level-one interrupt, etc. The appropriate branching addresses must be entered into these words by the program, and the addresses in the words can be altered by the program just as with any word in core.

Let us consider what happens during a level-zero interrupt. When the level-zero interrupt occurs, perhaps initiated by a device on the completion of some I/O function, the computer manufactures and executes a Branch and Store IAR (BSI) command, using the address for the level-zero interrupt, in word 9 in core, as the effective address. After execution of this BSI, the current IAR value is stored at this address, and the instruction in the next word is executed. What program is at the branching address (just after the storage word with address in word 9) will be determined either by what programming

system is in use (FORTRAN or assembler) or by what the programmer himself has placed there. The programmer can control the branching address and so decide where to branch for each of the interrupt levels. Often (always in FORTRAN) the programmer accepts the system-supplied subroutines for the interrupt.

The program at the branching address is designed to "service" the interrupt, that is, to take whatever action is necessary when the originally specified input or output operation has been completed. Since this servicing program is reached through a BSI, it can return control to the original program when its work has been completed. The flow of control is shown in Fig. 11–4.

Since there are many different things that can be done by the input/output devices, there are many possible interrupt causes. There are, for example, three interrupts, two of one level, one of another, that can be caused by the 1442 card read-punch. When a column of data has been read and is ready to be transferred to core memory, a level-zero interrupt is generated. When a column is ready to be punched, a level-zero interrupt allows for the necessary data transfer from core to the punch. A level-four interrupt occurs when column 80 of a card has passed the read station in the 1442, or when a machine malfunction occurs, such as a hopper check, when a card does not succeed in leaving the read hopper. Thus the card read-punch can cause an interrupt on two different levels and for several reasons. Appendix F-13 contains a list of conditions which produce interrupts in the 1130 and shows the corresponding interrupt levels.

Because there are many causes of interrupts, the interrupt service program must determine the cause of the interrupt before it can take the appropriate action. The *level* of the interrupt is the first piece of information that is available. In some situations this information determines the device, for with some 1130 configurations only one device may use a particular interrupt level. In other cases the servicing program must determine which device caused the interrupt.

With a level-four interrupt, both the card reader and the keyboard console (as well as the paper tape reader, if present) can create a level-four interrupt. To provide a quick way to see which device is responsible, the device sets a bit in a special central processor word, the *Interrupt Status Word*. The coding of the interrupt status word is:

Bit 0—Paper tape read/punch
Bit 1—Console/keyboard
Bit 2—Card read/punch

with a 1 in the appropriate bit identifying the device indicated. This word can be loaded in the accumulator by means of an XIO *Sense Interrupt* command (function code 011 in the IOCC).

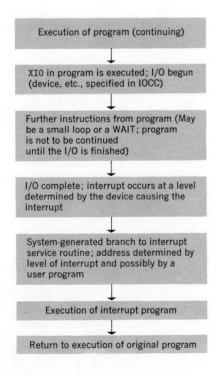

Execution of program (continuing)

↓

XIO in program is executed; I/O begun (device, etc., specified in IOCC)

↓

Further instructions from program (May be a small loop or a WAIT; program is not to be continued until the I/O is finished)

↓

I/O complete; interrupt occurs at a level determined by the device causing the interrupt

↓

System-generated branch to interrupt service routine; address determined by level of interrupt and possibly by a user program

↓

Execution of interrupt program

↓

Return to execution of original program

FIG. 11–4. Interrupt flow.

Multidisk systems and systems with a communications adapter for remote input or a storage access channel for user devices or high-speed input/output have interrupt level status words for use on all interrupt levels. Details of these facilities are given in the functional characteristics manual.

When the service program knows which device caused the interrupt, it must next determine why that device gave such a signal. The source of information on the cause of an interrupt is a special word stored for each device, the *Device Status Word*, which can be examined by the service program. A device status word in each device can be examined by the program and so the interrupt can be identified by the interrupt servicing program; it is loaded in the accumulator with an XIO *sense device* command (code 111 in the IOCC). Indeed, this determination of the precise reason for the interrupt is the first function that must be performed by the servicing program. The structure of the device status word for each device is specified in an IBM-supplied table, which is reprinted in Appendix F–11.

TRAFFIC CONTROL OF INTERRUPTS

There are difficulties and problems we have not yet covered. It is entirely possible for an interrupt to occur while the computer is already servicing another interrupt. This possibility is of such common and frequent occurrence that provision must be made for "nesting" interrupts. The situation is complicated by the timing requirements of the input/output devices.

When an interrupt occurs, the corresponding interrupt switch is set in the machine, and the appropriate light on the console goes on. After the interrupt, interrupts of higher priority can interrupt the interrupt, but the opposite is not true. Interrupts of equal or lower priority are constrained from interrupting. Thus interrupts can be nested; an interrupt servicing program can itself be interrupted by a higher priority interrupt. All active interrupts are completed before return to the main program.

It is the programmer's responsibility to "clear" the interrupt level after the completion of interrupt servicing and just before returning to the main program, thus allowing any equal or lower priority interrupts to be serviced. Clearing is done by a special form of the long BSC command; in machine language, a 1 in bit 9 of the first word clears the level, and in assembler the instruction BOSC replaces the usual BSC. The interrupt facility is a hardware facility in the central processor, so clearing the priority status is a hardware operation. The chart in Fig. 11–5 illustrates the general flow of operation in a level-zero interrupt.

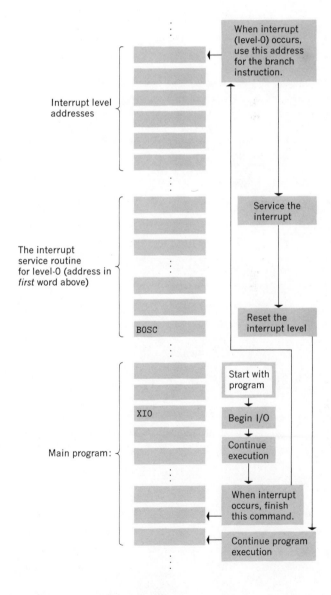

FIG. 11–5. Skeleton of memory and execution for a level-zero interrupt. Begin with the "Start with program" box in reading this example.

WHY USE INTERRUPTS?

The purpose of the interrupt system may be more apparent if it is seen as part of the progressive development of solutions to the problem of time usage. In early computer systems, when an input/output operation was started, the whole system had to wait for that operation to be finished. This limitation was often a waste of valuable time, for input/output operations use mechanical devices and are consequently much slower than the electronic operations of the central processor. Hence efforts were made to find other ways of dealing with the problem. One early solution, still used, is *buffering*, by which information for input or output is stored in a special separate memory or small auxiliary computer, thus enabling the main central processor to be used for other things while input/output operations are going on.

The interrupt facility is a more recently developed method of reducing the time for input/output, and it can be used both with and without buffering. After the XIO instruction is executed, the computer can continue to execute instructions in the program that are not concerned with the information being inputted or outputted; of course, one must be careful in the program not to change unintentionally the information going in or out. After some calculation the interrupt system signals that the machine is ready for more input or output operations. Thus considerable increase in speed is possible by the use of an interrupt system. The amount of gain actually realized depends on the design of the programs.

Most of the system-supplied input and output subroutines do not make full use of the interrupt facility. This is particularly true of the FORTRAN input/output subroutines, which complete input and output operations before returning to the main program. These subroutines have internal loops or waits to allow for the time needed to complete an input or output operation. Thus in a typical 1130 FORTRAN program no calculation goes on during input or output, just as with older input/output systems, as described above. It is not too hard to see why this is true in FORTRAN, a system designed for use by many persons at different levels of sophistication. Many of these users will be unaware of the nature of the interrupt system and its advantages. The unsophisticated FORTRAN programmer is likely to write a program in such a way that the instructions immediately following an input instruction alter the material just read in. If the program were to continue with these instructions during input/output, the results might be disastrous. But with experience the programmer learns how to exploit the interrupt facility to gain time.

THE LIFE HISTORY OF
A FORTRAN STATEMENT

You should already have a rough conception of what happens to a FORTRAN statement from its entry into the computer to its execution. The statement is first converted by the compiler into a series of computer words and then changed by stages into a string of instructions. This string of instructions is in turn adapted by the loader (or core load builder) into the actual program that is executed, command by command. For most users of the 1130 computer this knowledge is sufficient; it is not necessary to know the detailed structure of either the FORTRAN compiler or the loader in the monitor system of the 1130. Furthermore, in the space available here, it would be impossible to give a full account of their structure. Details are given in an IBM publication especially designed for use by system programmers, that is, programmers concerned with altering or extending the 1130 monitor system. This publication is the *IBM 1130 Monitor Programming System—Program Logic Manual*, and the reader interested in monitor program details beyond the scope of the present book is referred to that manual.

However, we may provide some insight into the operation of the various software packages within the system by tracing the history of a simple FORTRAN arithmetic statement through the entire process, from the entry of the statement to its execution. By this procedure we hope particularly to clarify the operation of the FORTRAN compiler. As you follow this history, you will probably discover that the process of compilation is more complex than you might have suspected thus far. Furthermore, you should bear in mind that you are learning only how one statement is handled. Remember that there are many other types!

This example can serve also as an introduction to language processors other than the FORTRAN compiler. A general survey of the sophisticated linguistic analysis used in constructing compilers is presented in an article by Ruth M. Davis, "Programming Language Processors" (ed. F. L. Alt and M. Rabinoff, *Advances in Computers*, Volume 7, Academic Press, New York, 1966).

THE SOURCE STATEMENT AND THE FORTRAN COMPILER

The FORTRAN statement we shall follow is

N = (N + M)*N − M

Our *source* language is FORTRAN, and our *target* language is 1130 machine language.

The first part of the system-supplied software that takes action is the FORTRAN compiler. In the 1130 version 1 monitor for a system with one disk, the FORTRAN compilation program comprises 28 separate phases. Each of these phases is brought into core individually from the

disk, one after the other. The FORTRAN program, entered from cards or paper tape, becomes a string of symbols in core memory. This symbol string is manipulated successively by each of the 28 phases of the FORTRAN compiler. A given statement may be affected by only certain phases. During this process the FORTRAN statement becomes, step by step, increasingly like a machine-language program. Certain auxiliary information, of which the most important is the symbol table, is also gathered during compilation. After compilation the symbol table will contain the variables in the program and their storage locations in memory relative to the beginning of the program. Thus the compilation process can be described as a string-manipulation operation, since the statement is converted by manipulation from the string of computer words that represent the statement as entered, into a corresponding string of machine-language instructions that will carry out the calculations specified in the statement.

Usually the compiler moves from phase to phase with no interruption, and the user is consequently not aware of successive phases going in and out of the core memory. But one can alter the usual operation of the compiler in order to obtain a printout of the string area following the execution of each phase. It is this technique which we use to study the history of a FORTRAN statement. (A user who wishes to trace the history of a statement of his own choosing can do so with the help of the program logic manual.)

FORTRAN—PHASE 3: INPUT

Phases 1 and 2 in the compiler program are initialization phases, independent of the particular FORTRAN program being compiled.

The internal symbol string that represents a source program is created in phase 3, during which the FORTRAN program card deck is read. On completion of phase 3, our FORTRAN statement is stored internally as 16-bit binary words, represented by the following hexadecimal string:

001C D57E 4DD5 4ED4 5D5C D560 D440

The internal coding for the symbols is 8-bit EBCDIC, packed two characters to a word. In hexadecimal notation, two digits represent one character in 8-bit EBCDIC. Thus in the second word, D5 is the EBCDIC coding for N, and the second half of that word, 7E, is the hexadecimal representation of the EBCDIC coding for =. The second half of the last word, 40, represents the EBCDIC coding for a blank, which was included because the total number of characters was odd. Note, however, that the blanks included in the source statement for clarity have been eliminated. By using the character code table, in Appendix C-8, we can ascertain that, except for the first word, the above string of hexadecimal words represents exactly the EBCDIC coding for the characters of the FORTRAN statement as those characters appeared on the entry card.

For each FORTRAN statement, the first word in the string plays a special role. The first five bits (0–4) in this ID word, will contain the code for the statement type when it is determined in phase 4. (For our statement these bits will remain five zeros, the code assigned to an arithmetic statement.) Bits 5–13 in the indicator word will change from phase to phase, however. They specify the number of *words*, including the ID word, in the string at the conclusion of each phase. If you expand into binary the first hexadecimal word, 001C, in the above phase-3 string, you will find that the number of words specified by bits 5–13 is seven, the number of words in the string. The last bit in the indicator word is set to 1 if the entered statement begins with a statement number.

The program is listed on the principal print device during phase 3, if the control records include a LIST SOURCE PROGRAM or LIST ALL card.

FORTRAN—PHASE 4: CLASSIFIER

After phase 4, the string is considerably altered in appearance.

0034   AA00   003E   000D   AA00   000E   A800   001D   001C   AA00   0020   A800   001E

Interpretation

     N   =   (N   +   M   )   *   N   −   M   ;

Again the first word in this string is the ID word; the statement type has been inserted, and there are 13 words in the sentence string. Although the new coding looks different, the alterations are not as great as they appear to be. The *order* of the symbols is unaltered.

Each symbol is allotted a full word in phase 4, and so the string is longer. The coding of the operators, such as plus and minus, is 6-bit rather than 8-bit EBCDIC. In 6-bit EBCDIC coding, only the rightmost 6 bits are used for the operator. This coding is at the right end of the word with 0's in the other bits, so an operator word has a 0 in bit 0. The 8-bit EBCDIC coding for an equals sign is 0111 1110. The rightmost 6 bits are 11 1110; with two 0's at the left end, the hex equivalent is 3E. Filling out the left end with 0's the word 003E stands for =. Similarly 000D indicates a left parenthesis, as you can check by using the EBCDIC coding. The symbols of the statement are indicated under their equivalent codings in the string.

A terminal operator, the semicolon, has been introduced into the string. This last word in the string, 001E, is included in the word count. There are now two indications of the string's end, the ID word with its count and the terminal operator.

The coding for the variables is also altered in phase 4. The hexadecimal coding for N in phase 3 was D5, while N is represented in the new string by the word AA00. Although these look different, their equivalence is more obvious when the two codings are examined in binary. Let us consider the two codes for N. AA is 10101010; D5 is 11010101. The new coding is again a variant of EBCDIC coding. Since the variable N is a single character, the rest of the word to the right is padded with 0's. A word containing a variable name in the string has a 1 in bit 0.

FORTRAN—PHASE 10:
VARIABLE AND STATEMENT FUNCTIONS

Phase 10 is the next compiler phase that operates on our string. After phase 10 the program string looks like this:

| 0034 | 8001 | 000E | 0010 | 8001 | 0004 | 8003 | 0002 | 000C | 8001 | 0006 | 8003 | 0000 |

Interpretation

| | N | = | (| N | + | M |) | * | N | — | M | ; |

In phase 10 the literal variable names N and M were removed from the string and replaced by *pointers*, which are codings that point to the location of the literal names in the symbol table, as well as in the string area. The pointer for N is 8001; for M, 8003.

The symbol table is a compiler-constructed list of the variables in a program. The variables are entered in the table during phase 10. A segment of the symbol table for our statement at the conclusion of phase 10 follows.

| C000 | 0062 | 0000 | 4000 | A800 | 8000 | C000 | 0001 | 0000 | 4000 | AA00 | 8000 |

One must read the symbol table from right to left, in groups of three; thus the "first" three words at the right are the entry for N, and the 1 at the end of the word 8001 in the program string points to this first group of three words. Hexadecimal AA00, the second word, is the already encountered coding for N. You should also be able to find the coding for M in the symbol table.

In phase 10 the arithmetic operators in our statement string are also changed. Later these operators are to be used in connection with a *forcing table*, and the values given here relate to that table. However, the string is still in the same order that it has been since the beginning; only the coding of the symbols has changed.

FORTRAN—PHASE 17: SCAN

Phase 17 in the compilation process is perhaps the most critical phase for arithmetic statements. The earlier changes have been leading up to the more complex pro-

cessing of phase 17, in which the order of the string is
completely changed. Here is the string representing our
statement after phase 17:

0036   0004   8001   8003   000C   8001   0006   8003   000E   8001   0000

Interpretation

+   N   M   *   N   –   M   =   N

If you compare this string and its interpretation with the
phase-10 string, you will see that all characters still present are represented by the same words, but that the order
is different. The ID word has changed, reflecting the fact
that two characters included earlier are now missing. The
left and right parentheses have dropped out of the string.
This dropping of the grouping symbols is an important
aspect of the rearrangement in phase 17. In the paren-
thesis-free string, there are no symbols which merely
group; all the operators are now true operators.

The purpose for this rearrangement is to bring the string
to an order more nearly like that in which the computation
will be performed. The phase-17 string,

$$+ N M * N - M = N$$

can be read as follows: add M to N; then multiply the sum
by N; then subtract M from the product; and, finally, place
the difference at N. This is the order we would follow in
carrying out the arithmetical operations specified in the
statement, and it corresponds to the order of the instructions in the final translated program. (The name of this
ordering, *modified Polish notation*, is derived from the fact
that such a notation, which eliminates the need for
parentheses, was used by the Polish logician, Jan Lukasie-
wicz. It was also used earlier for certain quaternion
operations. This rearranging is a critical stage in most
compilers.

The algorithm or procedure for rewriting the statement in
the new order is based on the use of the forcing values of
the operators and a forcing table. The details will not be
included here; they are covered in the *Program Logic
Manual*, in the discussion of an example (pp. 104–107).
Another similar method is described in the Davis article
cited.

For the statement we are considering, the work of phase
17 consists only of generating the symbol rearrangement
just described. However, the symbols in some statements
cannot simply be rearranged in computing order without
doing something else, because the statements call for
calculations in which the intermediate results of certain
steps must be stored temporarily for later use. For example, any method of computing the statement

$$N = N + (N*N + M*N)$$

will require temporary storage of one of the two products.
The compiler allocates any necessary temporary storage
by adding it to the symbol table, and by adding at the
same time whatever instructions are needed for storing a
value and for removing it. This means, in essence, that
the compiler itself defines a new variable, allocates
storage for it, and rewrites the sequence of instructions
using this new variable.

Thus the above statement containing two multiplications
might be approached by the compiler in the following
manner. Let the name J be given to the expression
$N \times N$, and allocate storage for J; compute $N \times N$, and
place the product at J. In other words, let

$$J = N * N.$$

Then the compiler could evaluate

$$N = N + (J + M*N)$$

according to the procedures outlined above. It should be
understood that at this phase the compiler is not working
with the FORTRAN symbols and that the example is intended only to illustrate the process.

FORTRAN—PHASE 19: EXPANDER II

Although the string was rearranged in phase 17, it was
still a string of codings for symbols, with each coded
word standing either for the location of a variable or for
an operator. The major step in phase 19 is the change
from a list of codings for symbols to a list that approaches
the coding of the final machine-language program. After
phase 19, each word corresponds to one instruction in
the final coding, and the resulting string is

001C   8801   9803   B001   3980   A003   9001

The first word, as before, is the ID word. The numbers
01 and 03 in each occurrence as the last two digits of a
word still point to N and M, respectively, in the symbol
table. We can identify each word (except the ID) by the
following "equivalent" assembler coding, provided we
bear in mind the fact that the machine-language equiva-

lents of this coding have not yet been completely
established.

```
27      35
|       |
LD      N
A       M
M       N
SLT     16
S       M
STO     N
```

The second parts of most of the words in the string still
contain pointers to locations of variables in the symbol
table. If we "translate" the first half of these words we
realize that the operation code is not yet being used.

FORTRAN—PHASE 27: OUTPUT II

The change in phase 19 is the last change of the string
that takes place *in core* during the compilation process.
If one examines the string after phase 28, the last phase
of compilation, the codings are those of phase 19. (These
other phases would affect other FORTRAN statements.)
Nevertheless, a significant alteration occurs in phase 27,
when the string is transferred from core to the working
storage area on disk. Phase 27 entails rewriting, not just
simple copying, and carries our statement another step
toward the final machine-language program that is to be
executed.

The program is transferred to working storage on disk in
disk system format, a format we have previously encountered. Programs are stored in both the user area and the
fixed area on disk in disk system format, unless the store
core image command is used. In disk system format all
addresses present in the instructions are specified relative to the beginning of the program, not as actual locations in storage.

Another important aspect of disk system format concerns
the handling of subprograms; any necessary subprograms
are indicated in the program by their names, in a special
coding known as name code. Since our statement has no
subprogram calls, this history shows no example of this
aspect. The two leftmost bits, not used in name code,
indicate the type of subprogram.

As an aid to understanding, we will list under the phase-27
string, which follows, the assembler mnemonics that correspond to the operation codes, which are now in place.
This string should be compared with that in phase 19.
Note the long instructions.

The addresses of the variables are still pointers, but the
locations are a little different, because the symbol table
has been slightly rearranged. These pointers are now
also relative addresses, referring to the storage area preceding the program during execution. We will see how
they are converted to actual addresses. The symbol table
at this stage reflects the relative placement of these
storage words in the final program. Variable storage
(except for COMMON) will precede the program.

A program in disk system format has a *header* (generated
in phase 26) stating the length of the program, the length
of the program header, the number of files defined, the
names and addresses of the entry points, and other
information.

In the phase-27 string there is one word, 0444, which has
neither a mnemonic nor a variable address associated
with it. It is not a machine-language instruction and will
not be converted into one. Instead it is another kind of
indicator word which occurs before every eight words in
a program in the disk system format. (Our statement is
only a piece of a program, so the location of this word
depends on what precedes our statement in the program.)
The role of this indicator word is to furnish information to
the loader program for the process of converting this
program into a working program. This process will be
described shortly. The 16 bits in this indicator word
correspond, in eight pairs, to each of the eight words
following. The first bit of each pair of bits indicates
whether the referenced word contains the name of a
called subprogram. The second bit indicates whether or
not the word is an address that needs to be relocated.
If we expand into binary the indicator word 0444, grouping the bits in pairs, we obtain

00 00 01 00 01 00 01 00

Since the first bit of each pair is 0, no subprograms are
involved; but the third, the fifth, and the seventh words
following this indicator word evidently contain addresses
requiring relocation, since the second bit of the pair
associated with each of these words contains a 1.
Checking the third and fifth words following the indicator
word shows that these are indeed addresses of variables.

The indicator word is not directly associated with individual instructions, but precedes each group of eight
words, as indicated above.

C400 0002	8400 0004	A400 0002	0444	1909	9400 0004	0400 0002
LD N	A M	M N		SLT 16	S M	STO N

THE LOADER

The final monitor program needed to bring our statement
to execution is the loader, or core load builder. As indicated above, the loader replaces subprogram names, if
any, by instructions branching to these subprograms, and
converts relative addresses to absolute addresses.

Replacing subprogram names with the necessary branches
is not a simple process. The subprograms may be stored
on disk either in the user area or in the fixed area. When
the loader finds a subprogram name in a program it is
converting for core usage, its first task is to look up the
name in LET or FLET to determine whether that subprogram is stored on disk. If not, an error message is
produced; but if the subprogram is on disk, the loader
"knows" its location on disk and its length. The loader
assigns a location for the subprogram in core memory
and then uses this location to determine the address in
the branching instruction for the subprogram. Each subprogram so established is also added to the transfer
vector, described in Chapter 8. A BSI replaces the name
of the subprogram.

Since subroutines are usually in disk system format, they
too must be converted by the loader. Furthermore, if
subprograms call other subprograms, a chain of operations
must be established whereby each subprogram called is
converted for core.

The loader's two-part process of converting and loading
involves a considerable amount of disk activity, and the
time it takes is not trivial. The tables by which subprograms are located, LET and FLET, are in one part of
the disk, and the subprograms themselves may be scat-
tered over many sectors. The process of gathering
information from the disk causes a buzzing sound from
the central processor after the XEQ instruction is encountered and before execution of the program is started.
The XEQ card can be considered as a call to the loader.
The loading process can be expedited in a system with
several disks if the working storage area, the core image
buffer, and the monitor system are all on separate disks,
as they may be with the version 2 monitor. After conversion the program is loaded into core, and control is
transferred to the first instruction.

Finally we have the machine-language instructions for
our statement as they are to be executed during the
running of the program of which the statement is a part.

C400 01C4	8400 01C6	A400 01C4	1090	9400 01C6	D400 01C4
LD N	A M	M N	SLT 16	S M	STO N

The actual addresses here (for example, the address
01C4 for N) are valid only for this particular core load;
the addresses would be different if the same statement

occurred in another FORTRAN program. By comparing these final addresses with those of the phase-27 string, you can see that the relocation process consisted in simply adding 01C2 to each phase-27 address; 01C2 is the usual location for the start of a FORTRAN or assembler program with the version 1 monitor.

HOW INSTRUCTIONS ARE EXECUTED

The final step in our life history of one FORTRAN statement is the execution of the instructions generated by the statement. Although a detailed explanation of the actions taken by the computer in executing a set of instructions is beyond the scope of this book, we can outline the process and explain a few of its salient features.

The first of two steps in the process of execution of an instruction is interpretation. (For a few instructions, in fact, interpretation is the only step.) Interpretation is accomplished by a series of *interpretation-* or *I-cycles*. The second step is the actual execution, which depends on information generated during interpretation. Execution is accomplished by several *execution-* or *E-cycles*. The number of cycles of both kinds varies from instruction to instruction. For example, at least one I-cycle *must* be and up to four *may* be used. All instructions require I-cycle 1, and all long instructions require I-2; the I-X cycle is required only when indexing is used in the instruction and the I-I cycle only when indirect addressing is used. When the mode switch is in the *Single Machine Cycle* (SMC) position, one cycle is carried out each time the START button is pressed. These cycles are indicated by the lights in the second row in the center of the console panel, starting with the light labeled I-1; there are lights in this row for the four possible I-cycles and for some of the E-cycles.

Each cycle is a series of steps. One can observe each step individually by putting the mode switch in the *Single Step* position (SS). The lights in the top row of the center group, those preceded by T, indicate the separate steps. Thus a given I-cycle, such as I-1, will include some of the T steps. You may be relieved to know that the average user almost never needs these two mode switch positions! However, they can be useful when one is trying to determine the cause of machine malfunctions. They can also provide a valuable tool for the student interested in learning how instructions are executed.

In the interpretation and execution of an instruction, the computer uses internal storage registers other than those already encountered. Most of these registers are represented by lights on the console display panel. The *Arithmetic Factor Register* always contains any number brought from memory to be combined arithmetically with the number in the accumulator. The *Storage Buffer Register* holds numbers initially when they are brought

from memory. The *Storage Address Register* is often used as a temporary home for the address in the instruction address register, particularly just before the IAR is to be incremented by 1. If the SAR is so used, the computer has available both the current address and the next consecutive address.

One register which has no corresponding lights is the *Temporary Accumulator*. During interpretation of an instruction, the accumulator may be employed for effective address computation. Hence the value in the accumulator must be stored for later use in execution of the instruction and for reloading the accumulator. The temporary accumulator provides this storage, and since it usually contains the same value that is in the accumulator, it requires no separate console lights.

Some uses of these registers during execution involve details that we have not yet covered. Reading a number from core is a destructive operation, an operation that results in the loss of that number. Heretofore we have always assumed that a number loaded from core memory is still in core memory after the loading is completed. However, the number will actually be lost unless, in addition to being loaded into the central processor registers, it is also later reloaded into core memory. The necessary reloading occurs during the first E-cycle for any instruction that accesses memory. The net effect of the complete execution is that the word is unaltered in core.

THE ADD INSTRUCTION

With this description in mind, we shall follow the interpretation and execution of an add instruction, giving only enough of the process to provide an understanding of the general flow. The instruction will be long and direct, and it will reference no index registers. Hence you might think of it as the add instruction in our "life history" statement, now as a machine-language instruction.

For interpretation a long instruction needs an I-1 and an I-2 cycle. During the I-1 cycle the computer stores the accumulator's value (one of the numbers to be added) in the temporary accumulator, stores the IAR in the storage address register, and increments the IAR by 1. Next the first word of the instruction is loaded into the storage buffer register. The first nine bits of this word are then separated into functional pieces (the operation code bits, the tag bits, etc.) and sent to a series of smaller registers —the operation register, the flag register, the tag register and the mode register—for temporary storage.

Since the instruction is long, an I-2 cycle is started. In the I-2 cycle the instruction address register is again loaded into its image, the SAR, and then the IAR is incremented by 1. Finally, the second word of the instruction is brought from memory into the SBR. For our add instruction this completes the I-cycles.

In E–1, the first execution cycle, the contents of the accumulator are transferred to the storage address register, and then the accumulator is restored to its initial value by loading it with the contents of the temporary accumulator. We did not need to use the accumulator for effective address computation.

Now the word whose address is in the storage address register is brought into both the storage buffer register and the arithmetic factor register. This word is also restored in memory by reading it back into the place from which it originally came. We are now prepared to carry out the add operation.

The two registers containing the quantities to be added are the accumulator and the arithmetic factor register. Addition is carried out by a repetitive process that works through both words a number of times until a certain condition is met. In each pass through the process, two actions are taken. *First*, if a particular bit of the AFR contains a 0, the corresponding bit in the accumulator is unaltered. On the other hand, if the bit of the AFR contains a 1, the corresponding accumulator bit is reversed. *Second*, whenever an accumulator bit is changed from a 1 to a 0—in other words, the carry situation—then the next higher-order position in the AFR is set equal to 1, a bit indicating a carry. All the other positions in the factor registers are set equal to 0. Thus after each pass there will still be two numbers, with the arithmetic factor register containing the carry bits. The process is repeated until all the bits in the arithmetic factor register are 0, indicating no further carry. Because of the use of the 2's complement for negative numbers, no special action needs to be taken in case one of the numbers is negative. The following example, using only 8-bit words for convenience, may make this description more transparent.

	Original contents	After first pass	After second pass	After third pass	After fourth pass (Operation complete)
ACC	00101101	00111010	00110000	00100100	01000100
AFR	00010111	00001010	00010100	00100000	00000000

Our discussion of how one machine-language instruction generated by our original FORTRAN statement, the add instruction, is executed by the 1130 is at an end. We have not considered the electronic circuitry to carry out the indicated steps, since the user need not be aware of the internal mechanism for execution of an instruction. Even apart from hardware consideration, our discussion is not complete. For example, we have had nothing to say about the Cycle Control Counter, nor about the carry and overflow bits. Other instructions will have to be implemented by procedures different from those for the direct, long-form, add instruction we have considered.

1130 INFORMATION

APPENDIXES

FORTRAN

APPENDIX A

1. **FORTRAN STATEMENT TYPES**

2. **FORTRAN DESCRIPTIONS FOR INPUT-OUTPUT DEVICES**

3. **TYPICAL DECK FOR RUNNING A FORTRAN (OR ASSEMBLER) PROGRAM**

4. **FORTRAN CONTROL RECORDS**

5. **FORTRAN SUPPLIED SUBPROGRAMS**

6. **FORTRAN ERROR CODES**

7. **FORTRAN INPUT/OUTPUT ERROR CODES**

8. **FORTRAN INDICATOR TESTS**

A-1. FORTRAN STATEMENT TYPES

Statement type	Executable	Example	Purpose
Arithmetic	Yes	A = B*C + SIN(D)	Calculates a value, stores it in memory
End	No	END	Last statement in program, signal to compiler
Subroutine header	No	SUBROUTINE HORSE (PIG, COW)	First statement of sub-routine
Call	Yes	CALL HORSE (3, 14, +J, DOG)	Transfers control to subroutine
Common	No	COMMON A,B,C	Stores variables in COMMON area
Dimension	No	DIMENSION Z(40), J(20,20)	Defines storage requirements for arrays
Real	No	REAL JOB, KUP(23)	Declares variables to be real
Integer	No	INTEGER COW, PIC	Declares variables to be integer
Do	Yes	DO 73 JOB = 1, JUP, 3	First statement of DO loop
Format	No	FORMAT ('A = 'F8.3, I5)	Controls form of input or output
Function sub-program header	No	FUNCTION FIG(PEA)	First statement of function subprogram
Go to	Yes	GO TO 64	Unconditional branch
Go to (computed)	Yes	GO TO (33, 78, 6), KOW	Conditional branch
If	Yes	IF (SQRT(C*D)−P) 10,20,20	Conditional branch
Return	Yes	RETURN	Returns from subprogram to calling program
Write	Yes	WRITE (3,5) JOB, COW	Causes output
Read	Yes	READ (6,8) AMT, GO, DO	Causes input
Pause	Yes	PAUSE	Computer waits within the program
Equivalence	No	EQUIVALENCE (A,B,C), (COW,DOG)	Stores several variables in the same location
Continue	No	CONTINUE	Dummy statement, does nothing except mark a place
Stop	Yes	STOP	Waits just before an exit
External	No	EXTERNAL COS, ABS	Identifies subprogram names as possible sub-program arguments
Find	Yes	FIND (2'I)	Positions the disk arm

A–1. (Continued)

Statement type	Executable	Example	Purpose
Define file	No	`DEFINE FILE (50,40,U, IR)`	Defines a data file on disk
Statement function	No	`DIST(X,Y) = SQRT(X*X + Y*Y)`	Defines function for use in the program
Data	No	`DATA A,B,C/3*0./, C,D/1.2,2.1/`	Stores values for variables during compilation
Backspace	Yes	`BACKSPACE 3`	Returns to previous disk record
Rewind	Yes	`REWIND 2`	Returns disk arm to first record
End file	Yes	`END FILE 4`	Writes an end-of-file record on disk

A–2. FORTRAN DESCRIPTIONS FOR INPUT-OUTPUT DEVICES

Unit number	Device	FORTRAN use	Number of characters allowed	IOCS card designation
1	Console printer	Write only	120	`TYPEWRITER`
2	1442 Card read punch (models 6 and 7)	Read or write	80	`CARD`
3	1132 Printer	Write only	120 + 1 carriage control	`1132 PRINTER`
4	1134–1055 Paper tape reader–punch	Read or write		`PAPER TAPE`
5	1403 Printer	Write only	120 + 1 carriage control	`1403 PRINTER`
6	Console keyboard	Read only	80	`KEYBOARD`
7	1627 Plotter	Write only	120	`PLOTTER`
8	2501 Card reader	Read only	80	`2501 READER`
9	1442 Card punch	Write only	80	`1442 PUNCH`
10	Disk	Read or write (no data conversion)	320	`DISK`

A-3. TYPICAL DECK FOR RUNNING A FORTRAN (OR ASSEMBLER) PROGRAM

b = blank space

Cards	Comment
//bJOB (With multidisk system, disk identifications go here.)	1) Used when the supervisor program is in control; otherwise a Cold Start card is needed. 2) Not always necessary but usually advisable. Erases JOB T and resets working storage indicator as well as error indicators.
//bFOR (The rest of card is available for identification purposes.)	Announces that the program is a FORTRAN program. (//bASM for an assembler program)
*IOCS (————)	Lists all devices used in the program, including subprograms (see previous table, A-2, for names).
*[Other FORTRAN (assembler) control cards]	Options: listings, tracing, precision, etc. (See Table A-4.)
FORTRAN (assembler) program cards	Last card must be END.
//bXEQ	Needed only if compiled program is to be executed.
Blank card	Saves some button-pushing and time, but not essential, especially if another job is stacked on top of this one. Omit if data cards follow.
Data cards	Requested by FORTRAN program.
Next JOB card, etc.	Programs may be stacked in the card reader.

A-4. FORTRAN CONTROL RECORDS

Record	Description
*NAME XXXXX	XXXXX represents program name to be printed on compiler-generated program listing. Used only in mainline programs.
*IOCS (Device list)	All input-output devices in program (including all subroutines) should be listed; commas between device names.
**(Header information)	Text after second asterisk will be printed on each *compiler* output page.
*ONE WORD INTEGERS	Allots one word of storage to integer variables; otherwise two words are set aside, but only one is used.
*EXTENDED PRECISION	Stores real variables and constants in three words instead of two, thus retaining more significant digits. Extended precision subroutines are used.
*ARITHMETIC TRACE	Switch 15 ON to print result of each assignment statement.
*TRANSFER TRACE	Switch 15 ON to print value of IF or Computed GO TO.
*LIST SOURCE PROGRAM	Lists source program on principal print device as it is read in.
*LIST SUBPROGRAM NAMES	Lists subprograms called directly by compiled program.
*LIST SYMBOL TABLE	Lists variable names, statement numbers, and constants; gives (in hexadecimal) relative address of each in program.
*LIST ALL	Lists source program, subprogram names, symbol table (equivalent to above three cards).

A-5. FORTRAN SUPPLIED SUBPROGRAMS

Name	Function Performed	No. of Arguments	Type of Argument(s)	Type of Function
SIN	Trigonometric sine	1	Real	Real
COS	Trigonometric cosine	1	Real	Real
ALOG	Natural logarithm	1	Real	Real
EXP	Argument power of e (i.e., e^x)	1	Real	Real
SQRT	Square root	1	Real	Real
ATAN	Arctangent	1	Real	Real
ABS	Absolute value	1	Real	Real
IABS	Absolute value	1	Integer	Integer
FLOAT	Convert integer argument to real	1	Integer	Real
IFIX	Convert real argument to integer	1	Real	Integer
SIGN	Transfer of sign (Sign of Arg_2 times Arg_1)	2	Real	Real
ISIGN	Transfer of sign (Sign of Arg_2 times Arg_1)	2	Integer	Integer
TANH	Hyperbolic tangent	1	Real	Real

A-6. FORTRAN ERROR CODES

Error Number*	Cause of Error
C 01	Non-numeric character in statement number.
C 02	More than five continuation cards, or continuation card out of sequence.
C 03	Syntax error in CALL LINK or CALL EXIT statement.
C 04	Undeterminable, misspelled, or incorrectly formed statement.
C 05	Statement out of sequence.
C 06	Statement following transfer statement or a STOP statement does not have statement number.
C 07	Name longer than five characters, or name not starting with an alphabetic character.
C 08	Incorrect or missing subscript within dimension information (DIMENSION, COMMON, or type).
C 09	Duplicate statement number.
C 10	Syntax error in COMMON statement.
C 11	Duplicate name in COMMON statement.
C 12	Syntax error in FUNCTION or SUBROUTINE statement.
C 13	Parameter (dummy argument) appears in COMMON statement.
C 14	Name appears twice as a parameter in SUBROUTINE or FUNCTION statement.
C 15	*IOCS control record in a subprogram.
C 16	Syntax error in DIMENSION statement.
C 17	Subprogram name in DIMENSION statement.
C 18	Name dimensioned more than once, or not dimensioned on first appearance of name.
C 19	Syntax error in REAL, INTEGER, or EXTERNAL statement.
C 20	Subprogram name in REAL or INTEGER statement.
C 21	Name in EXTERNAL which is also in a COMMON or DIMENSION statement.
C 22	IFIX or FLOAT in EXTERNAL statement.
C 23	Invalid real constant.
C 24	Invalid integer constant.
C 25	More than 15 dummy arguments, or duplicate dummy argument in statement function argument list.
C 26	Right parenthesis missing from a subscript expression.
C 27	Syntax error in FORMAT statement.
C 28	FORMAT statement without statement number.
C 29	Field width specification >145.
C 30	In a FORMAT statement specifying E or F conversion, $w > 127$, $d > 31$, or $d > w$, where w is an unsigned

*Printed at the conclusion of Compilation.

A-6. FORTRAN ERROR CODES (Continued)

Error Number*	Cause of Error
C 30 Cont.	integer constant specifying the total field length of the data, and d is an unsigned integer constant specifying the number of decimal places to the right of the decimal point.
C 31	Subscript error in EQUIVALENCE statement.
C 32	Subscripted variable in a statement function.
C 33	Incorrectly formed subscript expression.
C 34	Undefined variable in subscript expression.
C 35	Number of subscripts in a subscript expression does not agree with the dimension information.
C 36	Invalid arithmetic statement or variable; or, in a FUNCTION subprogram the left side of an arithmetic statement is a dummy argument (or in COMMON).
C 37	Syntax error in IF statement.
C 38	Invalid expression in IF statement.
C 39	Syntax error or invalid simple argument in CALL statement.
C 40	Invalid expression in CALL statement.
C 41	Invalid expression to the left of an equal sign in a statement function.
C 42	Invalid expression to the right of an equal sign in a statement function.
C 43	In an IF, GO TO, or DO statement a statement number is missing, invalid, incorrectly placed, or is the number of a FORMAT statement.
C 44	Syntax error in READ or WRITE statement.
C 45	*IOCS record missing with a READ or WRITE statement (mainline program only).
C 46	FORMAT statement number missing or incorrect in a READ or WRITE statement.
C 47	Syntax error in input/output list; or an invalid list element; or, in a FUNCTION subprogram, the input list element is a dummy argument or in COMMON.
C 48	Syntax error in GO TO statement.
C 49	Index of a computed GO TO is missing, invalid, or not preceded by a comma.
C 50	*TRANSFER TRACE or *ARITHMETIC TRACE control record present, with no *IOCS control record in a mainline program.
C 51	Incorrect nesting of DO statements; or the terminal statement of the associated DO statement is a GO TO, IF, RETURN, FORMAT, STOP, PAUSE, or DO statement.
C 52	More than 25 nested DO statements.
C 53	Syntax error in DO statement.
C 54	Initial value in DO statement is zero.

A-6. (Continued)

Error Number	Cause of Error
C 55	In a FUNCTION subprogram the index of DO is a dummy argument or in COMMON.
C 59	Syntax error in STOP statement.
C 60	Syntax error in PAUSE statement.
C 61	Integer constant in STOP or PAUSE statement is > 9999.
C 62	Last executable statement before END statement is not a STOP, GO TO, IF, CALL LINK, CALL EXIT, or RETURN statement.
C 63	Statement contains more than 15 different subscript expressions.
C 64	Statement too long to be scanned, because of compiler expansion of subscript expressions or compiler addition of generated temporary storage locations.
C 65*	All variables are undefined in an EQUIVALENCE list.
C 66*	Variable made equivalent to an element of an array, in such a manner as to cause the array to extend beyond the origin of the COMMON area.
C 67*	Two variables or array elements in COMMON are equated, or the relative locations of two variables or array elements are assigned more than once (directly or indirectly).
C 68	Syntax error in an EQUIVALENCE statement; or an illegal variable name in an EQUIVALENCE list.
C 69	Subprogram does not contain a RETURN statement, or a mainline program contains a RETURN statement.
C 70	No DEFINE FILE in a mainline program which has disk READ, WRITE, or FIND statements.
C 71	Syntax error in DEFINE FILE.
C 72	Duplicate DEFINE FILE, more than 75 DEFINE FILES, or DEFINE FILE in subprogram.
C 73	Syntax error in record number of READ, WRITE, or FIND statement.

*The detection of a code 65, 66, or 67 error prevents any subsequent detection of any of these three errors.

A-7. FORTRAN INPUT/OUTPUT ERROR CODES

Error Code*	Cause of Error
F000	No *IOCS control card appeared with the mainline program and I/O was attempted in a subroutine.
F001	1. Logical unit defined incorrectly. 2. No *IOCS control record for specified I/O device.
F002	Requested record exceeds allocated buffer size.
F003	Illegal character encountered in input record.
F004	Exponent too large or too small in input field.
F005	More than one E encountered in input field.
F006	More than one sign encountered in input field.
F007	More than one decimal point encountered in input field.
F008	1. Read of output-only device. 2. Write of input-only device.
F009	Real variable transmitted with an I format specification or integer variable transmitted with an E or F format specification.
F100	File not defined by DEFINE FILE statement.
F101	File record too large, equal to zero, or negative.
F103	Disk FIO (SDFIO) has not been initialized.
DISKZ Errors:	
F102	Read error.
F104	Write error.
F106	Read back check error.
F108	Seek error.
F10A	Forced read error (seek or find).

*Displayed in Accumulator

A-8. FORTRAN INDICATOR TESTS

Statement	Description
CALL SLITE (I)	I = 0 Turns off all sense lights I = 1 Turns on sense light 1 I = 2 Turns on sense light 2 I = 3 Turns on sense light 3 I = 4 Turns on sense light 4
CALL SLITET (I,J) CALL SLITT (I,J)	Returns J. If sense light I is on, J = 1; otherwise J = 2. Turns off sense light.
CALL OVERFL (J) CALL OVERF (J)	Returns J. If overflow indicator is on, J = 1. If no overflow, J = 2. If under- flow, J = 3. Real arithmetic only.
CALL DVCHK (J)	Returns J. If zero-divisor indicator is on, J = 1; otherwise J = 2. Turns off indicator. Real arithmetic only.
CALL DATSW (I,J)	Returns J. If console switch I is on, J = 1; if off, J = 2.
CALL TSTRT CALL TSTOP	If FORTRAN control trace cards were compiled and switch is on, these subroutines start and stop tracing.
CALL FCTST (I,J)	Tests subroutine error indicator word. If the indicator word has not been set, I = 2, J = 0. If set, I = 1, J = value of indicator.

MONITOR AND DISK UTILITY PROGRAMS

APPENDIX B

B-1. MONITOR CONTROL RECORDS

Record	Description
1　　8　12 |　　|　| //b* [comments]	Not allowed after XEQ, ASM, or FOR card.
//bJOB T　　[Disk label] (version 1)	Initializes a job sequence. T (if present) indicates a temporary job; any disk-stored material is deleted when the next JOB card is read. The label is optional. See next table for additional version 2 information.
//bASM	Assembler program follows. Remainder of card can be used for identification.
//bFOR	FORTRAN program follows. Remainder of card can be used for identification.
//bPAUS	Instructs computer to halt until START is pressed, then read cards or tape until next monitor control record is found in the input stream.
//bTYP	Changes control record input from principal input unit to keyboard/console printer for succeeding monitor control records.
//bTEND	Changes input mode from keyboard/console printer back to the principal unit for succeeding monitor control records.
//bDUP	Brings control section of disk utility program into core, and cards following will be DUP cards.
//bXEQ 　　Program name = columns 8–12 　　L = column 14 　　Count = columns 15–17 　　Disk 0, 1, N = column 19	If no program name given, executes program currently in working storage. If program name given, executes program stored on disk under that name. L produces a core map. Count = number (decimal, right-justified) of FILES, LOCAL and NOCAL cards following this card. Disk 0, 1, N for assembler programs specifies disk routine; blank for FORTRAN.

B-2. JOB CARD STRUCTURE IN DISK MONITOR SYSTEM, VERSION 2

Card columns	Use
8	A T indicates a temporary job; all programs stored on disk during the job are deleted at end of job. A blank in column 8 produces permanent storage.
11–14	Identification of the master cartridge, containing disk monitor system; logical drive 0.
16–19	Identification of cartridge on logical drive 1.
21–24	Identification of cartridge on logical drive 2.
26–29	Identification of cartridge on logical drive 3.
31–34	Identification of cartridge on logical drive 4.
36–39	Identification of cartridge containing the core image buffer for this job. Speed is increased if this is neither the master cartridge nor the working storage cartridge.
41–44	Identification of cartridge containing the working storage area for this job. Speed is increased if this is neither the master cartridge nor the CIB cartridge.
46–53	Heading printed at top of each page of the listing on principal print device.

The identification is a four-place hexadecimal number, stored in the fourth word of sector zero of each disk cartridge.

B-3. MONITOR SUPERVISOR ERROR MESSAGES

Error Message	Cause of Error
M 01 PHASE NONX	Execution is not permitted for this job.
M 02 INVALID	The above listed record is an invalid Supervisor record.
M 03 NON XEQ	The currently called execution is not permitted.
M 04 CHARACTER	A character in the name listed above is not permitted.
M 05 OFLO DISK	The records listed above were too many for the disk storage allocated.
M 06 NO PROGRAM	The mainline program name listed above is not in the LET or FLET table or is not a mainline program.
M 07 NON DUP	DUP is not allowed for the subjob.
M 09 RECORD TRAP	A system program detected a Supervisor record and returned control to the Supervisor.
M 11 NOT IDENT	The cartridge identifier on the cartridge is not identical to the one on the input record. The Supervisor waits to allow the operator to rectify the difference if desired.
M 12 SEQ ERROR	LOCAL, NOCAL, and/or FILES records are intermixed (they must be grouped).
M 13 T ERROR	Column 8 in the JOB record does not contain a blank or a T. An ampersand is printed in place of the illegal character. The Supervisor waits so that the operator can (1) correct the JOB record, reload it in the reader, and press PROGRAM START on the console; or (2) press PROGRAM START on the console. In either case the JOB record is processed completely before any other processing. The job is considered non-temporary if column 8 contains a blank or a character other than a T.

B-4. DUP CONTROL RECORDS

Card columns 1 2 3 4 5 6 7 8 9 10 11 12 13 14 15 16 17 18 19 20 21 22 23 24 25 26 27 28 29 30 31 32

Control record (cols 1–12)	From (13–16)	To (17–20)	Name (21–26)	Count (27–32)
* D U M P b	-From-	---To---	----------Name----------	
* D U M P D A T A b	-From-	---To---	----------Name----------	-------Sector count-------
* S T O R E	-From-	---To---	----------Name----------	
* S T O R E C I	-From-	---To---	----------Name----------	------Count of files------- records
* S T O R E D A T A	-From-	---To---	----------Name----------	------Sector, card, or------ record count
* S T O R E M O D b	WS	UA or FX	----------Name----------	
* D U M P L E T	[Print contents of LET (and FLET if there is one) on principal printing unit]			
* D U M P F L E T	(Print contents of FLET only on principal printing unit)			
* D W A D R	(Write sector addresses in working storage area)			
* D E L E T E			----------Name----------	
* D E F I N E b F I X E D b A R E A				------Cylinder count------
* D E F I N E b V O I D b A S S E M B L E R				
* D E F I N E b V O I D b F O R T R A N				

B-5. TO AND FROM FIELDS ON DUP CONTROL RECORDS

UA   User area on disk (Programs are repacked each time a program is deleted.)

FX   Fixed area on disk (Programs stay in a fixed disk location. A fixed area must be "defined.")

WS   Working storage (Programs are in working storage after compilation or assembly.)

CD   Cards

PT   Paper tape

PR   Principal print device

B–6. TO AND FROM IDENTIFICATION ON VERSION 2 DUP CONTROL RECORDS

DUP Control record	From ID columns 31–34	To ID columns 37–40	Remarks
DUMP	Yes	Yes	
DUMPDATA	Yes	Yes	Uses data format.
DUMPLET	Yes		If FROM ID is given, only that LET table is dumped; if no FROM ID, entire LET table is dumped.
DUMPFLET	Yes		As with DUMPLET, uses data format.
STORE	Yes	Yes	
STOREDATA	Yes	Yes	
STOREDATACI	Yes	Yes	
STORECI	Yes	Yes	Uses core load builder.
STOREMOD	Yes	Yes	Caution: new program *cannot* be longer than old program.
DELETE	Yes		UA repacked, FA not.
DEFINE			
FIXED AREA		Yes	– (minus sign) in column 31 indicates *reduction* of fixed area.
VOID ASSEMBLER			
VOID FORTRAN			
PRINCbPRINT			Columns 21–24 have device number.
PRINCINPUT			No number means console printer.
CORE SIZE			4K, 8K, 16K, or 32K, beginning in column 9.
DWADR		Yes	

B–7. RESTRICTIONS ON DUP FUNCTIONS IN TEMPORARY MODE (JOB T)

Functions	Restrictions (if any)	Functions	Restrictions (if any)
DUMP	None	Version 2	
DUMPDATA	None		
STORE	None	STOREDATACI	To UA only
STORECI	To UA only	DUMPFLET	None
STOREDATA	To UA and WS only	DEFINE PRINC PRINT	None
STOREMOD	Not allowed		
DUMPLET	None		
DWADR	Not allowed		
DELETE	Not allowed		
DEFINE FIXED AREA	Not allowed		
DEFINE VOID ASSEMBLER	Not allowed		
DEFINE VOID FORTRAN	Not allowed		

B-8. SUMMARY OF DUP DATA TRANSFER OPERATIONS

From \ To	UA (DSF)	UA (DDF)	UA (DCI)	FX (DSF)	FX (DDF)	FX (DCI)	WS (DSF)	WS (DDF)	CD (CDD)	CD (CDS)	PT (PTD)	PT (PTS)	PR (PRD)
UA (DSF)							DUMP**	DUMPDATA**	DUMPDATA**	DUMP**	DUMPDATA**	DUMP**	DUMP** DUMPDATA**
UA (DDF)								DUMP** DUMPDATA**	DUMP** DUMPDATA**		DUMP** DUMPDATA**		DUMP** DUMPDATA**
UA (DCI)								DUMP** DUMPDATA**	DUMP** DUMPDATA**		DUMP** DUMPDATA**		DUMP** DUMPDATA**
FX (DCI)								DUMP** DUMPDATA**	DUMP** DUMPDATA**		DUMP** DUMPDATA**		DUMP** DUMPDATA**
FX (DDF)								DUMP** DUMPDATA**	DUMP** DUMPDATA**		DUMP** DUMPDATA**		DUMP** DUMPDATA**
WS (DSF)	STORE* STOREMOD		STORECI*			STORECI			DUMPDATA	DUMP	DUMPDATA	DUMP	DUMP DUMPDATA
WS (DDF)		STOREDATA* STOREMOD			STOREDATA STOREMOD				DUMPDATA		DUMPDATA		DUMPDATA
CD (CDD)		STOREDATA*			STOREDATA**			STOREDATA**					
CD (CDS)	STORE*		STORECI			STORECI**	STORE**						
PT (PTD)		STOREDATA*			STOREDATA**			STOREDATA**					
PT (PTS)	STORE*		STORECI*			STORECI**	STORE**						

*Eliminates stored information from Working Storage

**Replaces current contents of Working Storage

127

B-9. DUP ERROR MESSAGES

Code and Printed Message*	Description
WS TOO LONG	An attempt is made with *STOREMOD to move an item from Working Storage that is longer than the item to be overlaid in the User or Fixed Area.
D 01 NOT PRIME ENTRY	The primary name of the program in Working Storage does not match the name on the DUP control record.
D 02 INVALID TYPE	One of the following is detected: non-DSF program, mispositioned header, foreign data, or erroneous subtype.
D 03 INVALID HEADER LENGTH	Word six of the DSF header is outside the range of 3-45. The causes are similar to D 02, except for subtype.
D 05 SECONDARY ENTRY POINT NAME ALREADY IN LET IS....	The specified name is already in LET. The name must be deleted before this subprogram can be stored.
D 13 DCTL, FUNCTION	An invalid DUP function specified in columns 1-12 of the DUP control record.
D 14 DCTL, FROM FLD	Unacceptable characters are in columns 13 and 14 of the DUP control record. If Working Storage is specified in columns 13 and 14, then there is no valid program in Working Storage, i.e., the Working Storage Indicator has been set to zero, thus inhibiting the movement of programs from Working Storage.
D 15 DCTL, TO FIELD	Unacceptable characters are in columns 17 and 18 of the DUP control record.
D 16 DCTL, NAME FLD	If this is a *STORE control record, then the name is already in LET/FLET. If this is a *DUMP control record, then the name is not found in LET or FLET. If this is a *DUMP control record of Working Storage to the principal I/O, then a name is required in columns 21 through 25 of the DUP control record. If this is a *DELETE control record, then the name is not found in LET or FLET. If this is a *STOREMOD control record, then the name is not found in LET or FLET.
D 17 DCTL, COUNT	Columns 27 through 30 are blank or include alphabetic characters. The count field requires a decimal number.
D 18 DCTL, TMP MODE	This function is not allowed during the JOB T mode.
D 41 FIXED AREA PRESENT	The FORTRAN compiler and/or assembler cannot be eliminated if a Fixed area has been previously defined.
D 42 ASSEMBLER NOT IN SYSTEM	The assembler has previously been eliminated from the system.
D 43 FORTRAN NOT IN SYSTEM	The FORTRAN compiler has previously been eliminated from the system.
D 44 INCREASE VALUE IN COUNT FIELD	The count field was read as a value of zero or one. The first DEFINE requires one cylinder for FLET plus one cylinder of Fixed area. Thereafter, as little as one cylinder of additional Fixed area can be defined.
D 45 EXCEEDS WORK STORAGE	The initiation or expansion of the Fixed area is limited to the Working Storage available.
D 61 DUPCO, EXCEEDS WORK STORAGE	This function requires more Working Storage than is available.

B-9. (Continued)

Code and Printed Message*	Description
D 62 EXCEEDS WORK STORAGE	The Working Storage area is not large enough to contain the program specified.
D 64 EXCEEDS FIXED AREA	There is insufficient room in the Fixed area for the program.
D 71 SEQUENCE OR CKSUM	The cards are out of sequence, or there was an erroneous checksum.
D 72 LOAD BLANK CARDS	More blank cards are required to complete the dump. The operator performs an NPRO and places blank cards between the two cards ejected, removes the first card, places the first card in the output stacker, places the remainder in front of the cards still in the reader hopper, and presses the reader START button.
D 82 NON FILES RECORD	The first six characters of records following *STORECI are not *FILES. The number of *FILES records is determined by the count field of DUP control record STORECI.
D 83 INVALID CHARACTER	The *FILES record following the *STORECI DUP control record has an invalid character.
D 84 EXCEEDS SECTOR ALLOCATION	Too many Files have been defined. More than two sectors are required to contain the information from the *FILES record.
D 92 INVALID CI CONVERT	The Loader has inhibited the continuation of *STORECI. The specific reason has been printed by the Loader.
D 94 LET/FLET OVERFLOW	A ninth sector of LET/FLET is required for the LET/FLET entry. A deletion of a program with a LET/FLET entry of similar size is required before this program can be stored.

*Printed upon detection of an erroneous DUP control record.

NOTE: DCTL means the error was detected in the DUP control record. DUPCO means the error was detected in the DUP common section.

B-10. DUP WAITS AND LOOPS

Address*	Explanation	Operator Action
Loops: 70FF@0287 (occurs after console printer prints first 320 core positions)	System check. LET/FLET, COMMA, and DCOM do not agree.	Reload entire Monitor System.
Wait at 092C	Paper tape reader not ready	Ready paper tape reader and press PROGRAM START.
Wait at 0005	Operator pressed PROGRAM STOP on console.	Do not alter core storage. To continue, press PROGRAM START.

*Displayed in Storage Address Register

B-11. LET AND FLET OUTPUT FORMATS

Line 1: LET

Line 2:
(Entries in comma—
base and adjusted
addresses — see
Appendix E)

XXXX XXXX,
Work Storage starting
sector address

XXXX XXXX,
Disk block address
available for next User
area program or data file

XXXX XXXX,
Number of words used
by LET

Line 3:
(LET sector header
words)

XXXX,
Relative sector
number (0-7)

XXXX,
0 if last sector
of LET; other-
wise non-zero

XXXX,
Number of disk
blocks referenced by
this sector of LET

XXXX,
Words available
in this sector
for more entries

XXXX,
Sector address of
next sector
(0 if last sector)

Line 4
.
.
Line n

XXXXX,
Program name

XXXX,
Program size
(disk blocks)

XXXX,
Starting address
(disk blocks)

} For DSF
programs

Line 4
.
.
.
Line n

XXXXX,
Program name

XXXX,
Program size
(disk blocks)

XXXX,
Starting address
in User area
(disk blocks)

XXXX,
Execute core
address
(absolute)

XXXX,
Program load
address in
core

XXXX,
Actual word count
of core image pro-
gram (includes a
60-word header)

} For core
image
programs

Line 4
.
.
.
Line n

XXXXX,
Data file name

XXXX,
Data file size
(disk blocks)

XXXX,
Starting address
in User area
(disk blocks)

0000   0000,
Reserved

XXXX,
Data file size
(disk blocks)

} For data
files

NOTE 1: The header words of the first sector are printed on line 3. Additional header words are printed for each following sector as required.

NOTE 2: For multi-entry subroutines, the Program Size and Starting Address fields for entry points subsequent to the first one will be blank.

NOTE 3: Program size is the disk block count of the program. This corresponds to word 3 of the actual LET entry (see Appendix G).

NOTE 4: Words 4, 5, and 6 of the printout reflect the actual LET entry words 4, 5, and 6.

NOTE 5: All numbers are in hexadecimal.

B-11. (Continued)

Line 1:	FLET			

Line 2:
(Entries in
COMMA)

XXXX XXXX — Sector address of CIB

XXXX XXXX — Sector address of FLET

XXXX XXXX — Number of words used by FLET

Line 3:
(FLET sector
header words)

XXXX — Relative sector number (first sector is numbered 16)

XXXX — 0 if last sector of FLET; otherwise non-zero

XXXX — Number of disk blocks referenced by this sector of FLET

XXXX — Words available in this sector for more entries

XXXX — Sector address of next sector (0 if last sector)

Line 4
⋮
Line n

FLET entries are the same as for LET except that DSF programs do not appear in the Fixed area; therefore, no three-word entries appear in FLET.

NOTE 1:   All references are in disk blocks unless otherwise indicated.

NOTE 2:   The header words of the first sector are printed on line 3. Additional header words are printed for each following sector as required; there is a header for each 52 FLET entries.

NOTE 3:   Program size is the disk block count of the program. This corresponds to word 3 of the actual FLET entry.

NOTE 4:   Words 4, 5, and 6 of the printout reflect the actual FLET entry words 4, 5, and 6.

NOTE 5:   All numbers are in hexadecimal.

B-12. SUPERVISOR CONTROL RECORDS

Follow the //bXEQ card.

Columns 16 and 17 in the //bXEQ card give the number (decimal, right-justified) of supervisor control cards.

No embedded blanks.

Continuation cards:

1) previous card ends in a comma.

2) New card does not list mainline program name.

Order of LOCAL, NOCAL, and FILES shown here must be followed.

Note: No brackets are used on record cards; they indicate syntax only in examples below.

---

*LOCAL [MAINLINE NAME] , [SUBPROGRAM 1] ,
  [SUBPROGRAM 2] , ...
*LOCAL, [SUBPROGRAM 1] , [SUBPROGRAM 2] ...

Second form lists no mainline program.

Result: Only one of the subprograms listed is in core at any one time. Others are in core image form in working storage and brought in when called.

---

*NOCAL [MAINLINE NAME] , [SUBPROGRAM 1] , ...
*NOCAL, [SUBPROGRAM 1] , [SUBPROGRAM 2] , ...

Result: The listed subprograms are prepared and loaded into core, even if they are not requested in the program.

---

*FILES (FILEN,NAMEN) , (FILEM,NAMEM) , ...

Result: The file with number FILEN in a FORTRAN DEFINE FILE statement is to be a file stored on disk under the name NAMEN. Any number of associations may be made.

In the version 2 monitor, each pair of parentheses can contain a third quantity, the disk cartridge identification; a comma follows the file name, and then the ID is listed. In a multidisk system, no third item in parentheses indicates that the master cylinder contains the file.

B-13. LOADER MESSAGES/ERROR MESSAGES

Code and Message	Explanation and Recovery Procedures
R 01 ORIGIN BELOW 1ST WORD OF MAINLINE	The Loader has been instructed to load a word into an address lower than that of the first word of the mainline program. The ORG statement which caused this situation must be removed, or the mainline program must start at a lower address.
*R 03 LOAD REQUIRES SYSTEM LOCALS, LEVEL 1	No error. The load was too long to fit into core. The Loader has made two overlays, and the program will be executed with these two groups of routines overlaying each other (refer to System Overlays).
*R 04 LOAD REQUIRES SYSTEM LOCALS, LEVEL 2	No error. The load was too long to fit into core. The Loader has made three overlays, and the program will be executed with these three groups of routines overlaying one another (refer to System Overlays).
R 06 FILE(S) TRUNCATED (SEE FILE MAP)	At least one defined file has been truncated either because the previously defined storage area in the User or Fixed area was inadequate or because there is inadequate Working Storage available to store the file. See Message R 12 for a possible remedy.
R 08 CORE LOAD EXCEEDS 32K	The Loader has been instructed to load a word into an address exceeding 32,767, which is a negative number. The loading process is immediately terminated, because the Loader cannot process negative addresses. This error was probably caused by bad data, i.e., the program being loaded from the disk has been destroyed.
R 10 LIBF TV REQUIRES 82 OR MORE ENTRIES	There are at'least 82 different entry points referenced in the load by LIBF statements. A possible remedy would be to subdivide the load into two or more links.
R 11 TOO MANY ENTRIES IN LOAD-TIME TV	There are more than 135 references to different entry points with CALL and/or LIBF statements in the load. A possible remedy would be to subdivide the load into two or more links.
R 12 LOCALS/SOCALS EXCEED WKNG. STORAGE	There is insufficient Working Storage remaining to accommodate the LOCAL and/or SOCAL overlays required in the load. A possible remedy would be to create more Working Storage by deleting subroutines, subprograms, and/or data no longer required by the installation.
R 13 DEFINED FILE(S) EXCEED WKNG. STORAGE	There is insufficient Working Storage remaining to accommodate even one record of the defined file(s). See Message R 12 for a possible remedy.
**R 16 XXXXX IS NOT IN LET OR FLET	The program or data file designated in the message cannot be found in LET or FLET. A possible remedy is to store the program or data file. If the name cannot be explained otherwise, the program being loaded has probably been destroyed.
**R 17 XXXXX CANNOT BE DESIGNATED A LOCAL	The routine named in this message is either a type which cannot appear on a LOCAL record, or this routine, which is a LOCAL, has been referenced, directly or indirectly, by another LOCAL, the name of which cannot be supplied by the Loader.
**R 18 XXXXX CANNOT BE DESIGNATED A NOCAL	The routine named in the message is either a mainline, an ILS, or it has an invalid type code. In any case, it may not appear on a *NOCAL record.
**R 19 XXXXX IS NOT ON A SECTOR BOUNDARY	The area named in this message does not begin at a sector boundary, which implies that it is not a storage area but a relocatable program, and thus a possible error. Choose another area for the storage of this file.
**R 20 XXXXX COMMON EXCEEDS THAT OF ML	The length of COMMON for the routine named in this message is longer than that of the mainline program. A possible remedy is to define more COMMON for the mainline program.
**R 21 XXXXX PRECISION DIFFERENT FROM ML	The precision for the routine named in this message is incompatible with that of the mainline program. Make the precisions compatible.
**R 22 XXXXX AND ANOTHER VERSION REFERENCED	At least two different versions of the same I/O routine have been referenced, e.g., both CARDZ and CARD0 (FORTRAN utilizes the "Z" version). If a disk routine is named in the message, it is possible that the XEQ record specifies one version, e.g., DISK0, whereas the program references another, e.g., DISK1 (a blank in col. 19 of the XEQ record causes DISKZ to be chosen).
**R 23 XXXXX IS A USER AREA FILE REFERENCE	The area named in this message is in the User area; references in DEFINE FILE and DSA statements for *STORECI functions must be to the Fixed area.

*FORTRAN mainline programs only
**XXXXX = the name of the program or disk file concerned

B-13. (Continued)

Code and Message	Explanation and Recovery Procedures
*R 24 XXXXX IS BOTH A LIBF AND A CALL	The routine named in this message has been either referenced improperly, i.e., CALL instead of LIBF or vice versa, or has been referenced in both CALL and LIBF statements. The only remedy is to reference the routine properly. NOTE: NOCALs must be CALL-type routines, i.e., type 4 or 6 routines (refer to Appendix B).
*R 25 XXXXX HAS MORE THAN 14 ENTRY POINTS	This message usually indicates that the routine has been destroyed since no routine is stored with more than 14 entry points.
*R 26 XXXXX HAS AN INVALID TYPE CODE	The routine named in this message has either been designated on an XEQ record and is not a mainline program, indicating a mistake has probably been made in preparing the XEQ record, or contains a type code other than 3 (subroutine), 4 (functional), 5 (ISS), or 6 (ILS), in which case the routine has probably been destroyed. This error could also be caused by a DSA statement referencing a program which is in Disk System format, or a CALL or LIBF referencing a program in Core Image or Disk Data format.
*R 27 XXXXX LOADING HAS BEEN TERMINATED	The loading of the mainline program named in this message has been terminated as a result of the detection of the error(s) listed in the messages preceding this one.
**R 32 XXXXX CANNOT REF'CE THE LOCAL XXXXX	The routine named first in this message has referenced the routine named second, which is a LOCAL. Either the first named routine is a LOCAL or it is entered (directly or indirectly) from a LOCAL. Neither case can be allowed for it could cause a LOCAL to be overlaid by another LOCAL before the first LOCAL has been completely executed.
R 40 XXXX (HEX) = ADDITIONAL CORE REQUIRED	If the load was executed, XXXX_{16} is the number of words by which it exceeded core storage before the Loader made it fit by creating special overlays (SOCALs); if the load was not executed, the first occurrence of the message is as described and the record indicates the number of words by which it exceeds core storage even after creating the deepest level of special overlays. A possible solution to the latter problem is to create two or more links or LOCALs.
R 41 XXXX (HEX) TOO MANY WDS IN COMMON	The length of COMMON specified in the mainline program plus the length of the core load exceeds core storage by XXXX_{16} words.
R 42 XXXX (HEX) IS THE EXECUTION ADDR	No error. This message follows every successful conversion from Disk System format to Core Image format provided a core map is requested.
R 43 XXXX (HEX) = ARITH/FUNC OVERLAY SIZE	No error. It has been necessary to employ the special overlays (SOCALs), and XXXX_{16} is the length of the arithmetic/functional overlay (refer to System Overlays).
R 44 XXXX (HEX) = FI/O + I/O OVERLAY SIZE	No error. It has been necessary to employ the special overlays (SOCALs), and XXXX_{16} is the length of the FORTRAN I/O, I/O, and conversion routine overlay (refer to System Overlays).
R 45 XXXX (HEX) = DISK FI/O OVERLAY SIZE	No error. It has been necessary to employ the special overlays (SOCALs), and XXXX_{16} is the length of the Disk FORTRAN I/O overlay, including the 320-word buffer.
R 46 XXXX (HEX) = AN ILLEGAL ML LOAD ADDR	XXXX_{16} is the address at which the loader has been requested to start loading the mainline program, but this address is lower than the highest address occupied by the version of Disk I/O requested for this load. Either make the mainline origin higher or request a shorter version of Disk.
R 47 XXXX (HEX) WORDS AVAILABLE	No error. XXXX_{16} is the number of words of core storage not occupied by this core load.

*XXXXX = the name of the program or disk file concerned
**XXXXX = the name of the program concerned

CODING

APPENDIX C

C-1. VALUE RANGES—SINGLE PRECISION WORD

Positive Binary Values	Powers of 2	Absolute Values		Negative Binary Values
Bit Positions 11 1111 0123 4567 8901 2345		Decimal Notation Base-10	Hexa- decimal Notation Base-16	Bit Positions 11 1111 0123 4567 8901 2345
0000 0000 0000 0000	–	0	0	No negative zero
0000 0000 0000 0001	0	1	1	1111 1111 1111 1111
0000 0000 0000 0010	1	2	2	1111 1111 1111 1110
0000 0000 0000 0100	2	4	4	1111 1111 1111 1100
0000 0000 0000 1000	3	8	8	1111 1111 1111 1000
0000 0000 0001 0000	4	16	10	1111 1111 1111 0000
0000 0000 0010 0000	5	32	20	1111 1111 1110 0000
0000 0000 0100 0000	6	64	40	1111 1111 1100 0000
0000 0000 1000 0000	7	128	80	1111 1111 1000 0000
0000 0001 0000 0000	8	256	100	1111 1111 0000 0000
0000 0010 0000 0000	9	512	200	1111 1110 0000 0000
0000 0100 0000 0000	10	1,024	400	1111 1100 0000 0000
0000 1000 0000 0000	11	2,048	800	1111 1000 0000 0000
0001 0000 0000 0000	12	4,096	1,000	1111 0000 0000 0000
0010 0000 0000 0000	13	8,192	2,000	1110 0000 0000 0000
0100 0000 0000 0000	14	16,384	4,000	1100 0000 0000 0000
0111 1111 1111 1111	–	32,767	7,FFF	1000 0000 0000 0001
No positive equivalent	15	32,768	8,000	1000 0000 0000 0000

VALUE RANGES—DOUBLE PRECISION WORD

Positive Binary Values	Powers of 2	Absolute Values		Negative Binary Values
Bit Positions 11 1111 1111 2222 2222 2233 0123 4567 8901 2345 6789 0123 4567 8901		Decimal Notation Base - 10	Hexidecimal Notation Base - 16	Bit Positions 11 1111 1111 2222 2222 2233 0123 4567 8901 2345 6789 0123 4567 8901
0000 0000 0000 0000 0000 0000 0000 0000	–	0	0	No negative zero
0000 0000 0000 0000 0000 0000 0000 0001	0	1	1	1111 1111 1111 1111 1111 1111 1111 1111
0000 0000 0000 0000 0000 0000 0000 0010	1	2	2	1111 1111 1111 1111 1111 1111 1111 1110
0000 0000 0000 0000 0000 0000 0000 0100	2	4	4	1111 1111 1111 1111 1111 1111 1111 1100
0000 0000 0000 0000 0000 0000 0000 1000	3	8	8	1111 1111 1111 1111 1111 1111 1111 1000
0000 0000 0000 0000 0000 0000 0001 0000	4	16	10	1111 1111 1111 1111 1111 1111 1111 0000
0000 0000 0000 0000 0000 0000 0010 0000	5	32	20	1111 1111 1111 1111 1111 1111 1110 0000
0000 0000 0000 0000 0000 0000 0100 0000	6	64	40	1111 1111 1111 1111 1111 1111 1100 0000
0000 0000 0000 0000 0000 0000 1000 0000	7	128	80	1111 1111 1111 1111 1111 1111 1000 0000
0000 0000 0000 0000 0000 0001 0000 0000	8	256	100	1111 1111 1111 1111 1111 1111 0000 0000
0000 0000 0000 0000 0000 0010 0000 0000	9	512	200	1111 1111 1111 1111 1111 1110 0000 0000
0000 0000 0000 0000 0000 0100 0000 0000	10	1,024	400	1111 1111 1111 1111 1111 1100 0000 0000
0000 0000 0000 0000 0000 1000 0000 0000	11	2,048	800	1111 1111 1111 1111 1111 1000 0000 0000
0000 0000 0000 0000 0001 0000 0000 0000	12	4,096	1,000	1111 1111 1111 1111 1111 0000 0000 0000
0000 0000 0000 0000 0010 0000 0000 0000	13	8,192	2,000	1111 1111 1111 1111 1110 0000 0000 0000
0000 0000 0000 0000 0100 0000 0000 0000	14	16,384	4,000	1111 1111 1111 1111 1100 0000 0000 0000
0000 0000 0000 0000 1000 0000 0000 0000	15	32,768	8,000	1111 1111 1111 1111 1000 0000 0000 0000
0000 0000 0000 0001 0000 0000 0000 0000	16	65,536	10,000	1111 1111 1111 1111 0000 0000 0000 0000
0000 0000 0000 0010 0000 0000 0000 0000	17	131,072	20,000	1111 1111 1111 1110 0000 0000 0000 0000
0000 0000 0000 0100 0000 0000 0000 0000	18	262,144	40,000	1111 1111 1111 1100 0000 0000 0000 0000
0000 0000 0000 1000 0000 0000 0000 0000	19	524,288	80,000	1111 1111 1111 1000 0000 0000 0000 0000
0000 0000 0001 0000 0000 0000 0000 0000	20	1,048,576	100,000	1111 1111 1111 0000 0000 0000 0000 0000
0000 0000 0010 0000 0000 0000 0000 0000	21	2,097,152	200,000	1111 1111 1110 0000 0000 0000 0000 0000
0000 0000 0100 0000 0000 0000 0000 0000	22	4,194,304	400,000	1111 1111 1100 0000 0000 0000 0000 0000
0000 0000 1000 0000 0000 0000 0000 0000	23	8,388,608	800,000	1111 1111 1000 0000 0000 0000 0000 0000
0000 0001 0000 0000 0000 0000 0000 0000	24	16,777,216	1,000,000	1111 1111 0000 0000 0000 0000 0000 0000
0000 0010 0000 0000 0000 0000 0000 0000	25	33,554,432	2,000,000	1111 1110 0000 0000 0000 0000 0000 0000
0000 0100 0000 0000 0000 0000 0000 0000	26	67,108,864	4,000,000	1111 1100 0000 0000 0000 0000 0000 0000
0000 1000 0000 0000 0000 0000 0000 0000	27	134,217,728	8,000,000	1111 1000 0000 0000 0000 0000 0000 0000
0001 0000 0000 0000 0000 0000 0000 0000	28	268,435,456	10,000,000	1111 0000 0000 0000 0000 0000 0000 0000
0010 0000 0000 0000 0000 0000 0000 0000	29	536,870,912	20,000,000	1110 0000 0000 0000 0000 0000 0000 0000
0100 0000 0000 0000 0000 0000 0000 0000	30	1,073,741,824	40,000,000	1100 0000 0000 0000 0000 0000 0000 0000
0111 1111 1111 1111 1111 1111 1111 1111	–	2,147,483,647	7F,FFF,FFF	1000 0000 0000 0000 0000 0000 0000 0001
No positive equivalent	31	2,147,483,648	80,000,000	1000 0000 0000 0000 0000 0000 0000 0000

C-2. POWERS OF TWO TABLE

2^n	n	2^{-n}
1	0	1.0
2	1	0.5
4	2	0.25
8	3	0.125
16	4	0.062 5
32	5	0.031 25
64	6	0.015 625
128	7	0.007 812 5
256	8	0.003 906 25
512	9	0.001 953 125
1 024	10	0.000 976 562 5
2 048	11	0.000 488 281 25
4 096	12	0.000 244 140 625
8 192	13	0.000 122 070 312 5
16 384	14	0.000 061 035 156 25
32 768	15	0.000 030 517 578 125
65 536	16	0.000 015 258 789 062 5
131 072	17	0.000 007 629 394 531 25
262 144	18	0.000 003 814 697 265 625
524 288	19	0.000 001 907 348 632 812 5
1 048 576	20	0.000 000 953 674 316 406 25
2 097 152	21	0.000 000 476 837 158 203 125
4 194 304	22	0.000 000 238 418 579 101 562 5
8 388 608	23	0.000 000 119 209 289 550 781 25
16 777 216	24	0.000 000 059 604 644 775 390 625
33 554 432	25	0.000 000 029 802 322 387 695 312 5
67 108 864	26	0.000 000 014 901 161 193 847 656 25
134 217 728	27	0.000 000 007 450 580 596 923 828 125
268 435 456	28	0.000 000 003 725 290 298 461 914 062 5
536 870 912	29	0.000 000 001 862 645 149 230 957 031 25
1 073 741 824	30	0.000 000 000 931 322 574 615 478 515 625
2 147 483 648	31	0.000 000 000 465 661 287 307 739 257 812 5
4 294 967 296	32	0.000 000 000 232 830 643 653 869 628 906 25
8 589 934 592	33	0.000 000 000 116 415 321 826 934 814 453 125
17 179 869 184	34	0.000 000 000 058 207 660 913 467 407 226 562 5
34 359 738 368	35	0.000 000 000 029 103 830 456 733 703 613 281 25
68 719 476 736	36	0.000 000 000 014 551 915 228 366 851 806 640 625
137 438 953 472	37	0.000 000 000 007 275 957 614 183 425 903 320 312 5
274 877 906 944	38	0.000 000 000 003 637 978 807 091 712 951 660 156 25
549 755 813 888	39	0.000 000 000 001 818 989 403 545 856 475 830 078 125

C–3. CONVERTING HEXADECIMAL FRACTIONS TO DECIMAL FRACTIONS

	$\times 16^{-1}$	$\times 16^{-2}$	$\times 16^{-3}$	$\times 16^{-4}$	$\times 16^{-5}$	$\times 16^{-6}$	$\times 16^{-7}$
1	0.06250000	0.00390625	0.00024414	0.00001525	0.00000095	0.00000005	0.00000000
2	0.12500000	0.00781250	0.00048828	0.00003051	0.00000190	0.00000011	0.00000000
3	0.18750000	0.01171875	0.00073242	0.00004577	0.00000286	0.00000017	0.00000001
4	0.25000000	0.01562500	0.00097656	0.00006103	0.00000381	0.00000023	0.00000001
5	0.31250000	0.01953125	0.00122070	0.00007629	0.00000476	0.00000029	0.00000001
6	0.37500000	0.02343750	0.00146484	0.00009155	0.00000572	0.00000035	0.00000002
7	0.43750000	0.02734375	0.00170898	0.00010681	0.00000667	0.00000041	0.00000002
8	0.50000000	0.03125000	0.00195312	0.00012207	0.00000762	0.00000047	0.00000002
9	0.56250000	0.03515625	0.00219726	0.00013732	0.00000858	0.00000053	0.00000003
A–10	0.62500000	0.03906250	0.00244140	0.00015258	0.00000953	0.00000059	0.00000003
B–11	0.68750000	0.04296875	0.00268554	0.00016784	0.00001049	0.00000065	0.00000004
C–12	0.75000000	0.04687500	0.00292968	0.00018310	0.00001144	0.00000071	0.00000004
D–13	0.81250000	0.05078125	0.00317382	0.00019836	0.00001239	0.00000077	0.00000004
E–14	0.87500000	0.05468750	0.00341796	0.00021362	0.00001335	0.00000083	0.00000005
F–15	0.93750000	0.05859375	0.00366210	0.00022888	0.00001430	0.00000089	0.00000005

C–4. HEXADECIMAL NUMBERS—BASIC SYMBOLS

Hexadecimal	Decimal	Four-place binary coding
1	1	0001
2	2	0010
3	3	0011
4	4	0100
5	5	0101
6	6	0110
7	7	0110
8	8	1000
9	9	1001
A	10	1010
B	11	1011
C	12	1100
D	13	1101
E	14	1110
F	15	1111

C-5. HEXADECIMAL/DECIMAL CONVERSION CHART

The tables printed below are used to convert decimal numbers to hexadecimal and hexadecimal numbers to decimal. In the descriptions that follow, the explanation of each step is followed by an example in parentheses.

Decimal to Hexadecimal Conversion. Locate the decimal number (0489) in the body of the table. The two high-order digits (1E) of the hexadecimal number are in the left column on the same line, and the low-order digit (9) is at the top of the column. Thus, the hexadecimal number 1E9 is equal to the decimal number 0489.

Hexadecimal to Decimal Conversion. Locate the first two digits (1E) of the hexadecimal number (1E9) in the left column. Follow the line of figures across the page to the column headed by the low-order digit (9). The decimal number (0489) located at the junction of the horizontal line and the vertical column is the equivalent of the hexadecimal number.

	0	1	2	3	4	5	6	7	8	9	A	B	C	D	E	F
00	0000	0001	0002	0003	0004	0005	0006	0007	0008	0009	0010	0011	0012	0013	0014	0015
01	0016	0017	0018	0019	0020	0021	0022	0023	0024	0025	0026	0027	0028	0029	0030	0031
02	0032	0033	0034	0035	0036	0037	0038	0039	0040	0041	0042	0043	0044	0045	0046	0047
03	0048	0049	0050	0051	0052	0053	0054	0055	0056	0057	0058	0059	0060	0061	0062	0063
04	0064	0065	0066	0067	0068	0069	0070	0071	0072	0073	0074	0075	0076	0077	0078	0079
05	0080	0081	0082	0083	0084	0085	0086	0087	0088	0089	0090	0091	0092	0093	0094	0095
06	0096	0097	0098	0099	0100	0101	0102	0103	0104	0105	0106	0107	0108	0109	0110	0111
07	0112	0113	0114	0115	0116	0117	0118	0119	0120	0121	0122	0123	0124	0125	0126	0127
08	0128	0129	0130	0131	0132	0133	0134	0135	0136	0137	0138	0139	0140	0141	0142	0143
09	0144	0145	0146	0147	0148	0149	0150	0151	0152	0153	0154	0155	0156	0157	0158	0159
0A	0160	0161	0162	0163	0164	0165	0166	0167	0168	0169	0170	0171	0172	0173	0174	0175
0B	0176	0177	0178	0179	0180	0181	0182	0183	0184	0185	0186	0187	0188	0189	0190	0191
0C	0192	0193	0194	0195	0196	0197	0198	0199	0200	0201	0202	0203	0204	0205	0206	0207
0D	0208	0209	0210	0211	0212	0213	0214	0215	0216	0217	0218	0219	0220	0221	0222	0223
0E	0224	0225	0226	0227	0228	0229	0230	0231	0232	0233	0234	0235	0236	0237	0238	0239
0F	0240	0241	0242	0243	0244	0245	0246	0247	0248	0249	0250	0251	0252	0253	0254	0255
10	0256	0257	0258	0259	0260	0261	0262	0263	0264	0265	0266	0267	0268	0269	0270	0271
11	0272	0273	0274	0275	0276	0277	0278	0279	0280	0281	0282	0283	0284	0285	0286	0287
12	0288	0289	0290	0291	0292	0293	0294	0295	0296	0297	0298	0299	0300	0301	0302	0303
13	0304	0305	0306	0307	0308	0309	0310	0311	0312	0313	0314	0315	0316	0317	0318	0319
14	0320	0321	0322	0323	0324	0325	0326	0327	0328	0329	0330	0331	0332	0333	0334	0335
15	0336	0337	0338	0339	0340	0341	0342	0343	0344	0345	0346	0347	0348	0349	0350	0351
16	0352	0353	0354	0355	0356	0357	0358	0359	0360	0361	0362	0363	0364	0365	0366	0367
17	0368	0369	0370	0371	0372	0373	0374	0375	0376	0377	0378	0379	0380	0381	0382	0383
18	0384	0385	0386	0387	0388	0389	0390	0391	0392	0393	0394	0395	0396	0397	0398	0399
19	0400	0401	0402	0403	0404	0405	0406	0407	0408	0409	0410	0411	0412	0413	0414	0415
1A	0416	0417	0418	0419	0420	0421	0422	0423	0424	0425	0426	0427	0428	0429	0430	0431
1B	0432	0433	0434	0435	0436	0437	0438	0439	0440	0441	0442	0443	0444	0445	0446	0447
1C	0448	0449	0450	0451	0452	0453	0454	0455	0456	0457	0458	0459	0460	0461	0462	0463
1D	0464	0465	0466	0467	0468	0469	0470	0471	0472	0473	0474	0475	0476	0477	0478	0479
1E	0480	0481	0482	0483	0484	0485	0486	0487	0488	0489	0490	0491	0492	0493	0494	0495
1F	0496	0497	0498	0499	0500	0501	0502	0503	0504	0505	0506	0507	0508	0509	0510	0511
20	0512	0513	0514	0515	0516	0517	0518	0519	0520	0521	0522	0523	0524	0525	0526	0527
21	0528	0529	0530	0531	0532	0533	0534	0535	0536	0537	0538	0539	0540	0541	0542	0543
22	0544	0545	0546	0547	0548	0549	0550	0551	0552	0553	0554	0555	0556	0557	0558	0559
23	0560	0561	0562	0563	0564	0565	0566	0567	0568	0569	0570	0571	0572	0573	0574	0575
24	0576	0577	0578	0579	0580	0581	0582	0583	0584	0585	0586	0587	0588	0589	0590	0591
25	0592	0593	0594	0595	0596	0597	0598	0599	0600	0601	0602	0603	0604	0605	0606	0607
26	0608	0609	0610	0611	0612	0613	0614	0615	0616	0617	0618	0619	0620	0621	0622	0623
27	0624	0625	0626	0627	0628	0629	0630	0631	0632	0633	0634	0635	0636	0637	0638	0639
28	0640	0641	0642	0643	0644	0645	0646	0647	0648	0649	0650	0651	0652	0653	0654	0655
29	0656	0657	0658	0659	0660	0661	0662	0663	0664	0665	0666	0667	0668	0669	0670	0671
2A	0672	0673	0674	0675	0676	0677	0678	0679	0680	0681	0682	0683	0684	0685	0686	0687
2B	0688	0689	0690	0691	0692	0693	0694	0695	0696	0697	0698	0699	0700	0701	0702	0703
2C	0704	0705	0706	0707	0708	0709	0710	0711	0712	0713	0714	0715	0716	0717	0718	0719
2D	0720	0721	0722	0723	0724	0725	0726	0727	0728	0729	0730	0731	0732	0733	0734	0735
2E	0736	0737	0738	0739	0740	0741	0742	0743	0744	0745	0746	0747	0748	0749	0750	0751
2F	0752	0753	0754	0755	0756	0757	0758	0759	0760	0761	0762	0763	0764	0765	0766	0767
30	0768	0769	0770	0771	0772	0773	0774	0775	0776	0777	0778	0779	0780	0781	0782	0783
31	0784	0785	0786	0787	0788	0789	0790	0791	0792	0793	0794	0795	0796	0797	0798	0799
32	0800	0801	0802	0803	0804	0805	0806	0807	0808	0809	0810	0811	0812	0813	0814	0815
33	0816	0817	0818	0819	0820	0821	0822	0823	0824	0825	0826	0827	0828	0829	0830	0831
34	0832	0833	0834	0835	0836	0837	0838	0839	0840	0841	0842	0843	0844	0845	0846	0847
35	0848	0849	0850	0851	0852	0853	0854	0855	0856	0857	0858	0859	0860	0861	0862	0863
36	0864	0865	0866	0867	0868	0869	0870	0871	0872	0873	0874	0875	0876	0877	0878	0879
37	0880	0881	0882	0883	0884	0885	0886	0887	0888	0889	0890	0891	0892	0893	0894	0895
38	0896	0897	0898	0899	0900	0901	0902	0903	0904	0905	0906	0907	0908	0909	0910	0911
39	0912	0913	0914	0915	0916	0917	0918	0919	0920	0921	0922	0923	0924	0925	0926	0927
3A	0928	0929	0930	0931	0932	0933	0934	0935	0936	0937	0938	0939	0940	0941	0942	0943
3B	0944	0945	0946	0947	0948	0949	0950	0951	0952	0953	0954	0955	0956	0957	0958	0959
3C	0960	0961	0962	0963	0964	0965	0966	0967	0968	0969	0970	0971	0972	0973	0974	0975
3D	0976	0977	0978	0979	0980	0981	0982	0983	0984	0985	0986	0987	0988	0989	0990	0991
3E	0992	0993	0994	0995	0996	0997	0998	0999	1000	1001	1002	1003	1004	1005	1006	1007
3F	1008	1009	1010	1011	1012	1013	1014	1015	1016	1017	1018	1019	1020	1021	1022	1023

	0	1	2	3	4	5	6	7	8	9	A	B	C	D	E	F
40	1024	1025	1026	1027	1028	1029	1030	1031	1032	1033	1034	1035	1036	1037	1038	1039
41	1040	1041	1042	1043	1044	1045	1046	1047	1048	1049	1050	1051	1052	1053	1054	1055
42	1056	1057	1058	1059	1060	1061	1062	1063	1064	1065	1066	1067	1068	1069	1070	1071
43	1072	1073	1074	1075	1076	1077	1078	1079	1080	1081	1082	1083	1084	1085	1086	1087
44	1088	1089	1090	1091	1092	1093	1094	1095	1096	1097	1098	1099	1100	1101	1102	1103
45	1104	1105	1106	1107	1108	1109	1110	1111	1112	1113	1114	1115	1116	1117	1118	1119
46	1120	1121	1122	1123	1124	1125	1126	1127	1128	1129	1130	1131	1132	1133	1134	1135
47	1136	1137	1138	1139	1140	1141	1142	1143	1144	1145	1146	1147	1148	1149	1150	1151
48	1152	1153	1154	1155	1156	1157	1158	1159	1160	1161	1162	1163	1164	1165	1166	1167
49	1168	1169	1170	1171	1172	1173	1174	1175	1176	1177	1178	1179	1180	1181	1182	1183
4A	1184	1185	1186	1187	1188	1189	1190	1191	1192	1193	1194	1195	1196	1197	1198	1199
4B	1200	1201	1202	1203	1204	1205	1206	1207	1208	1209	1210	1211	1212	1213	1214	1215
4C	1216	1217	1218	1219	1220	1221	1222	1223	1224	1225	1226	1227	1228	1229	1230	1231
4D	1232	1233	1234	1235	1236	1237	1238	1239	1240	1241	1242	1243	1244	1245	1246	1247
4E	1248	1249	1250	1251	1252	1253	1254	1255	1256	1257	1258	1259	1260	1261	1262	1263
4F	1264	1265	1266	1267	1268	1269	1270	1271	1272	1273	1274	1275	1276	1277	1278	1279
50	1280	1281	1282	1283	1284	1285	1286	1287	1288	1289	1290	1291	1292	1293	1294	1295
51	1296	1297	1298	1299	1300	1301	1302	1303	1304	1305	1306	1307	1308	1309	1310	1311
52	1312	1313	1314	1315	1316	1317	1318	1319	1320	1321	1322	1323	1324	1325	1326	1327
53	1328	1329	1330	1331	1332	1333	1334	1335	1336	1337	1338	1339	1340	1341	1342	1343
54	1344	1345	1346	1347	1348	1349	1350	1351	1352	1353	1354	1355	1356	1357	1358	1359
55	1360	1361	1362	1363	1364	1365	1366	1367	1368	1369	1370	1371	1372	1373	1374	1375
56	1376	1377	1378	1379	1380	1381	1382	1383	1384	1385	1386	1387	1388	1389	1390	1391
57	1392	1393	1394	1395	1396	1397	1398	1399	1400	1401	1402	1403	1404	1405	1406	1407
58	1408	1409	1410	1411	1412	1413	1414	1415	1416	1417	1418	1419	1420	1421	1422	1423
59	1424	1425	1426	1427	1428	1429	1430	1431	1432	1433	1434	1435	1436	1437	1438	1439
5A	1440	1441	1442	1443	1444	1445	1446	1447	1448	1449	1450	1451	1452	1453	1454	1455
5B	1456	1457	1458	1459	1460	1461	1462	1463	1464	1465	1466	1467	1468	1469	1470	1471
5C	1472	1473	1474	1475	1476	1477	1478	1479	1480	1481	1482	1483	1484	1485	1486	1487
5D	1488	1489	1490	1491	1492	1493	1494	1495	1496	1497	1498	1499	1500	1501	1502	1503
5E	1504	1505	1506	1507	1508	1509	1510	1511	1512	1513	1514	1515	1516	1517	1518	1519
5F	1520	1521	1522	1523	1524	1525	1526	1527	1528	1529	1530	1531	1532	1533	1534	1535
60	1536	1537	1538	1539	1540	1541	1542	1543	1544	1545	1546	1547	1548	1549	1550	1551
61	1552	1553	1554	1555	1556	1557	1558	1559	1560	1561	1562	1563	1564	1565	1566	1567
62	1568	1569	1570	1571	1572	1573	1574	1575	1576	1577	1578	1579	1580	1581	1582	1583
63	1584	1585	1586	1587	1588	1589	1590	1591	1592	1593	1594	1595	1596	1597	1598	1599
64	1600	1601	1602	1603	1604	1605	1606	1607	1608	1609	1610	1611	1612	1613	1614	1615
65	1616	1617	1618	1619	1620	1621	1622	1623	1624	1625	1626	1627	1628	1629	1630	1631
66	1632	1633	1634	1635	1636	1637	1638	1639	1640	1641	1642	1643	1644	1645	1646	1647
67	1648	1649	1650	1651	1652	1653	1654	1655	1656	1657	1658	1659	1660	1661	1662	1663
68	1664	1665	1666	1667	1668	1669	1670	1671	1672	1673	1674	1675	1676	1677	1678	1679
69	1680	1681	1682	1683	1684	1685	1686	1687	1688	1689	1690	1691	1692	1693	1694	1695
6A	1696	1697	1698	1699	1700	1701	1702	1703	1704	1705	1706	1707	1708	1709	1710	1711
6B	1712	1713	1714	1715	1716	1717	1718	1719	1720	1721	1722	1723	1724	1725	1726	1727
6C	1728	1729	1730	1731	1732	1733	1734	1735	1736	1737	1738	1739	1740	1741	1742	1743
6D	1744	1745	1746	1747	1748	1749	1750	1751	1752	1753	1754	1755	1756	1757	1758	1759
6E	1760	1761	1762	1763	1764	1765	1766	1767	1768	1769	1770	1771	1772	1773	1774	1775
6F	1776	1777	1778	1779	1780	1781	1782	1783	1784	1785	1786	1787	1788	1789	1790	1791
70	1792	1793	1794	1795	1796	1797	1798	1799	1800	1801	1802	1803	1804	1805	1806	1807
71	1808	1809	1810	1811	1812	1813	1814	1815	1816	1817	1818	1819	1820	1821	1822	1823
72	1824	1825	1826	1827	1828	1829	1830	1831	1832	1833	1834	1835	1836	1837	1838	1839
73	1840	1841	1842	1843	1844	1845	1846	1847	1848	1849	1850	1851	1852	1853	1854	1855
74	1856	1857	1858	1859	1860	1861	1862	1863	1864	1865	1866	1867	1868	1869	1870	1871
75	1872	1873	1874	1875	1876	1877	1878	1879	1880	1881	1882	1883	1884	1885	1886	1887
76	1888	1889	1890	1891	1892	1893	1894	1895	1896	1897	1898	1899	1900	1901	1902	1903
77	1904	1905	1906	1907	1908	1909	1910	1911	1912	1913	1914	1915	1916	1917	1918	1919
78	1920	1921	1922	1923	1924	1925	1926	1927	1928	1929	1930	1931	1932	1933	1934	1935
79	1936	1937	1938	1939	1940	1941	1942	1943	1944	1945	1946	1947	1948	1949	1950	1951
7A	1952	1953	1954	1955	1956	1957	1958	1959	1960	1961	1962	1963	1964	1965	1966	1967
7B	1968	1969	1970	1971	1972	1973	1974	1975	1976	1977	1978	1979	1980	1981	1982	1983
7C	1984	1985	1986	1987	1988	1989	1990	1991	1992	1993	1994	1995	1996	1997	1998	1999
7D	2000	2001	2002	2003	2004	2005	2006	2007	2008	2009	2010	2011	2012	2013	2014	2015
7E	2016	2017	2018	2019	2020	2021	2022	2023	2024	2025	2026	2027	2028	2029	2030	2031
7F	2032	2033	2034	2035	2036	2037	2038	2039	2040	2041	2042	2043	2044	2045	2046	2047

The table to the left gives the decimal, binary, and hexadecimal coding for the full range of four binary bits, from zero through F_{16} and 15_{10}.

To convert a four-digit hexadecimal number to decimal, determine the decimal value of the three low-order hexadecimal digits in the main table, and add the value for the high-order digit, as shown in the extended chart to the right.

For conversion of decimal values beyond the main table, deduct the largest number in the table at the right that will yield a positive result. The related digit is the high-order hexadecimal digit. Determine the three remaining hexadecimal digits by converting the product of the above subtraction in the main table.

Hex	Dec
1000	4096
2000	8192
3000	12288
4000	16384
5000	20480
6000	24576
7000	28672
8000	32768

Hex	Dec
9000	36864
A000	40960
B000	45056
C000	49152
D000	53248
E000	57344
F000	61440

Dec	Bin	Hex	Dec	Bin	Hex
0	0000	0	8	1000	8
1	0001	1	9	1001	9
2	0010	2	10	1010	A
3	0011	3	11	1011	B
4	0100	4	12	1100	C
5	0101	5	13	1101	D
6	0110	6	14	1110	E
7	0111	7	15	1111	F

C-6. DECIMAL/HEXADECIMAL CONVERSION CHART—FRACTIONS

Decimal to Hexadecimal Conversion. Locate the decimal fraction (.1973) in the table. If the exact figure is not shown, locate the next higher and lower fractions (.19726563, .19750977). The first two digits of the hexadecimal fraction are at the top of the column (.32). To locate the third digit, determine by observation or subtraction the smaller difference between the known fraction and each of the found fractions. The smaller difference identifies the correct line (.008). The hexadecimal equivalent is .328.

If the hexadecimal fraction is required to more places, multiply the decimal fraction by 16 and develop integers as successive terms of the hexadecimal fraction. Using the previous sample decimal fraction:

```
      .1973
       x16
  3.1568
       x16
  2.5085
       x16
  8.1360
       x16
  2.1760
```

$.1973_{10} = .328_{16}$

Hexadecimal to Decimal Conversion. Locate the first two digits (.1E) of the hexadecimal fraction (.1E9) in the horizontal row of column headings. Locate the third digit (.009) in the leftmost column of the table. Follow the .009 line horizontally to the right to the .1E column. The decimal equivalent is .11938477. The decimal fractions in the table were carried to eight places and rounded. If 12 places are required, or if the hexadecimal fraction exceeds the capacity of the table, express the hexadecimal fraction as powers of 16 (expansion). For example:

$$.1E9_{16} = 1(16^{-1}) + 14(16^{-2}) + 9(16^{-3}) + 4(16^{-4})$$
$$= 1(.0625) + 14(.00390625) + 9(.000244140625) + 4(.00001525878906250)$$
$$= .11944580078125_{10}$$

	.00	.01	.02	.03	.04	.05	.06	.07	.08	.09	.0A	.0B	.0C	.0D	.0E	.0F
.000	.00000000	.00390625	.00781250	.01171875	.01562500	.01953125	.02343750	.02734375	.03125000	.03515625	.03906250	.04296875	.04687500	.05078125	.05468750	.05859375
.001	.00024414	.00415039	.00805664	.01196289	.01586914	.01977539	.02368164	.02758789	.03149414	.03540039	.03930664	.04321289	.04711914	.05102539	.05493164	.05883789
.002	.00048828	.00439453	.00830078	.01220703	.01611328	.02001953	.02392578	.02783203	.03173828	.03564453	.03955078	.04345703	.04736328	.05126953	.05517578	.05908203
.003	.00073242	.00463867	.00854492	.01245117	.01635742	.02026367	.02416992	.02807617	.03198242	.03588867	.03979492	.04370117	.04760742	.05151367	.05541992	.05932617
.004	.00097656	.00488281	.00878906	.01269531	.01660156	.02050781	.02441406	.02832031	.03222656	.03613281	.04003906	.04394531	.04785156	.05175781	.05566406	.05957031
.005	.00122070	.00512695	.00903320	.01293945	.01684570	.02075195	.02465820	.02856445	.03247070	.03637695	.04028320	.04418945	.04809570	.05200195	.05590820	.05981445
.006	.00146484	.00537109	.00927734	.01318359	.01708984	.02099609	.02490234	.02880859	.03271484	.03662109	.04052734	.04443359	.04833984	.05224609	.05615234	.06005859
.007	.00170898	.00561523	.00952148	.01342773	.01733398	.02124023	.02514648	.02905273	.03295898	.03686523	.04077148	.04467773	.04858398	.05249023	.05639648	.06030273
.008	.00195313	.00585938	.00976563	.01367188	.01757813	.02148438	.02539063	.02929688	.03320313	.03710938	.04101563	.04492188	.04882813	.05273438	.05664063	.06054688
.009	.00219727	.00610352	.01000977	.01391602	.01782227	.02172852	.02563477	.02954102	.03344727	.03735352	.04125977	.04516602	.04907227	.05297852	.05688477	.06079102
.00A	.00244141	.00634766	.01025391	.01416016	.01806641	.02197266	.02587891	.02978516	.03369141	.03759766	.04150391	.04541016	.04931641	.05322266	.05712891	.06103516
.00B	.00268555	.00659180	.01049805	.01440430	.01831055	.02221680	.02612305	.03002930	.03393555	.03784180	.04174805	.04565430	.04956055	.05346680	.05737305	.06127930
.00C	.00292969	.00683594	.01074219	.01464844	.01855469	.02246094	.02636719	.03027344	.03417969	.03808594	.04199219	.04589844	.04980469	.05371094	.05761719	.06152344
.00D	.00317383	.00708008	.01098633	.01489258	.01879883	.02270508	.02661133	.03051758	.03442383	.03833008	.04223633	.04614258	.05004883	.05395508	.05786133	.06176758
.00E	.00341797	.00732422	.01123047	.01513672	.01904297	.02294922	.02685547	.03076172	.03466797	.03857422	.04248047	.04638672	.05029297	.05419922	.05810547	.06201172
.00F	.00366211	.00756836	.01147461	.01538086	.01928711	.02319336	.02709961	.03100586	.03491211	.03881836	.04272461	.04663086	.05053711	.05444336	.05834961	.06225586

	.10	.11	.12	.13	.14	.15	.16	.17	.18	.19	.1A	.1B	.1C	.1D	.1E	.1F
.000	.06250000	.06640625	.07031250	.07421875	.07812500	.08203125	.08593750	.08984375	.09375000	.09765625	.10156250	.10546875	.10937500	.11328125	.11718750	.12109375
.001	.06274414	.06665039	.07055664	.07446289	.07836914	.08227539	.08618164	.09008789	.09399414	.09790039	.10180664	.10571289	.10961914	.11352539	.11743164	.12133789
.002	.06298828	.06689453	.07080078	.07470703	.07861328	.08251953	.08642578	.09033203	.09423828	.09814453	.10205078	.10595703	.10986328	.11376953	.11767578	.12158203
.003	.06323242	.06713867	.07104492	.07495117	.07885742	.08276367	.08666992	.09057617	.09448242	.09838867	.10229492	.10620117	.11010742	.11401367	.11791992	.12182617
.004	.06347656	.06738281	.07128906	.07519531	.07910156	.08300781	.08691406	.09082031	.09472656	.09863281	.10253906	.10644531	.11035156	.11425781	.11816406	.12207031
.005	.06372070	.06762695	.07153320	.07543945	.07934570	.08325195	.08715820	.09106445	.09497070	.09887695	.10278320	.10668945	.11059570	.11450195	.11840820	.12231445
.006	.06396484	.06787109	.07177734	.07568359	.07958984	.08349609	.08740234	.09130859	.09521484	.09912109	.10302734	.10693359	.11083984	.11474609	.11865234	.12255859
.007	.06420898	.06811523	.07202148	.07592773	.07983398	.08374023	.08764648	.09155273	.09545898	.09936523	.10327148	.10717773	.11108398	.11499023	.11889648	.12280273
.008	.06445313	.06835938	.07226563	.07617188	.08007813	.08398438	.08789063	.09179688	.09570313	.09960938	.10351563	.10742188	.11132813	.11523438	.11914063	.12304688
.009	.06469727	.06860352	.07250977	.07641602	.08032227	.08422852	.08813477	.09204102	.09594727	.09985352	.10375977	.10766602	.11157227	.11547852	.11938477	.12329102
.00A	.06494141	.06884766	.07275391	.07666016	.08056641	.08447266	.08837891	.09228516	.09619141	.10009766	.10400391	.10791016	.11181641	.11572266	.11962891	.12353516
.00B	.06518555	.06909180	.07299805	.07690430	.08081055	.08471680	.08862305	.09252930	.09643555	.10034180	.10424805	.10815430	.11206055	.11596680	.11987305	.12377930
.00C	.06542969	.06933594	.07324219	.07714844	.08105469	.08496094	.08886719	.09277344	.09667969	.10058594	.10449219	.10839844	.11230469	.11621094	.12011719	.12402344
.00D	.06567383	.06958008	.07348633	.07739258	.08129883	.08520508	.08911133	.09301758	.09692383	.10083008	.10473633	.10864258	.11254883	.11645508	.12036133	.12426758
.00E	.06591797	.06982422	.07373047	.07763672	.08154297	.08544922	.08935547	.09326172	.09716797	.10107422	.10498047	.10888672	.11279297	.11669922	.12060547	.12451172
.00F	.06616211	.07006836	.07397461	.07788086	.08178711	.08569336	.08959961	.09350586	.09741211	.10131836	.10522461	.10913086	.11303711	.11694336	.12084961	.12475586

	.20	.21	.22	.23	.24	.25	.26	.27	.28	.29	.2A	.2B	.2C	.2D	.2E	.2F
.000	.12500000	.12890625	.13281250	.13671875	.14062500	.14453125	.14843750	.15234375	.15625000	.16015625	.16406250	.16796875	.17187500	.17578125	.17968750	.18359375
.001	.12524414	.12915039	.13305664	.13696289	.14086914	.14477539	.14868164	.15258789	.15649414	.16040039	.16430664	.16821289	.17211914	.17602539	.17993164	.18383789
.002	.12548828	.12939453	.13330078	.13720703	.14111328	.14501953	.14892578	.15283203	.15673828	.16064453	.16455078	.16845703	.17236328	.17626953	.18017578	.18408203
.003	.12573242	.12963867	.13354492	.13745117	.14135742	.14526367	.14916992	.15307617	.15698242	.16088867	.16479492	.16870117	.17260742	.17651367	.18041992	.18432617
.004	.12597656	.12988281	.13378906	.13769531	.14160156	.14550781	.14941406	.15332031	.15722656	.16113281	.16503906	.16894531	.17285156	.17675781	.18066406	.18457031
.005	.12622070	.13012695	.13403320	.13793945	.14184570	.14575195	.14965820	.15356445	.15747070	.16137695	.16528320	.16918945	.17309570	.17700195	.18090820	.18481445
.006	.12646484	.13037109	.13427734	.13818359	.14208984	.14599609	.14990234	.15380859	.15771484	.16162109	.16552734	.16943359	.17333984	.17724609	.18115234	.18505859
.007	.12670898	.13061523	.13452148	.13842773	.14233398	.14624023	.15014648	.15405273	.15795898	.16186523	.16577148	.16967773	.17358398	.17749023	.18139648	.18530273
.008	.12695313	.13085938	.13476563	.13867188	.14257813	.14648438	.15039063	.15429688	.15820313	.16210938	.16601563	.16992188	.17382813	.17773438	.18164063	.18554688
.009	.12719727	.13110352	.13500977	.13891602	.14282227	.14672852	.15063477	.15454102	.15844727	.16235352	.16625977	.17016602	.17407227	.17797852	.18188477	.18579102
.00A	.12744141	.13134766	.13525391	.13916016	.14306641	.14697266	.15087891	.15478516	.15869141	.16259766	.16650391	.17041016	.17431641	.17822266	.18212891	.18603516
.00B	.12768555	.13159180	.13549805	.13940430	.14331055	.14721680	.15112305	.15502930	.15893555	.16284180	.16674805	.17065430	.17456055	.17846680	.18237305	.18627930
.00C	.12792969	.13183594	.13574219	.13964844	.14355469	.14746094	.15136719	.15527344	.15917969	.16308594	.16699219	.17089844	.17480469	.17871094	.18261719	.18652344
.00D	.12817383	.13208008	.13598633	.13989258	.14379883	.14770508	.15161133	.15551758	.15942383	.16333008	.16723633	.17114258	.17504883	.17895508	.18286133	.18676758

	.30	.31	.32	.33	.34	.35	.36	.37	.38	.39	.3A	.3B	.3C	.3D	.3E	.3F
.000	.18750000	.19140625	.19531250	.19921875	.20312500	.20703125	.21093750	.21484375	.21875000	.22265625	.22656250	.23046875	.23437500	.23828125	.24218750	.24609375
.001	.18774414	.19165039	.19555664	.19946289	.20336914	.20727539	.21118164	.21508789	.21899414	.22290039	.22680664	.23071289	.23461914	.23852539	.24243164	.24633789
.002	.18798828	.19189453	.19580078	.19970703	.20361328	.20751953	.21142578	.21533203	.21923828	.22314453	.22705078	.23095703	.23486328	.23876953	.24267578	.24658203
.003	.18823242	.19213867	.19604492	.19995117	.20385742	.20776367	.21166992	.21557617	.21948242	.22338867	.22729492	.23120117	.23510742	.23901367	.24291992	.24682617
.004	.18847656	.19238281	.19628906	.20019531	.20410156	.20800781	.21191406	.21582031	.21972656	.22363281	.22753906	.23144531	.23535156	.23925781	.24316406	.24707031
.005	.18872070	.19262695	.19653320	.20043945	.20434570	.20825195	.21215820	.21606445	.21997070	.22387695	.22778320	.23168945	.23559570	.23950195	.24340820	.24731445
.006	.18896484	.19287109	.19677734	.20068359	.20458984	.20849609	.21240234	.21630859	.22021484	.22412109	.22802734	.23193359	.23583984	.23974609	.24365234	.24755859
.007	.18920898	.19311523	.19702148	.20092773	.20483398	.20874023	.21264648	.21655273	.22045898	.22436523	.22827148	.23217773	.23608398	.23999023	.24389648	.24780273
.008	.18945313	.19335938	.19726563	.20117188	.20507813	.20898438	.21289063	.21679688	.22070313	.22460938	.22851563	.23242188	.23632813	.24023438	.24414063	.24804688
.009	.18969727	.19360352	.19750977	.20141602	.20532227	.20922852	.21313477	.21704102	.22094727	.22485352	.22875977	.23266602	.23657227	.24047852	.24438477	.24829102
.00A	.18994141	.19384766	.19775391	.20166016	.20556641	.20947266	.21337891	.21728516	.22119141	.22509766	.22900391	.23291016	.23681641	.24072266	.24462891	.24853516
.00B	.19018555	.19409180	.19799805	.20190430	.20581055	.20971680	.21362305	.21752930	.22143555	.22534180	.22924805	.23315430	.23706055	.24096680	.24487305	.24877930
.00C	.19042969	.19433594	.19824219	.20214844	.20605469	.20996094	.21386719	.21777344	.22167969	.22558594	.22949219	.23339844	.23730469	.24121094	.24511719	.24902344
.00D	.19067383	.19458008	.19848633	.20239258	.20629883	.21020508	.21411133	.21801758	.22192383	.22583008	.22973633	.23364258	.23754883	.24145508	.24536133	.24926758
.00E	.19091797	.19482422	.19873047	.20263672	.20654297	.21044922	.21435547	.21826172	.22216797	.22607422	.22998047	.23388672	.23779297	.24169922	.24560547	.24951172
.00F	.19116211	.19506836	.19897461	.20288086	.20678711	.21069336	.21459961	.21850586	.22241211	.22631836	.23022461	.23413086	.23803711	.24194336	.24584961	.24975586

	.40	.41	.42	.43	.44	.45	.46	.47	.48	.49	.4A	.4B	.4C	.4D	.4E	.4F
.000	.25000000	.25390625	.25781250	.26171875	.26562500	.26953125	.27343750	.27734375	.28125000	.28515625	.28906250	.29296875	.29687500	.30078125	.30468750	.30859375
.001	.25024414	.25415039	.25805664	.26196289	.26586914	.26977539	.27368164	.27758789	.28149414	.28540039	.28930664	.29321289	.29711914	.30102539	.30493164	.30883789
.002	.25048828	.25439453	.25830078	.26220703	.26611328	.27001953	.27392578	.27783203	.28173828	.28564453	.28955078	.29345703	.29736328	.30126953	.30517578	.30908203
.003	.25073242	.25463867	.25854492	.26245117	.26635742	.27026367	.27416992	.27807617	.28198242	.28588867	.28979492	.29370117	.29760742	.30151367	.30541992	.30932617
.004	.25097656	.25488281	.25878906	.26269531	.26660156	.27050781	.27441406	.27832031	.28222656	.28613281	.29003906	.29394531	.29785156	.30175781	.30566406	.30957031
.005	.25122070	.25512695	.25903320	.26293945	.26684570	.27075195	.27465820	.27856445	.28247070	.28637695	.29028320	.29418945	.29809570	.30200195	.30590820	.30981445
.006	.25146484	.25537109	.25927734	.26318359	.26708984	.27099609	.27490234	.27880859	.28271484	.28662109	.29052734	.29443359	.29833984	.30224609	.30615234	.31005859
.007	.25170898	.25561523	.25952148	.26342773	.26733398	.27124023	.27514648	.27905273	.28295898	.28686523	.29077148	.29467773	.29858398	.30249023	.30639648	.31030273
.008	.25195313	.25585938	.25976563	.26367188	.26757813	.27148438	.27539063	.27929688	.28320313	.28710938	.29101563	.29492188	.29882813	.30273438	.30664063	.31054688
.009	.25219727	.25610352	.26000977	.26391602	.26782227	.27172852	.27563477	.27954102	.28344727	.28735352	.29125977	.29516602	.29907227	.30297852	.30688477	.31079102
.00A	.25244141	.25634766	.26025391	.26416016	.26806641	.27197266	.27587891	.27978516	.28369141	.28759766	.29150390	.29541016	.29931641	.30322266	.30712891	.31103516
.00B	.25268555	.25659180	.26049805	.26440430	.26831055	.27221680	.27612305	.28002930	.28393555	.28784180	.29174805	.29565430	.29956055	.30346680	.30737305	.31127930
.00C	.25292969	.25683594	.26074219	.26464844	.26855469	.27246094	.27636719	.28027344	.28417969	.28808594	.29199219	.29589844	.29980469	.30371094	.30761719	.31152344
.00D	.25317383	.25708008	.26098633	.26489258	.26879883	.27270508	.27661133	.28051758	.28442383	.28833008	.29223633	.29614258	.30004883	.30395508	.30786133	.31176758
.00E	.25341797	.25732422	.26123047	.26513672	.26904297	.27294922	.27685547	.28076172	.28466797	.28857422	.29248047	.29638672	.30029297	.30419922	.30810547	.31201172
.00F	.25366211	.25756836	.26147461	.26538086	.26928711	.27319336	.27709961	.28100586	.28491211	.28881836	.29272461	.29663086	.30053711	.30444336	.30834961	.31225586

	.50	.51	.52	.53	.54	.55	.56	.57	.58	.59	.5A	.5B	.5C	.5D	.5E	.5F
.000	.31250000	.31640625	.32031250	.32421875	.32812500	.33203125	.33593750	.33984375	.34375000	.34765625	.35156250	.35546875	.35937500	.36328125	.36718750	.37109375
.001	.31274414	.31665039	.32055664	.32446289	.32836914	.33227539	.33618164	.34008789	.34399414	.34790039	.35180664	.35571289	.35961914	.36352539	.36743164	.37133789
.002	.31298828	.31689453	.32080078	.32470703	.32861328	.33251953	.33642578	.34033203	.34423828	.34814453	.35205078	.35595703	.35986328	.36376953	.36767578	.37158203
.003	.31323242	.31713867	.32104492	.32495117	.32885742	.33276367	.33666992	.34057617	.34448242	.34838867	.35229492	.35620117	.36010742	.36401367	.36791992	.37182617
.004	.31347656	.31738281	.32128906	.32519531	.32910156	.33300781	.33691406	.34082031	.34472656	.34863281	.35253906	.35644531	.36035156	.36425781	.36816406	.37207031
.005	.31372070	.31762695	.32153320	.32543945	.32934570	.33325195	.33715820	.34106445	.34497070	.34887695	.35278320	.35668945	.36059570	.36450195	.36840820	.37231445
.006	.31396484	.31787109	.32177734	.32568359	.32958984	.33349609	.33740234	.34130859	.34521484	.34912109	.35302734	.35693359	.36083984	.36474609	.36865234	.37255859
.007	.31420898	.31811523	.32202148	.32592773	.32983398	.33374023	.33764648	.34155273	.34545898	.34936523	.35327148	.35717773	.36108398	.36499023	.36889648	.37280273
.008	.31445313	.31835938	.32226563	.32617188	.33007813	.33398438	.33789063	.34179688	.34570313	.34960938	.35351563	.35742188	.36132813	.36523438	.36914063	.37304688
.009	.31469727	.31860352	.32250977	.32641602	.33032227	.33422852	.33813477	.34204102	.34594727	.34985352	.35375977	.35766602	.36157227	.36547852	.36938477	.37329102
.00A	.31494141	.31884766	.32275391	.32666016	.33056641	.33447266	.33837891	.34228516	.34619141	.35009766	.35400391	.35791016	.36181641	.36572266	.36962891	.37353516
.00B	.31518555	.31909180	.32299805	.32690430	.33081055	.33471680	.33862305	.34252930	.34643555	.35034180	.35424805	.35815430	.36206055	.36596680	.36987305	.37377930
.00C	.31542969	.31933594	.32324219	.32714844	.33105469	.33496094	.33886719	.34277344	.34667969	.35058594	.35449219	.35839844	.36230469	.36621094	.37011719	.37402344
.00D	.31567383	.31958008	.32348633	.32739258	.33129883	.33520508	.33911133	.34301758	.34692383	.35083008	.35473633	.35864258	.36254883	.36645508	.37036133	.37426758
.00E	.31591797	.31982422	.32373047	.32763672	.33154297	.33544922	.33935547	.34326172	.34716797	.35107422	.35498047	.35888672	.36279297	.36669922	.37060547	.37451172
.00F	.31616211	.32006836	.32397461	.32788086	.33178711	.33569336	.33959961	.34350586	.34741211	.35131836	.35522461	.35913086	.36303711	.36694336	.37084961	.37475586

	.60	.61	.62	.63	.64	.65	.66	.67	.68	.69	.6A	.6B	.6C	.6D	.6E	.6F
.000	.37500000	.37890625	.38281250	.38671875	.39062500	.39453125	.39843750	.40234375	.40625000	.41015625	.41406250	.41796875	.42187500	.42578125	.42968750	.43359375
.001	.37524414	.37915039	.38305664	.38696289	.39086914	.39477539	.39868164	.40258789	.40649414	.41040039	.41430664	.41821289	.42211914	.42602539	.42993164	.43383789
.002	.37548828	.37939453	.38330078	.38720703	.39111328	.39501953	.39892578	.40283203	.40673828	.41064453	.41455078	.41845703	.42236328	.42626953	.43017578	.43408203
.003	.37573242	.37963867	.38354492	.38745117	.39135742	.39526367	.39916992	.40307617	.40698242	.41088867	.41479492	.41870117	.42260742	.42651367	.43041992	.43432617
.004	.37597656	.37988281	.38378906	.38769531	.39160156	.39550781	.39941406	.40332031	.40722656	.41113281	.41503906	.41894531	.42285156	.42675781	.43066406	.43457031
.005	.37622070	.38012695	.38403320	.38793945	.39184570	.39575195	.39965820	.40356445	.40747070	.41137695	.41528320	.41918945	.42309570	.42700195	.43090820	.43481445
.006	.37646484	.38037109	.38427734	.38818359	.39208984	.39599609	.39990234	.40380859	.40771484	.41162109	.41552734	.41943359	.42333984	.42724609	.43115234	.43505859
.007	.37670898	.38061523	.38452148	.38842773	.39233398	.39624023	.40014648	.40405273	.40795898	.41186523	.41577148	.41967773	.42358398	.42749023	.43139648	.43530273
.008	.37695313	.38085938	.38476563	.38867188	.39257813	.39648438	.40039063	.40429688	.40820313	.41210938	.41601563	.41992188	.42382813	.42773438	.43164063	.43554688
.009	.37719727	.38110352	.38500977	.38891602	.39282227	.39672852	.40063477	.40454102	.40844727	.41235352	.41625977	.42016602	.42407227	.42797852	.43188477	.43579102
.00A	.37744141	.38134766	.38525391	.38916016	.39306641	.39697266	.40087891	.40478516	.40869141	.41259766	.41650391	.42041016	.42431641	.42822266	.43212891	.43603516
.00B	.37768555	.38159180	.38549805	.38940430	.39331055	.39721680	.40112305	.40502930	.40893555	.41284180	.41674805	.42065430	.42456055	.42846680	.43237305	.43627930
.00C	.37792969	.38183594	.38574219	.38964844	.39355469	.39746094	.40136719	.40527344	.40917969	.41308594	.41699219	.42089844	.42480469	.42871094	.43261719	.43652344
.00D	.37817383	.38208008	.38598633	.38989258	.39379883	.39770508	.40161133	.40551758	.40942383	.41333008	.41723633	.42114258	.42504883	.42895508	.43286133	.43676758
.00E	.37841797	.38232422	.38623047	.39013672	.39404297	.39794922	.40185547	.40576172	.40966797	.41357422	.41748047	.42138672	.42529297	.42919922	.43310547	.43701172
.00F	.37866211	.38256836	.38647461	.39038086	.39428711	.39819336	.40209961	.40600586	.40991211	.41381836	.41772461	.42163086	.42553711	.42944336	.43334961	.43725586

C-6. DECIMAL/HEXADECIMAL CONVERSION CHART—FRACTIONS (Continued)

	.70	.71	.72	.73	.74	.75	.76	.77	.78	.79	.7A	.7B	.7C	.7D	.7E	.7F
.000	.43750000	.44140625	.44531250	.44921875	.45312500	.45703125	.46093750	.46484375	.46875000	.47265625	.47656250	.48046875	.48437500	.48828125	.49218750	.49609375
.001	.43774414	.44165039	.44555664	.44946289	.45336914	.45727539	.46118164	.46508789	.46899414	.47290039	.47680664	.48071289	.18461914	.48852539	.49243164	.49633789
.002	.43798828	.44189453	.44580078	.44970703	.45361328	.45751953	.46142578	.46533203	.46923828	.47314453	.47705078	.48095703	.48486328	.48876953	.49267578	.49658203
.003	.43823242	.44213867	.44604492	.44995117	.45385742	.45776367	.46166992	.46557617	.46948242	.47338867	.47729492	.48120117	.48510742	.48901367	.49291992	.49682617
.004	.43847656	.44238281	.44628906	.45019531	.45410156	.45800781	.46191406	.46582031	.46972656	.47363281	.47753906	.48144531	.48535156	.48925781	.49316406	.49707031
.005	.43872070	.44262695	.44653320	.45043945	.45434570	.45825195	.46215820	.46606445	.46997070	.47387695	.47778320	.48168945	.48559570	.48950195	.49340820	.49731445
.006	.43896484	.44287109	.44677734	.45068359	.45458984	.45849609	.46240234	.46630859	.47021484	.47412109	.47802734	.48193359	.48583984	.48974609	.49365234	.49755859
.007	.43920898	.44311523	.44702148	.45092773	.45483398	.45874023	.46264648	.46655273	.47045898	.47436523	.47827148	.48217773	.48608398	.48999023	.49389648	.49780273
.008	.43945313	.44335938	.44726563	.45117188	.45507813	.45898438	.46289063	.46679688	.47070313	.47460938	.47851563	.48242188	.48632813	.49023438	.49414063	.49804688
.009	.43969727	.44360352	.44750977	.45141602	.45532227	.45922852	.46313477	.46704102	.47094727	.47485352	.47875977	.48266602	.48657227	.49047852	.49438477	.49829102
.00A	.43994141	.44384766	.44775391	.45166016	.45556641	.45947266	.46337891	.46728516	.47119141	.47509766	.47900391	.48291016	.48681641	.49072266	.49462891	.49853516
.00B	.44018555	.44409180	.44799805	.45190430	.45581055	.45971680	.46362305	.46752930	.47143555	.47534180	.47924805	.48315430	.48706055	.49096680	.49487305	.49877930
.00C	.44042969	.44433594	.44824219	.45214844	.45605469	.45996094	.46386719	.46777344	.47167969	.47558594	.47949219	.48339844	.48730469	.49121094	.49511719	.49902344
.00D	.44067383	.44458008	.44848633	.45239258	.45629883	.46020508	.46411133	.46801758	.47192383	.47583008	.47973633	.48364258	.48754883	.49145508	.49536133	.49926758
.00E	.44091797	.44482422	.44873047	.45263672	.45654297	.46044922	.46435547	.46826172	.47216797	.47607422	.47998047	.48388672	.48779297	.49169922	.49560547	.49951172
.00F	.44116211	.44506836	.44897461	.45288086	.45678711	.46069336	.46459961	.46850586	.47241211	.47631836	.48022461	.48413086	.48803711	.49194336	.49584961	.49975586

	.80	.81	.82	.83	.84	.85	.86	.87	.88	.89	.8A	.8B	.8C	.8D	.8E	.8F
.000	.50000000	.50390625	.50781250	.51171875	.51562500	.51953125	.52343750	.52734375	.53125000	.53515625	.53906250	.54296875	.54687500	.55078125	.55468750	.55859375
.001	.50024414	.50415039	.50805664	.51196289	.51586914	.51977539	.52368164	.52758789	.53149414	.53540039	.53930664	.54321289	.54711914	.55102539	.55493164	.55883789
.002	.50048828	.50439453	.50830078	.51220703	.51611328	.52001953	.52392578	.52783203	.53173828	.53564453	.53955078	.54345703	.54736328	.55126953	.55517578	.55908203
.003	.50073242	.50463867	.50854492	.51245117	.51635742	.52026367	.52416992	.52807617	.53198242	.53588867	.53979492	.54370117	.54760742	.55151367	.55541992	.55932617
.004	.50097656	.50488281	.50878906	.51269531	.51660156	.52050781	.52441406	.52832031	.53222656	.53613281	.54003906	.54394531	.54785156	.55175781	.55566406	.55957031
.005	.50122070	.50512695	.50903320	.51293945	.51684570	.52075195	.52465820	.52856445	.53247070	.53637695	.54028320	.54418945	.54809570	.55200195	.55590820	.55981445
.006	.50146484	.50537109	.50927734	.51318359	.51708984	.52099609	.52490234	.52880859	.53271484	.53662109	.54052734	.54443359	.54833984	.55224609	.55615234	.56005859
.007	.50170898	.50561523	.50952148	.51342773	.51733398	.52124023	.52514648	.52905273	.53295898	.53686523	.54077148	.54467773	.54858398	.55249023	.55639648	.56030273
.008	.50195313	.50585938	.50976563	.51367188	.51757813	.52148438	.52539063	.52929688	.53320313	.53710938	.54101563	.54492188	.54882813	.55273438	.55664063	.56054688
.009	.50219727	.50610352	.51000977	.51391602	.51782227	.52172852	.52563477	.52954102	.53344727	.53735352	.54125977	.54516602	.54907227	.55297852	.55688477	.56079102
.00A	.50244141	.50634766	.51025391	.51416016	.51806641	.52197266	.52587891	.52978516	.53369141	.53759766	.54150391	.54541016	.54931641	.55322266	.55712891	.56103516
.00B	.50268555	.50659180	.51049805	.51440430	.51831055	.52221680	.52612305	.53002930	.53393555	.53784180	.54174805	.54565430	.54956055	.55346680	.55737305	.56127930
.00C	.50292969	.50683594	.51074219	.51464844	.51855469	.52246094	.52636719	.53027344	.53417969	.53808594	.54199219	.54589844	.54980469	.55371094	.55761719	.56152344
.00D	.50317383	.50708008	.51098633	.51489258	.51879883	.52270508	.52661133	.53051758	.53442383	.53833008	.54223633	.54614258	.55004883	.55395508	.55786133	.56176758
.00E	.50341797	.50732422	.51123047	.51513672	.51904297	.52294922	.52685547	.53076172	.53466797	.53857422	.54248047	.54638672	.55029297	.55419922	.55810547	.56201172
.00F	.50366211	.50756836	.51147461	.51538086	.51928711	.52319336	.52709961	.53100586	.53491211	.53881836	.54272461	.54663086	.55053711	.55444336	.55834961	.56225586

	.90	.91	.92	.93	.94	.95	.96	.97	.98	.99	.9A	.9B	.9C	.9D	.9E	.9F
.000	.56250000	.56640625	.57031250	.57421875	.57812500	.58203125	.58593750	.58984375	.59375000	.59765625	.60156250	.60546875	.60937500	.61328125	.61718750	.62109375
.001	.56274414	.56665039	.57055664	.57446289	.57836914	.58227539	.58618164	.59008789	.59399414	.59790039	.60180664	.60571289	.60961914	.61352539	.61743164	.62133789
.002	.56298828	.56689453	.57080078	.57470703	.57861328	.58251953	.58642578	.59033203	.59423828	.59814453	.60205078	.60595703	.60986328	.61376953	.61767578	.62158203
.003	.56323242	.56713867	.57104492	.57495117	.57885742	.58276367	.58666992	.59057617	.59448242	.59838867	.60229492	.60620117	.61010742	.61401367	.61791992	.62182617
.004	.56347656	.56738281	.57128906	.57519531	.57910156	.58300781	.58691406	.59082031	.59472656	.59863281	.60253906	.60644531	.61035156	.61425781	.61816406	.62207031
.005	.56372070	.56762695	.57153320	.57543945	.57934570	.58325195	.58715820	.59106445	.59497070	.59887695	.60278320	.60668945	.61059570	.61450195	.61840820	.62231445
.006	.56396484	.56787109	.57177734	.57568359	.57958984	.58349609	.58740234	.59130859	.59521484	.59912109	.60302734	.60693359	.61083984	.61474609	.61865234	.62255859
.007	.56420898	.56811523	.57202148	.57592773	.57983398	.58374023	.58764648	.59155273	.59545898	.59936523	.60327148	.60717773	.61108398	.61499023	.61889648	.62280273
.008	.56445313	.56835938	.57226563	.57617188	.58007813	.58398438	.58789063	.59179688	.59570313	.59960938	.60351563	.60742188	.61132813	.61523438	.61914063	.62304688
.009	.56469727	.56860352	.57250977	.57641602	.58032227	.58422852	.58813477	.59204102	.59594727	.59985352	.60375977	.60766602	.61157227	.61547852	.61938477	.62329102
.00A	.56494141	.56884766	.57275391	.57666016	.58056641	.58447266	.58837891	.59228516	.59619141	.60009766	.60400391	.60791016	.61181641	.61572266	.61962891	.62353516
.00B	.56518555	.56909180	.57299805	.57690430	.58081055	.58471680	.58862305	.59252930	.59643555	.60034180	.60424805	.60815430	.61206055	.61596680	.61987305	.62377930
.00C	.56542969	.56933594	.57324219	.57714844	.58105469	.58496094	.58886719	.59277344	.59667969	.60058594	.60449219	.60839844	.61230469	.61621094	.62011719	.62402344
.00D	.56567383	.56958008	.57348633	.57739258	.58129883	.58520508	.58911133	.59301758	.59692383	.60083008	.60473633	.60864258	.61254883	.61645508	.62036133	.62426758
.00E	.56591797	.56982422	.57373047	.57763672	.58154297	.58544922	.58935547	.59326172	.59716797	.60107422	.60498047	.60888672	.61279297	.61669922	.62060547	.62451172
.00F	.56616211	.57006836	.57397461	.57788086	.58178711	.58569336	.58959961	.59350586	.59741211	.60131836	.60522461	.60913086	.61303711	.61694336	.62084961	.62475586

C-6. (Continued)

	.A0	.A1	.A2	.A3	.A4	.A5	.A6	.A7	.A8	.A9	.AA	.AB	.AC	.AD	.AE	.AF
.000	62500000	62890625	63281250	63671875	64062500	64453125	64843750	65234375	65625000	66015625	66406250	66796875	67187500	67578125	67968750	68359375
.001	62524414	62915039	63305664	63696289	64086914	64477539	64868164	65258789	65649414	66040039	66430664	66821289	67211914	67602539	67993164	68383789
.002	62548828	62939453	63330078	63720703	64111328	64501953	64892578	65283203	65673828	66064453	66455078	66845703	67236328	67626953	68017578	68408203
.003	62573242	62963867	63354492	63745117	64135742	64526367	64916992	65307617	65698242	66088867	66479492	66870117	67260742	67651367	68041992	68432617
.004	62597656	62988281	63378906	63769531	64160156	64550781	64941406	65332031	65722656	66113281	66503906	66894531	67285156	67675781	68066406	68457031
.005	62622070	63012695	63403320	63793945	64184570	64575195	64965820	65356445	65747070	66137695	66528320	66918945	67309570	67700195	68090820	68481445
.006	62646484	63037109	63427734	63818359	64208984	64599609	64990234	65380859	65771484	66162109	66552734	66943359	67333984	67724609	68115234	68505859
.007	62670898	63061523	63452148	63842773	64233398	64624023	65014648	65405273	65795898	66186523	66577148	66967773	67358398	67749023	68139648	68530273
.008	62695313	63085938	63476563	63867188	64257813	64648438	65039063	65429688	65820313	66210938	66601563	66992188	67382813	67773438	68164063	68554688
.009	62719727	63110352	63500977	63891602	64282227	64672852	65063477	65454102	65844727	66235352	66625977	67016602	67407227	67797852	68188477	68579102
.00A	62744141	63134766	63525391	63916016	64306641	64697266	65087891	65478516	65869141	66259766	66650391	67041016	67431641	67822266	68212891	68603516
.00B	62768555	63159180	63549805	63940430	64331055	64721680	65112305	65502930	65893555	66284180	66674805	67065430	67456055	67846680	68237305	68627930
.00C	62792969	63183594	63574219	63964844	64355469	64746094	65136719	65527344	65917969	66308594	66699219	67089844	67480469	67871094	68261719	68652344
.00D	62817383	63208008	63598633	63989258	64379883	64770508	65161133	65551758	65942383	66333008	66723633	67114258	67504883	67895508	68286133	68676758
.00E	62841797	63232422	63623047	64013672	64404297	64794922	65185547	65576172	65966797	66357422	66748047	67138672	67529297	67919922	68310547	68701172
.00F	62866211	63256836	63647461	64038086	64428711	64819336	65209961	65600586	65991211	66381836	66772461	67163086	67553711	67944336	68334961	68725586

	.B0	.B1	.B2	.B3	.B4	.B5	.B6	.B7	.B8	.B9	.BA	.BB	.BC	.BD	.BE	.BF
.000	68750000	69140625	69531250	69921875	70312500	70703125	71093750	71484375	71875000	72265625	72656250	73046875	73437500	73828125	74218750	74609375
.001	68774414	69165039	69555664	69946289	70336914	70727539	71118164	71508789	71899414	72290039	72680664	73071289	73461914	73852539	74243164	74633789
.002	68798828	69189453	69580078	69970703	70361328	70751953	71142578	71533203	71923828	72314453	72705078	73095703	73486328	73876953	74267578	74658203
.003	68823242	69213867	69604492	69995117	70385742	70776367	71166992	71557617	71948242	72338867	72729492	73120117	73510742	73901367	74291992	74682617
.004	68847656	69238281	69628906	70019531	70410156	70800781	71191406	71582031	71972656	72363281	72753906	73144531	73535156	73925781	74316406	74707031
.005	68872070	69262695	69653320	70043945	70434570	70825195	71215820	71606445	71997070	72387695	72778320	73168945	73559570	73950195	74340820	74731445
.006	68896484	69287109	69677734	70068359	70458984	70849609	71240234	71630859	72021484	72412109	72802734	73193359	73583984	73974609	74365234	74755859
.007	68920898	69311523	69702148	70092773	70483398	70874023	71264648	71655273	72045898	72436523	72827148	73217773	73608398	73999023	74389648	74780273
.008	68945313	69335938	69726563	70117188	70507813	70898438	71289063	71679688	72070313	72460938	72851563	73242188	73632813	74023438	74414063	74804688
.009	68969727	69360352	69750977	70141602	70532227	70922852	71313477	71704102	72094727	72485352	72875977	73266602	73657227	74047852	74438477	74829102
.00A	68994141	69384766	69775391	70166016	70556641	70947266	71337891	71728516	72119141	72509766	72900391	73291016	73681641	74072266	74462891	74853516
.00B	69018555	69409180	69799805	70190430	70581055	70971680	71362305	71752930	72143555	72534180	72924805	73315430	73706055	74096680	74487305	74877930
.00C	69042969	69433594	69824219	70214844	70605469	70996094	71386719	71777344	72167969	72558594	72949219	73339844	73730469	74121094	74511719	74902344
.00D	69067383	69458008	69848633	70239258	70629883	71020508	71411133	71801758	72192383	72583008	72973633	73364258	73754883	74145508	74536133	74926758
.00E	69091797	69482422	69873047	70263672	70654297	71044922	71435547	71826172	72216797	72607422	72998047	73388672	73779297	74169922	74560547	74951172
.00F	69116211	69506836	69897461	70288086	70678711	71069336	71459961	71850586	72241211	72631836	73022461	73413086	73803711	74194336	74584961	74975586

	.C0	.C1	.C2	.C3	.C4	.C5	.C6	.C7	.C8	.C9	.CA	.CB	.CC	.CD	.CE	.CF
.000	75000000	75390625	75781250	76171875	76562500	76953125	77343750	77734375	78125000	78515625	78906250	79296875	79687500	80078125	80468750	80859375
.001	75024414	75415039	75805664	76196289	76586914	76977539	77368164	77758789	78149414	78540039	78930664	79321289	79711914	80102539	80493164	80883789
.002	75048828	75439453	75830078	76220703	76611328	77001953	77392578	77783203	78173828	78564453	78955078	79345703	79736328	80126953	80517578	80908203
.003	75073242	75463867	75854492	76245117	76635742	77026367	77416992	77807617	78198242	78588867	78979492	79370117	79760742	80151367	80541992	80932617
.004	75097656	75488281	75878906	76269531	76660156	77050781	77441406	77832031	78222656	78613281	79003906	79394531	79785156	80175781	80566406	80957031
.005	75122070	75512695	75903320	76293945	76684570	77075195	77465820	77856445	78247070	78637695	79028320	79418945	79809570	80200195	80590820	80981445
.006	75146484	75537109	75927734	76318359	76708984	77099609	77490234	77880859	78271484	78662109	79052734	79443359	79833984	80224609	80615234	81005859
.007	75170898	75561523	75952148	76342773	76733398	77124023	77514648	77905273	78295898	78686523	79077148	79467773	79858398	80249023	80639648	81030273
.008	75195313	75585938	75976563	76367188	76757813	77148438	77539063	77929688	78320313	78710938	79101563	79492188	79882813	80273438	80664063	81054688
.009	75219727	75610352	76000977	76391602	76782227	77172852	77563477	77954102	78344727	78735352	79125977	79516602	79907227	80297852	80688477	81079102
.00A	75244141	75634766	76025391	76416016	76806641	77197266	77587891	77978516	78369141	78759766	79150391	79541016	79931641	80322266	80712891	81103516
.00B	75268555	75659180	76049805	76440430	76831055	77221680	77612305	78002930	78393555	78784180	79174805	79565430	79956055	80346680	80737305	81127930
.00C	75292969	75683594	76074219	76464844	76855469	77246094	77636719	78027344	78417969	78808594	79199219	79589844	79980469	80371094	80761719	81152344
.00D	75317383	75708008	76098633	76489258	76879883	77270508	77661133	78051758	78442383	78833008	79223633	79614258	80004883	80395508	80786133	81176758
.00E	75341797	75732422	76123047	76513672	76904297	77294922	77685547	78076172	78466797	78857422	79248047	79638672	80029297	80419922	80810547	81201172
.00F	75366211	75756836	76147461	76538086	76928711	77319336	77709961	78100586	78491211	78881836	79272461	79663086	80053711	80444336	80834961	81225586

C-6. DECIMAL/HEXADECIMAL CONVERSION CHART—FRACTIONS (Continued)

	.D0	.D1	.D2	.D3	.D4	.D5	.D6	.D7	.D8	.D9	.DA	.DB	.DC	.DD	.DE	.DF
.000	.81250000	.81640625	.82031250	.82421875	.82812500	.83203125	.83593750	.83984375	.84375000	.84765625	.85156250	.85546875	.85937500	.86328125	.86718750	.87109375
.001	.81274414	.81665039	.82055664	.82446289	.82836914	.83227539	.83618164	.84008789	.84399414	.84790039	.85180664	.85571289	.85961914	.86352539	.86743164	.87133789
.002	.81298828	.81689453	.82080078	.82470703	.82861328	.83251953	.83642578	.84033203	.84423828	.84814453	.85205078	.85595703	.85986328	.86376953	.86767578	.87158203
.003	.81323242	.81713867	.82104492	.82495117	.82885742	.83276367	.83666992	.84057617	.84448242	.84838867	.85229492	.85620117	.86010742	.86401367	.86791992	.87182617
.004	.81347656	.81738281	.82128906	.82519531	.82910156	.83300781	.83691406	.84082031	.84472656	.84863281	.85253906	.85644531	.86035156	.86425781	.86816406	.87207031
.005	.81372070	.81762695	.82153320	.82543945	.82934570	.83325195	.83715820	.84106445	.84497070	.84887695	.85278320	.85668945	.86059570	.86450195	.86840820	.87231445
.006	.81396484	.81787109	.82177734	.82568359	.82958984	.83349609	.83740234	.84130859	.84521484	.84912109	.85302734	.85693359	.86083984	.86474609	.86865234	.87255859
.007	.81420898	.81811523	.82202148	.82592773	.82983398	.83374023	.83764648	.84155273	.84545898	.84936523	.85327148	.85717773	.86108398	.86499023	.86889648	.87280273
.008	.81445313	.81835938	.82226563	.82617188	.83007813	.83398438	.83789063	.84179688	.84570313	.84960938	.85351563	.85742188	.86132813	.86523438	.86914063	.87304688
.009	.81469727	.81860352	.82250977	.82641602	.83032227	.83422852	.83813477	.84204102	.84594727	.84985352	.85375977	.85766602	.86157227	.86547852	.86938477	.87329102
.00A	.81494141	.81884766	.82275391	.82666016	.83056641	.83447266	.83837891	.84228516	.84619141	.85009766	.85400391	.85791016	.86181641	.86572266	.86962891	.87353516
.00B	.81518555	.81909180	.82299805	.82690430	.83081055	.83471680	.83862305	.84252930	.84643555	.85034180	.85424805	.85815430	.86206055	.86596680	.86987305	.87377930
.00C	.81542969	.81933594	.82324219	.82714844	.83105469	.83496094	.83886719	.84277344	.84667969	.85058594	.85449219	.85839844	.86230469	.86621094	.87011719	.87402344
.00D	.81567383	.81958008	.82348633	.82739258	.83129883	.83520508	.83911133	.84301758	.84692383	.85083008	.85473633	.85864258	.86254883	.86645508	.87036133	.87426758
.00E	.81591797	.81982422	.82373047	.82763672	.83154297	.83544922	.83935547	.84326172	.84716797	.85107422	.85498047	.85888672	.86279297	.86669922	.87060547	.87451172
.00F	.81616211	.82006836	.82397461	.82788086	.83178711	.83569336	.83959961	.84350586	.84741211	.85131836	.85522461	.85913086	.86303711	.86694336	.87084961	.87475586

	.E0	.E1	.E2	.E3	.E4	.E5	.E6	.E7	.E8	.E9	.EA	.EB	.EC	.ED	.EE	.EF
.000	.87500000	.87890625	.88281250	.88671875	.89062500	.89453125	.89843750	.90234375	.90625000	.91015625	.91406250	.91796875	.92187500	.92578125	.92968750	.93359375
.001	.87524414	.87915039	.88305664	.88696289	.89086914	.89477539	.89868164	.90258789	.90649414	.91040039	.91430664	.91821289	.92211914	.92602539	.92993164	.93383789
.002	.87548828	.87939453	.88330078	.88720703	.89111328	.89501953	.89892578	.90283203	.90673828	.91064453	.91455078	.91845703	.92236328	.92626953	.93017578	.93408203
.003	.87573242	.87963867	.88354492	.88745117	.89135742	.89526367	.89916992	.90307617	.90698242	.91088867	.91479492	.91870117	.92260742	.92651367	.93041992	.93432617
.004	.87597656	.87988281	.88378906	.88769531	.89160156	.89550781	.89941406	.90332031	.90722656	.91113281	.91503906	.91894531	.92285156	.92675781	.93066406	.93457031
.005	.87622070	.88012695	.88403320	.88793945	.89184570	.89575195	.89965820	.90356445	.90747070	.91137695	.91528320	.91918945	.92309570	.92700195	.93090820	.93481445
.006	.87646484	.88037109	.88427734	.88818359	.89208984	.89599609	.89990234	.90380859	.90771484	.91162109	.91552734	.91943359	.92333984	.92724609	.93115234	.93505859
.007	.87670898	.88061523	.88452148	.88842773	.89233398	.89624023	.90014648	.90405273	.90795898	.91186523	.91577148	.91967773	.92358398	.92749023	.93139648	.93530273
.008	.87695313	.88085938	.88476563	.88867188	.89257813	.89648438	.90039063	.90429688	.90820313	.91210938	.91601563	.91992188	.92382813	.92773438	.93164063	.93554688
.009	.87719727	.88110352	.88500977	.88891602	.89282227	.89672852	.90063477	.90454102	.90844727	.91235352	.91625977	.92016602	.92407227	.92797852	.93188477	.93579102
.00A	.87744141	.88134766	.88525391	.88916016	.89306641	.89697266	.90087891	.90478516	.90869141	.91259766	.91650391	.92041016	.92431641	.92822266	.93212891	.93603516
.00B	.87768555	.88159180	.88549805	.88940430	.89331055	.89721680	.90112305	.90502930	.90893555	.91284180	.91674805	.92065430	.92456055	.92846680	.93237305	.93627930
.00C	.87792969	.88183594	.88574219	.88964844	.89355469	.89746094	.90136719	.90527344	.90917969	.91308594	.91699219	.92089844	.92480469	.92871094	.93261719	.93652344
.00D	.87817383	.88208008	.88598633	.88989258	.89379883	.89770508	.90161133	.90551758	.90942383	.91333008	.91723633	.92114258	.92504883	.92895508	.93286133	.93676758
.00E	.87841797	.88232422	.88623047	.89013672	.89404297	.89794922	.90185547	.90576172	.90966797	.91357422	.91748047	.92138672	.92529297	.92919922	.93310547	.93701172
.00F	.87866211	.88256836	.88647461	.89038086	.89428711	.89819336	.90209961	.90600586	.90991211	.91381836	.91772461	.92163086	.92553711	.92944336	.93334961	.93725586

	.F0	.F1	.F2	.F3	.F4	.F5	.F6	.F7	.F8	.F9	.FA	.FB	.FC	.FD	.FE	.FF
.000	.93750000	.94140625	.94531250	.94921875	.95312500	.95703125	.96093750	.96484375	.96875000	.97265625	.97656250	.98046875	.98437500	.98828125	.99218750	.99609375
.001	.93774414	.94165039	.94555664	.94946289	.95336914	.95727539	.96118164	.96508789	.96899414	.97290039	.97680664	.98071289	.98461914	.98852539	.99243164	.99633789
.002	.93798828	.94189453	.94580078	.94970703	.95361328	.95751953	.96142578	.96533203	.96923828	.97314453	.97705078	.98095703	.98486328	.98876953	.99267578	.99658203
.003	.93823242	.94213867	.94604492	.94995117	.95385742	.95776367	.96166992	.96557617	.96948242	.97338867	.97729492	.98120117	.98510742	.98901367	.99291992	.99682617
.004	.93847656	.94238281	.94628906	.95019531	.95410156	.95800781	.96191406	.96582031	.96972656	.97363281	.97753906	.98144531	.98535156	.98925781	.99316406	.99707031
.005	.93872070	.94262695	.94653320	.95043945	.95434570	.95825195	.96215820	.96606445	.96997070	.97387695	.97778320	.98168945	.98559570	.98950195	.99340820	.99731445
.006	.93896484	.94287109	.94677734	.95068359	.95458984	.95849609	.96240234	.96630859	.97021484	.97412109	.97802734	.98193359	.98583984	.98974609	.99365234	.99755859
.007	.93920898	.94311523	.94702148	.95092773	.95483398	.95874023	.96264648	.96655273	.97045898	.97436523	.97827148	.98217773	.98608398	.98999023	.99389648	.99780273
.008	.93945313	.94335938	.94726563	.95117188	.95507813	.95898438	.96289063	.96679688	.97070313	.97460938	.97851563	.98242188	.98632813	.99023438	.99414063	.99804688
.009	.93969727	.94360352	.94750977	.95141602	.95532227	.95922852	.96313477	.96704102	.97094727	.97485352	.97875977	.98266602	.98657227	.99047852	.99438477	.99829102
.00A	.93994141	.94384766	.94775391	.95166016	.95556641	.95947266	.96337891	.96728516	.97119141	.97509766	.97900391	.98291016	.98681641	.99072266	.99462891	.99853516
.00B	.94018555	.94409180	.94799805	.95190430	.95581055	.95971680	.96362305	.96752930	.97143555	.97534180	.97924805	.98315430	.98706055	.99096680	.99487305	.99877930
.00C	.94042969	.94433594	.94824219	.95214844	.95605469	.95996094	.96386719	.96777344	.97167969	.97558594	.97949219	.98339844	.98730469	.99121094	.99511719	.99902344
.00D	.94067383	.94458008	.94848633	.95239258	.95629883	.96020508	.96411133	.96801758	.97192383	.97583008	.97973633	.98364258	.98754883	.99145508	.99536133	.99926758
.00E	.94091797	.94482422	.94873047	.95263672	.95654297	.96044922	.96435547	.96826172	.97216797	.97607422	.97998047	.98388672	.98779297	.99169922	.99560547	.99951172
.00F	.94116211	.94506836	.94897461	.95288086	.95678711	.96069336	.96459961	.96850586	.97241211	.97631836	.98022461	.98413086	.98803711	.99194336	.99584961	.99975586

C–7. DEVICE CHARACTER CODES

Device	Characters per word	Bits used	Code in core (see Appendix C–9)
Console printer	one	0–7 (7 control)	Console printer code
Keyboard	one	0–11 12–EOF 13–Backspace 14–Scan field	Card code
Console entry switches		0–15	Binary word as in the switches
Card reader, normal mode	one	0–11	Card image (Punch = 1; no punch = 0, beginning at top of card)
Card reader, load mode	one	0–4 (12, 11, 0, and 1 on card) 8–15 (3–9 on card)	Card image
Card punch	one	0–11 12–operation complete	Card image
Paper tape	one	0–7	PTTC/8 (tape image)
1132 Printer			No code set. Characters printed in print-chain order. Words 32_{10}–39_{10} are the print scan field. The current character is printed if there is a 1 in the corresponding position in the scan field. The program "loads" the scan field.
1403 Printer	two	1–7, 9–15 (1 and 8 parity bits)	1403 Printer code

C–8. CHARACTER CODE CHART

Ref No.	EBCDIC Binary 0123 4567	EBCDIC Hex	12	11	0	9	8	7-1	IBM Card Code Hex	Graphics	and Control Names	1132 Printer EBCDIC Subset Hex	PTTC/8 Hex U–Upper Case L–Lower Case	Console Printer Hex	Notes
0	0000 0000	00	12		0	9	8	1	B030	NUL					
1	0000 0001	01	12			9		1	9010						
2	0000 0010	02	12			9		2	8810						
3	0000 0011	03	12			9		3	8410						
4	0000 0100	04	12			9		4	8210	PF	Punch Off				
5*	0000 0101	05	12			9		5	8110	HT	Horiz. Tab		6D (U/L)	41	①
6*	0000 0110	06	12			9		6	8090	LC	Lower Case		6E (U/L)		
7*	0000 0111	07	12			9		7	8050	DEL	Delete		7F (U/L)		
8	0000 1000	08	12			9	8		8030						
9	0000 1001	09	12			9	8	1	9030						
10	0000 1010	0A	12			9	8	2	8830						
11	0000 1011	0B	12			9	8	3	8430						
12	0000 1100	0C	12			9	8	4	8230						
13	0000 1101	0D	12			9	8	5	8130						
14	0000 1110	0E	12			9	8	6	80B0						
15	0000 1111	0F	12			9	8	7	8070						
16	0001 0000	10	12	11		9	8	1	D030						
17	0001 0001	11		11		9		1	5010						
18	0001 0010	12		11		9		2	4810						
19	0001 0011	13		11		9		3	4410						
20*	0001 0100	14		11		9		4	4210	RES	Restore		4C (U/L)	05	②
21*	0001 0101	15		11		9		5	4110	NL	New Line		DD (U/L)	81	③
22*	0001 0110	16		11		9		6	4090	BS	Backspace		5E (U/L)	11	
23	0001 0111	17		11		9		7	4050	IDL	Idle				
24	0001 1000	18		11		9	8		4030						
25	0001 1001	19		11		9	8	1	5030						
26	0001 1010	1A		11		9	8	2	4830						
27	0001 1011	1B		11		9	8	3	4430						
28	0001 1100	1C		11		9	8	4	4230						
29	0001 1101	1D		11		9	8	5	4130						
30	0001 1110	1E		11		9	8	6	40B0						
31	0001 1111	1F		11		9	8	7	4070						
32	0010 0000	20		11	0	9	8	1	7030						
33	0010 0001	21			0	9		1	3010						
34	0010 0010	22			0	9		2	2810						
35	0010 0011	23			0	9		3	2410						
36	0010 0100	24			0	9		4	2210	BYP	Bypass				
37*	0010 0101	25			0	9		5	2110	LF	Line Feed		3D (U/L)	03	
38*	0010 0110	26			0	9		6	2090	EOB	End of Block		3E (U/L)		
39	0010 0111	27			0	9		7	2050	PRE	Prefix				
40	0010 1000	28			0	9	8		2030						
41	0010 1001	29			0	9	8	1	3030						
42	0010 1010	2A			0	9	8	2	2830						
43	0010 1011	2B			0	9	8	3	2430						
44	0010 1100	2C			0	9	8	4	2230						
45	0010 1101	2D			0	9	8	5	2130						
46	0010 1110	2E			0	9	8	6	20B0						
47	0010 1111	2F			0	9	8	7	2070						
48	0011 0000	30	12	11	0	9	8	1	F030						
49	0011 0001	31				9		1	1010						
50	0011 0010	32				9		2	0810						
51	0011 0011	33				9		3	0410						
52	0011 0100	34				9		4	0210	PN	Punch On				
53*	0011 0101	35				9		5	0110	RS	Reader Stop		0D (U/L)	09	④
54*	0011 0110	36				9		6	0090	UC	Upper Case		0E (U/L)		
55	0011 0111	37				9		7	0050	EOT	End of Trans.				
56	0011 1000	38				9	8		0030						
57	0011 1001	39				9	8	1	1030						
58	0011 1010	3A				9	8	2	0830						
59	0011 1011	3B				9	8	3	0430						
60	0011 1100	3C				9	8	4	0230						
61	0011 1101	3D				9	8	5	0130						
62	0011 1110	3E				9	8	6	00B0						
63	0011 1111	3F				9	8	7	0070						

NOTES: Typewriter Output
① Tabulate
② Shift to black
③ Carrier Return
④ Shift to red
* Recognized by all Conversion subroutines
Codes that are not asterisked are recognized only by the SPEED subroutine

C-8. (Continued)

Ref No.	EBCDIC Binary 0123	4567	Hex	IBM Card Code Rows 12	11	0	9	8	7-1	Hex	Graphics and Control Names	1132 Printer EBCDIC Subset Hex	PTTC/8 Hex U-Upper Case L-Lower Case	Console Printer Hex
64*	0100	0000	40	no punches						0000	(space)	‡	10 (U/L)	21
65		0001	41	12		0	9		1	B010				
66		0010	42	12		0	9		2	A810				
67		0011	43	12		0	9		3	A410				
68		0100	44	12		0	9		4	A210				
69		0101	45	12		0	9		5	A110				
70		0110	46	12		0	9		6	A090				
71		0111	47	12		0	9		7	A050				
72		1000	48	12		0	9	8		A030				
73		1001	49	12				8	1	9020				
74*		1010	4A	12				8	2	8820	¢		20 (U)	02
75*		1011	4B	12				8	3	8420	. (period)	4B	6B (L)	00
76*		1100	4C	12				8	4	8220	<		02 (U)	DE
77*		1101	4D	12				8	5	8120	(	4D	19 (U)	FE
78*		1110	4E	12				8	6	80A0	+	4E	70 (U)	DA
79*		1111	4F	12				8	7	8060	I (logical OR)		3B (U)	C6
80*	0101	0000	50	12						8000	&	50	70 (L)	44
81		0001	51	12	11		9		1	D010				
82		0010	52	12	11		9		2	C810				
83		0011	53	12	11		9		3	C410				
84		0100	54	12	11		9		4	C210				
85		0101	55	12	11		9		5	C110				
86		0110	56	12	11		9		6	C090				
87		0111	57	12	11		9		7	C050				
88		1000	58	12	11		9	8		C030				
89*		1001	59		11			8	1	5020				
90*		1010	5A		11			8	2	4820	!		5B (U)	42
91*		1011	5B		11			8	3	4420	$	5B	5B (L)	40
92*		1100	5C		11			8	4	4220	*	5C	08 (U)	D6
93*		1101	5D		11			8	5	4120	)	5D	1A (U)	F6
94*		1110	5E		11			8	6	40A0	;		13 (U)	D2
95*		1111	5F		11			8	7	4060	¬ (logical NOT)		6B (U)	F2
96*	0110	0000	60		11					4000	- (dash)	60	40 (L)	84
97*		0001	61			0			1	3000	/	61	31 (L)	BC
98		0010	62		11	0	9		2	6810				
99		0011	63		11	0	9		3	6410				
100		0100	64		11	0	9		4	6210				
101		0101	65		11	0	9		5	6110				
102		0110	66		11	0	9		6	6090				
103		0111	67		11	0	9		7	6050				
104		1000	68		11	0	9	8		6030				
105		1001	69			0		8	1	3020				
106		1010	6A	12	11					C000				
107*		1011	6B			0		8	3	2420	, (comma)	6B	3B (L)	80
108*		1100	6C			0		8	4	2220	%		15 (U)	06
109*		1101	6D			0		8	5	2120	_ (underscore)		40 (U)	BE
110*		1110	6E			0		8	6	20A0	>		07 (U)	46
111*		1111	6F			0		8	7	2060	?		31 (U)	86
112	0111	0000	70	12	11	0				E000				
113		0001	71	12	11	0	9		1	F010				
114		0010	72	12	11	0	9		2	E810				
115		0011	73	12	11	0	9		3	E410				
116		0100	74	12	11	0	9		4	E210				
117		0101	75	12	11	0	9		5	E110				
118		0110	76	12	11	0	9		6	E090				
119		0111	77	12	11	0	9		7	E050				
120		1000	78	12	11	0	9	8		E030				
121		1001	79					8	1	1020				
122*		1010	7A					8	2	0820	:		04 (U)	82
123*		1011	7B					8	3	0420	#		0B (L)	C0
124*		1100	7C					8	4	0220	@		20 (L)	04
125*		1101	7D					8	5	0120	' (apostrophe)	7D	16 (U)	E6
126*		1110	7E					8	6	00A0	=	7E	01 (U)	C2
127*		1111	7F					8	7	0060	"		0B (U)	E2

‡ Any code other than those defined will be interpreted by PRNT1 as a space.

C–8. CHARACTER CODE CHART (Continued)

Ref No.	EBCDIC Binary 0123	EBCDIC Binary 4567	EBCDIC Hex	Card 12	Card 11	Card 0	Card 9	Card 8	Card 7-1	Card Hex	Graphics and Control Names	1132 Printer EBCDIC Subset Hex	PTTC/8 Hex U-Upper/L-Lower	Console Printer Hex
128	1000	0000	80	12		0		8	1	B020				
129		0001	81	12		0			1	B000	a			
130		0010	82	12		0			2	A800	b			
131		0011	83	12		0			3	A400	c			
132		0100	84	12		0			4	A200	d			
133		0101	85	12		0			5	A100	e			
134		0110	86	12		0			6	A080	f			
135		0111	87	12		0			7	A040	g			
136		1000	88	12		0		8		A020	h			
137		1001	89	12		0	9			A010	i			
138		1010	8A	12		0		8	2	A820				
139		1011	8B	12		0		8	3	A420				
140		1100	8C	12		0		8	4	A220				
141		1101	8D	12		0		8	5	A120				
142		1110	8E	12		0		8	6	A0A0				
143		1111	8F	12		0		8	7	A060				
144	1001	0000	90	12	11			8	1	D020				
145		0001	91	12	11				1	D000	j			
146		0010	92	12	11				2	C800	k			
147		0011	93	12	11				3	C400	l			
148		0100	94	12	11				4	C200	m			
149		0101	95	12	11				5	C100	n			
150		0110	96	12	11				6	C080	o			
151		0111	97	12	11				7	C040	p			
152		1000	98	12	11			8		C020	q			
153		1001	99	12	11		9			C010	r			
154		1010	9A	12	11			8	2	C820				
155		1011	9B	12	11			8	3	C420				
156		1100	9C	12	11			8	4	C220				
157		1101	9D	12	11			8	5	C120				
158		1110	9E	12	11			8	6	C0A0				
159		1111	9F	12	11			8	7	C060				
160	1010	0000	A0		11	0		8	1	7020				
161		0001	A1		11	0			1	7000				
162		0010	A2		11	0			2	6800	s			
163		0011	A3		11	0			3	6400	t			
164		0100	A4		11	0			4	6200	u			
165		0101	A5		11	0			5	6100	v			
166		0110	A6		11	0			6	6080	w			
167		0111	A7		11	0			7	6040	x			
168		1000	A8		11	0		8		6020	y			
169		1001	A9		11	0	9			6010	z			
170		1010	AA		11	0		8	2	6820				
171		1011	AB		11	0		8	3	6420				
172		1100	AC		11	0		8	4	6220				
173		1101	AD		11	0		8	5	6120				
174		1110	AE		11	0		8	6	60A0				
175		1111	AF		11	0		8	7	6060				
176	1011	0000	B0	12	11	0		8	1	F020				
177		0001	B1	12	11	0			1	F000				
178		0010	B2	12	11	0			2	E800				
179		0011	B3	12	11	0			3	E400				
180		0100	B4	12	11	0			4	E200				
181		0101	B5	12	11	0			5	E100				
182		0110	B6	12	11	0			6	E080				
183		0111	B7	12	11	0			7	E040				
184		1000	B8	12	11	0		8		E020				
185		1001	B9	12	11	0	9			E010				
186		1010	BA	12	11	0		8	2	E820				
187		1011	BB	12	11	0		8	3	E420				
188		1100	BC	12	11	0		8	4	E220				
189		1101	BD	12	11	0		8	5	E120				
190		1110	BE	12	11	0		8	6	E0A0				
191		1111	BF	12	11	0		8	7	E060				

C–8. (Continued)

Ref No.	EBCDIC Binary 0123	4567	Hex	IBM Card Code Rows 12	11	0	9	8	7-1	Hex	Graphics and Control Names	1132 Printer EBCDIC Subset Hex	PTTC/8 Hex U-Upper Case L-Lower Case	Console Printer Hex
192	1100	0000	C0	12		0				A000	(+ zero)			
193*		0001	C1	12					1	9000	A	C1	61 (U)	3C or 3E
194*		0010	C2	12					2	8800	B	C2	62 (U)	18 or 1A
195*		0011	C3	12					3	8400	C	C3	73 (U)	1C or 1E
196*		0100	C4	12					4	8200	D	C4	64 (U)	30 or 32
197*		0101	C5	12					5	8100	E	C5	75 (U)	34 or 36
198*		0110	C6	12					6	8080	F	C6	76 (U)	10 or 12
199*		0111	C7	12					7	8040	G	C7	67 (U)	14 or 16
200*		1000	C8	12				8		8020	H	C8	68 (U)	24 or 26
201*		1001	C9	12			9			8010	I	C9	79 (U)	20 or 22
202		1010	CA	12		0	9	8	2	A830				
203		1011	CB	12		0	9	8	3	A430				
204		1100	CC	12		0	9	8	4	A230				
205		1101	CD	12		0	9	8	5	A130				
206		1110	CE	12		0	9	8	6	A0B0				
207		1111	CF	12		0	9	8	7	A070				
208	1101	0000	D0		11	0				6000	(– zero)			
209*		0001	D1		11				1	5000	J	D1	51 (U)	7C or 7 E
210*		0010	D2		11				2	4800	K	D2	52 (U)	58 or 5A
211*		0011	D3		11				3	4400	L	D3	43 (U)	5C or 5E
212*		0100	D4		11				4	4200	M	D4	54 (U)	70 or 72
213*		0101	D5		11				5	4100	N	D5	45 (U)	74 or 76
214*		0110	D6		11				6	4080	O	D6	46 (U)	50 or 52
215*		0111	D7		11				7	4040	P	D7	57 (U)	54 or 56
216*		1000	D8		11			8		4020	Q	D8	58 (U)	64 or 66
217*		1001	D9		11		9			4010	R	D9	49 (U)	60 or 62
218		1010	DA	12	11		9	8	2	C830				
219		1011	DB	12	11		9	8	3	C430				
220		1100	DC	12	11		9	8	4	C230				
221		1101	DD	12	11		9	8	5	C130				
222		1110	DE	12	11		9	8	6	C0B0				
223		1111	DF	12	11		9	8	7	C070				
224	1110	0000	E0			0		8	2	2820				
225		0001	E1		11	0	9		1	7010				
226*		0010	E2			0			2	2800	S	E2	32 (U)	98 or 9A
227*		0011	E3			0			3	2400	T	E3	23 (U)	9C or 9E
228*		0100	E4			0			4	2200	U	E4	34 (U)	B0 or B2
229*		0101	E5			0			5	2100	V	E5	25 (U)	B4 or B6
230*		0110	E6			0			6	2080	W	E6	26 (U)	90 or 92
231*		0111	E7			0			7	2040	X	E7	37 (U)	94 or 96
232*		1000	E8			0		8		2020	Y	E8	38 (U)	A4 or A6
233*		1001	E9			0	9			2010	Z	E9	29 (U)	A0 or A2
234		1010	EA		11	0	9	8	2	6830				
235		1011	EB		11	0	9	8	3	6430				
236		1100	EC		11	0	9	8	4	6230				
237		1101	ED		11	0	9	8	5	6130				
238		1110	EE		11	0	9	8	6	60B0				
239		1111	EF		11	0	9	8	7	6070				
240*	1111	0000	F0			0				2000	0	F0	1A (L)	C4
241*		0001	F1						1	1000	1	F1	01 (L)	FC
242*		0010	F2						2	0800	2	F2	02 (L)	D8
243*		0011	F3						3	0400	3	F3	13 (L)	DC
244*		0100	F4						4	0200	4	F4	04 (L)	F0
245*		0101	F5						5	0100	5	F5	15 (L)	F4
246*		0110	F6						6	0080	6	F6	16 (L)	D0
247*		0111	F7						7	0040	7	F7	07 (L)	D4
248*		1000	F8					8		0020	8	F8	08 (L)	E4
249*		1001	F9				9			0010	9	F9	19 (L)	E0
250		1010	FA	12	11	0	9	8	2	E830				
251		1011	FB	12	11	0	9	8	3	E430				
252		1100	FC	12	11	0	9	8	4	E230				
253		1101	FD	12	11	0	9	8	5	E130				
254		1110	FE	12	11	0	9	8	6	E0B0				
255		1111	FF	12	11	0	9	8	7	E070				

ASSEMBLER

APPENDIX D

D-1. ASSEMBLER CONTROL RECORDS

Record	Description
*TWO PASS MODE	Reads source deck twice; must be specified when LIST DECK or LIST DECK E is specified, or when intermediate output fills working storage.
*LIST	Prints a listing on the principal printing device, giving error codes.
*LIST DECK	Punches a list deck on the principal I/O device if it is the card reader (requires TWO PASS MODE).
*LIST DECK E	Punches only error codes (columns 18–19) into source program list deck (requires TWO PASS MODE).
*PRINT SYMBOL TABLE	Prints a listing of the symbol table on the principal printing device.
*PUNCH SYMBOL TABLE	Punches a list deck of the symbol table (in the form of EQU commands).
*SAVE SYMBOL TABLE	Saves symbol table on disk as a system symbol table.
*SYSTEM SYMBOL TABLE	Uses system symbol table to initialize symbol table for this assembly.
*LEVEL n	n = interrupt level; required for ISS subroutines.
*COMMON n	n = number (decimal) of words of COMMON to be saved between links.
*FILE n	n = number (decimal) of sectors of working storage required at execution time by the program being assembled.

Version 2

*OVERFLOW SECTORS nn	nn = number of sectors assigned to symbol table overflow.

D-2. ASSEMBLER ERROR DETECTION CODES

Flag	Cause	Assembler Action
A	Address Error Attempt made to specify displacement field, directly or indirectly, outside range of −128 to +127.	Displacement set to zero
C	Condition Code Error Character other than +, −, Z, E, C, or O detected in first operand of short branch or second operand of long BSC, BOSC, or BSI statement.	Displacement set to zero
F	Format Code Error Character other than L, I, X, or blank detected in col. 32, or L or I format specified for instruction valid only in short form.	Instruction processed as if L format were specified, unless that instruction is valid only in short form, in which case it is processed as if the X format were specified
L	Label Error Invalid symbol detected in label field.	Label ignored
M	Multiply Defined Label Error Duplicate symbol encountered in operand.	First occurrence of symbol in label field defines its value; subsequent occurrences of symbol in label field cause a multiply defined indicator to be inserted in symbol table entry (Bit 0 of first word).
R	Relocation Error Expression does not have valid relocation.	Expression set to zero
	Non-absolute displacement specified.	Displacement set to zero
	Absolute origin specified in relocatable program.	Origin ignored
	Non-absolute operand specified in BSS or BES.	Operand assumed to be zero
	Non-relocatable operand in END statement of relocatable mainline program.	Card columns 9–12 left blank; entry assumed to be relative zero
	ENT operand non-relocatable.	Statement ignored
S	Syntax Error Invalid expression (e.g., invalid symbol, adjacent operators, illegal constant)	Expression set to zero
	Illegal character in record.	If illegal character appears in expression, label, op code, format, or tag field, additional errors may be caused.
	Main program entry point not specified in END operand.	Card columns 9–12 left blank; entry assumed to be relative zero. Card columns 9–12 not punched; address counter incremented by 17.
	Incorrect syntax in EBC statement (e.g., no delimiter in card column 35, zero character count).	
	Invalid label in ENT or ISS operand.	Statement ignored
T	Tag Error Card column 33 contains character other than blank, 0, 1, 2, or 3 in instruction statement.	Tag of zero assumed
U	Undefined Symbol Undefined symbol in expression	Expression set to absolute zero
O	Op Code Unrecognized	Statement ignored and address counter incremented by 2.
	ISS, ILS, ENT, LIBR, SPR, EPR, or ABS incorrectly placed.	Statement ignored

D-3. ASSEMBLER ERROR MESSAGES

Error Code and Error Message	Cause of Error	Corrective Action
A 01 MINIMUM W. S. NOT AVAILABLE--- ASSEMBLY TERMINATED	Less than 33 sectors of Working Storage are available at the beginning of the assembly.	Perform a DUP DELETE to expand Working Storage to a minimum of 33 sectors before attempting further assemblies.
A 02 SYMBOL TABLE OVERFLOW EXCEEDS 4 CYLINDERS	Symbol table overflow exceeds 3392 symbols (refer to <u>Assembler Messages and Error Codes</u> to compute number of symbols allowed in a program).	1. Reduce number of symbols and reassemble. 2. Divide program into segments and assemble each separately.
A 03 DISK OUTPUT EXCEEDS W.S.	Disk output is greater than Working Storage.	1. If error occured during pass 1, the assembler will wait at 0AD6. When PROGRAM START is pressed, the assembly will continue in the two-pass mode. Therefore, the operator should first insure that the source statements can be read a second time without encountering the next monitor control record. 2. If error occurred during pass 2, object output exceeds Working Storage. Perform a DUP DELETE to enlarge Working Storage.
A 04 SAVE SYMBOL TABLE INHIBITED	With SAVE SYMBOL TABLE option, symbol table exceeds the allowable System Symbol Table size of 100 symbols, or at least one assembly error was detected.	Reduce number of symbols and/or correct the erroneous statements and reassemble.

D-4. CARD FORMAT AND OTHER DETAILS FOR AN ASSEMBLER INSTRUCTION

Card column	Contents
21-25	Label, which begins with number and is "name" of this word. Five places allowed.
27	Operation, a mnemonic (or pseudo-assembler mnemonic), which indicates type of instruction.
32	Blank for short instruction; L for long; I for indirect.
33	1, 2, or 3 for index register (blank for none) referenced by instruction.
35-	Operands, usually one, but long BSC, BSI, or MDX may have second operand after a comma. No embedded blanks in operands. Blank before comment material.

D-5. LIST DECK FORMAT

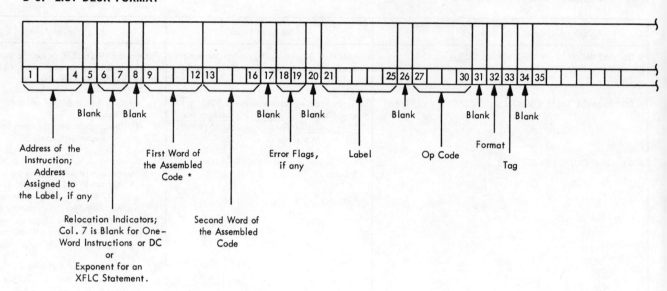

Address of the Instruction; Address Assigned to the Label, if any

Blank

Relocation Indicators; Col. 7 is Blank for One-Word Instructions or DC or Exponent for an XFLC Statement.

Blank

First Word of the Assembled Code *

Second Word of the Assembled Code

Blank

Error Flags, if any

Blank

Label

Blank

Op Code

Blank

Format

Tag

Blank

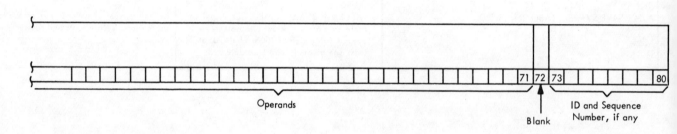

Operands

Blank

ID and Sequence Number, if any

* For EBC Statements, Col. 9-12 Contains the Number of EBC Characters

For BSS and BES Statements, Col. 9-12 Contains the Number of Words Reserved for the Block.

D–6. INSTRUCTION CODES AND EXECUTION TIMES

Instruction	Mnemonic	Binary OP Code	Execution Times (in microseconds) for 3.6 μsec Core Only**							
			Single Word (F = 0)				Double Word (F = 1)			
			T = 00		T = 01, 10, or 11		T = 00		T = 01, 10, or 11	
			Avg.	Max.	Avg.	Max.	Avg.①	Max.①	Avg.①	Max.①
Load and Store										
Load ACC	LD	11000	7.6	–	11.2	–	10.8	–	14.8	–
Load Double	LDD	11001	11.2	–	14.9	–	14.4	–	18.0	–
Store ACC	STO	11010	7.6	–	11.2	–	10.8	–	14.8	–
Store Double	STD	11011	11.2	–	14.9	–	14.4	–	18.0	–
Load Index	LDX	01100	4.5	–	7.2	–	7.2	–	11.8	–
Store Index	STX	01101	7.6	–	11.2	–	11.8	–	15.4	–
Load Status*	LDS ⑦	00100	3.6	–	3.6	–	–	–	–	–
Store Status	STS	00101	7.6	–	11.2	–	10.8	–	14.8	–
Arithmetic										
Add	A	10000	8.0	13.0	11.7	16.6	11.2	16.2	15.3	20.3
Add Double	AD	10001	12.2	22.0	15.8	25.6	15.3	25.2	19.3	29.5
Subtract	S	10010	8.0	13.0	11.7	16.6	11.2	16.2	15.3	20.3
Subtract Double	SD	10011	12.2	22.0	15.8	25.6	15.3	25.2	19.3	29.5
Multiply	M	10100	25.7	40.0	29.3	43.6	29.3	43.6	32.9	47.2
Divide	D	10101	76.0	150.8	79.6	154.4	79.6	154.4	83.2	150.0
And	AND	11100	7.6	–	11.2	–	10.8	–	14.8	–
Or	OR	11101	7.6	–	11.2	–	10.8	–	14.8	–
Exclusive Or	EOR	11110	7.6	–	11.2	–	10.8	–	14.8	–
Shift Left* Modifier Bits 8 & 9:										
Shift Left ACC 00	SLA ⑦	00010								
Shift Left ACC and EXT 10	SLT ⑦	00010								
Shift Left and Count ACC 01 ⑧	SLCA ⑦	00010								
Shift Left and Count ACC and EXT 11 ⑧	SLC ⑦	00010	③	–	④	–	–	–	–	–
Shift Right* Modifier Bits 8 & 9:										
Shift Right ACC 00 or 01	SRA ⑦	00011								
Shift Right ACC and EXT 10	SRT ⑦	00011								
Rotate Right 11	RTE ⑦	00011	⑤		⑥					
Branch										
Branch and Store IAR	BSI	01000	7.6	–	11.2	–	10.8②	–	14.8	–
Branch or Skip on Condition	BSC	01001	3.6	–	3.6	–	7.2②	–	11.2	–
Modify Index and Skip	MDX	01110	4.5	9.9	11.2	16.2	18.5	23.4	18.5	23.4
Wait*	WAIT ⑦	00110 ⑨	3.6	–	3.6	–	–	–	–	–
Input/Output										
Execute I/O	XIO ⑩	00001	11.2	–	14.8	–	14.8	–	18.4	–

* Valid in short format only   ** For 2.2 μsec core, multiply figures shown by 61%.

NOTES:

1. Indirect addressing, where applicable, adds 3.6μsec to execution time
2. If branch is taken
3. $3.6 + .45(N-4)$
4. $7.2 + .45(N-4)$
5. $N > 16$: $3.6 + .45(N-19)$
   $N = 16$: 3.6
   $N < 16$: $3.6 + .45(N-4)$
6. $N > 16$: $7.2 + .45(N-19)$
   $N = 16$: 7.2
   $N < 16$: $7.2 + .45(N-4)$
   where N = number of positions shifted
7. Indirect addressing not allowed
8. If T = 00, functions as SLA or SLT
9. All unassigned OP codes are defined as Wait operations
10. If XIO Read or Write, add 3.6μsec

D-7. BSC, BOSC, AND BSI CONDITION CODES

Unique character	Condition	Description	Bit position set to 1
θ	Overflow	Skip or do not branch if overflow indicator *off*	15
C	Carry	Skip or do not branch if carry indicator *off*	14
E	Even	Skip or do not branch if bit 15 of accumulator = 0	13
+ or &	Plus	Skip or do not branch if bit 0 of accumulator = 0, but not all bits of accumulator = 0	12
−	Minus	Skip or do not branch if bit 0 of accumulator = 1	11
Z	Zero	Skip or do not branch if all bits of accumulator = 0	10

D-8. EXAMPLES OF ASSEMBLER INSTRUCTIONS

G0—Label of an instruction word
NUM—Label of a data word

Load Instructions

LD		NUM⎫	Loads word stored in NUM into accumulator.
LD	L	NUM⎭	
LD	L	/1873	Loads word with hexadecimal address 1873 into accumulator.
LD	I	NUM	Loads word with address stored in NUM into accumulator.
STO		NUM⎫	Stores accumulator in NUM.
STO	L	NUM⎭	
STO	I	NUM	Stores accumulator in word whose address is in NUM.

Arithmetic Instructions

A		NUM⎫	Adds 16-bit binary word stored in NUM to word in accumulator; result is in accumulator.
A	L	NUM⎭	
A	I	NUM	Adds 16-bit binary word whose *address* is stored in NUM to word in accumulator; result is in accumulator.
A	L	/1687	Adds word with address 1687 (hex) to word in accumulator; result is in accumulator.
S		NUM⎫	Subtracts word stored in NUM from word in accumulator; result is in accumulator.
S	L	NUM⎭	

S I NUM Subtracts word whose *address* is in NUM from word in accumulator; result is in accumulator.

M NUM Multiplies word in accumulator and word in NUM. Result is in accumulator extension and accumulator, as follows:

Accumulator	Accumulator extension

Rightmost bit of product

M I NUM Multiplies word in accumulator and word whose *address* is in NUM. Result as above.

D NUM Divide instruction. Dividend is in accumulator extension, divisor in NUM. Result is in accumulator, remainder in accumulator extension.

D L NUM

D I NUM Indirect version of divide instruction.

Store and Load Double Instructions

LDD NUM
LDD L NUM

1. NUM an *even* address:
   Contents of NUM in accumulator, NUM + 1 in accumulator extension.

Accumulator	Accumulator extension		NUM	NUM+1

Core memory

2. NUM an *odd* address:
   Contents of NUM in *both* accumulator and accumulator extension.

STD NUM
STD L NUM

1. NUM an *even* address:
   Contents of accumulator and accumulator extension stored in NUM and NUM + 1.
2. NUM an *odd* address:
   Contents of accumulator stored in NUM; extension not stored.

Double Arithmetic Instructions

AD NUM
AD L NUM

1. NUM an *even* address: The 32-bit word in NUM and NUM + 1 is added to 32-bit word in accumulator and accumulator extension; result in accumulator and accumulator extension.
2. NUM an *odd* address: The 16-bit word in NUM is added to both accumulator and accumulator extension.

Similar structure for subtract double instructions.

(Continued)

157

D–8. EXAMPLES OF ASSEMBLER INSTRUCTIONS (Continued)

Logical Instruction

Assume for all:

Contents of accumulator before execution is

0000 0000 1111 1111,

and of the word symbolically addressed as VAR is

0000 1111 0000 1111.

AND		VAR	Accumulator after execution contains 0000 0000 0000 1111
AND	L	VAR	
OR		VAR	Accumulator after execution contains 0000 1111 1111 1111
OR	L	VAR	
EOR		VAR	Accumulator after execution contains 0000 1111 1111 0000
EOR	L	VAR	

Load and Store Index Registers

LDX		/0038	Unconditional branch to hexadecimal address 38 (38 is loaded in IAR).
LDX	L	/0038	
LDX	2	/0014	Hexadecimal 14 is loaded in index register 2.
LDX	L2	/0014	
LDX	1	16	Decimal 16 is loaded in index register 1.
LDX	L1	16	
LDX	L1	NUM	Address of NUM is loaded in index register 1.
LDX	I3	NUM	Word whose address is NUM is loaded in index register 3.
STX		NUM	Contents of IAR are placed in NUM.
STX	2	NUM	Contents of index register 2 are placed in NUM.
STX	L2	NUM	
STX	I3	NUM	Index register 3 is stored in word whose address is in NUM.

Branch or Skip Instructions

MDX		GO	The next instruction to be executed is that labeled GO.
MDX	2	–3	Subtracts 3 from contents of index register 2. If resulting number is zero, or if contents change sign, skips next word; if neither, continues with next instruction.
MDX	L1	NUM	Contents of NUM are added to index register 1. If contents of register change sign or equal zero, next word is skipped.
MDX	I2	NUM	Contents of word whose address is in NUM are added to index register 3. Word skipped or not, as in previous MDX instructions.

Instruction		Operand	Description
MDX	I	NUM,2	Adds 2 to contents of NUM. If result is zero, or changes sign, skips next word (as above); if result is nonzero, uses next word (or two) as next instruction. If zero result is possible, this instruction should be followed by a short instruction.
BSC		+−	Skips next word if accumulator is either positive or negative.
BSC		E	Skips next word if accumulator is even.
BSC	L	GO	Unconditional branch to instruction labeled GO.
BSC	I	NUM	Unconditional branch to instruction whose address is in NUM.
BSC	L	GO,+Z	Branch to instruction labeled GO if word in accumulator is negative (i.e., not positive or zero); otherwise continue with next instruction.
BSC	I	GO,−	Branch to instruction whose address is stored in GO if accumulator is zero or positive; otherwise continue with the next instruction.
BSI		NUM	Stores current value of IAR in word labeled NUM, and starts executing instructions beginning at NUM + 1.
BSI	L	NUM	
BSI	I	NUM	Stores value of IAR in word whose address is in NUM, and executes following instructions.
BSI	L	NUM,Z	If accumulator is zero, continues with next instruction; if not zero, stores IAR in word labeled NUM and starts executing instructions at NUM + 1.

Branch and Skip Instructions—Version 2, extended instruction mnemonics

Instruction		Operand	Description
SKP		Z+	Skips next word if accumulator is zero or positive; equivalent to BSC Z+
B		GO	Next instruction to be executed is that labeled GO; equivalent to MDX GO
B	L	GO	BSC L GO
BZ		GO	Branches to GO if accumulator is zero; an implicit long instruction equivalent to BSC L GO, +−
BNZ	I	NUM	Branches to address in NUM if accumulator is not zero; equivalent to BSC I NUM, Z
BN		GO	Branches to GO if accumulator is negative. Long instruction equivalent to BSC L GO, Z+
BNN		GO	Branches to GO if accumulator is not negative; equivalent to BSC L GO, −
BP		GO	Branches to GO if accumulator is positive; equivalent to BSC L GO, −Z
BNP		GO	Branches to GO if accumulator is not positive; equivalent to BSC L GO, +
BC		GO	Branches to GO if carry indicator is on; equivalent to BSC L GO, C

(Continued)

159

D-8. EXAMPLES OF ASSEMBLER INSTRUCTIONS (Continued)

BO	GO	Branches to GO if overflow indicator is on; equivalent to BSC L GO, O
BOD	GO	Branches to GO if accumulator is *odd*; equivalent to BSC L GO,E
MDM	NUM,83	Adds 83 to the quantity stored in NUM; equivalent to MDX L NUM,83

Shift Instructions

SLA	3	Shifts number in accumulator left three places, adding zeros at right. For example, 1101 becomes 1101000.
SLA	1	Shifts left one place (a convenient way of multiplying by 2).
SRA	2	Shifts accumulator right two places (e.g., 11001 becomes 110). Fills vacated spaces with zeros.
SLT	4	Considers contents of accumulator and accumulator extension to be a single 32-bit number, shifts it left four places, adding zeros at right.

Accumulator	Accumulator extension
0000 0100 0000 0010	1111 0000 1010 1001

becomes

0100 0000 0010 1111	0000 1010 1001 0000

SRT	8	Shifts paired registers right eight places; duplicates original zero-bit of accumulator in all vacated bits.
RTE	16	Shifts both accumulator and extension 16 places right, putting each bit shifted out of right end of extension into left end of accumulator. This instruction interchanges the accumulator and extension.
XCH		Version 2 only. Exchange accumulator and extension; equivalent to RTE 16

SLCA 1

	Before instruction		After instruction		
	Accumulator	Index register 1	Accumulator	Index register 1	Carry
Case 1.	1XXXXXXXXXXXXXXX	0000000000000011	Unaltered	Unaltered	Unaltered
Case 2.	001XXXXXXXXXXXXX	0000000000000111	1XXXXXXXXXXXXX00	0000000000000101	Turned on
			(Terminated by a 1 in leftmost bit of accumulator)		
Case 3.	0000000001XXXXXX	0000000000000111	001XXXXX0000000	0000000000000000	Turned off
			(Terminated by count in register 1 going to zero)		

X = either 0 or 1
SLC uses accumulator and extension as a double register, but functions otherwise like SLCA.

Assembler Storage and Data Definition Statements

DC	27	Puts binary equivalent of 27_{10} into a word: `0000 0000 0001 1011`
DC	/004E	Puts binary equivalent of $4E_{16}$ into a word: `0000 0000 0100 1110`
DC	.F	Stores 8-bit EBCDIC code for F in a word.
DC	G0+1	Stores one more than the value of G0.
DEC	16	Establishes two words and stores binary equivalent of 16_{10}. `0000000000000000` `0000000000010000` The label, if any, refers to leftmost word.
DEC	3.5	Stores in two words the standard precision floating point representation for 3.5. The label, if any, refers to leftmost word.
DEC	4.3E10	Stores in two words the standard precision floating point representation for 4.3×10^{10}. The label, if any, refers to leftmost word.
XFLC	2.783	Stores in three words the extended precision floating point representation for 2.783. The label, if any, refers to leftmost word.
EBC	.HORSE.	Stores H and 0 in first word, R and S in second, and E in third. The character code is 8-bit EBCDIC. The label, if any, refers to first word. EBC can store up to 35 characters.
BSS	43	Reserves 43 words in storage. The label, if any, refers to leftmost word.
BSS E	0	Sets address counter even.
BES	16	Reserves 16 words in storage. The label, if any, refers to one word past rightmost word.

D–9. SPECIAL ASSEMBLER INSTRUCTIONS

Program control

ABS	Assembles with absolute (instead of relocatable) addresses.
LIBR	Identifies subroutine to be called by LIBF; first instruction of subroutine.
SPR	Uses only standard precision subroutines.
EPR	Uses only extended precision subroutines.
ORG	Assigns an address for next instruction.
END	Specifies end of program; always required.

Program linking

ENT	Specifies subroutine entry point. At least one required with a subroutine.
ISS	Specifies Interrupt Service Subroutine entry point.
CALL	Call for CALL subroutines.
LIBF	Call for LIBF subroutines.
ILS	Specifies that a subroutine is an Interrupt Level Subroutine.
LINK	Requests that another program on disk be loaded into core and executed.
EXIT	Returns control to skeleton supervisor; exits from current program.

Miscellaneous

EQU	Equates two symbols in program.
DSA	Identifies a named file on disk.
HDNG	Specifies a page heading for a listing; skips to a new page.

D–10. SPECIAL ASSEMBLER INSTRUCTIONS— VERSION 2 ONLY

Miscellaneous

DN	Converts name in operand field (up to five characters, first a letter) into name code, stored in two words.
DMES	Stores operand as a message for use in an output subroutine; tag field (column 33) specifies device and code (e.g., 0 = console, 1 = 1403, 2 = 1132).
LIST	By using ON or OFF as an operand, allows selective listing of only part of an assembler program.
SPAC	Integer in operand is number of blank spaces desired at this point in listing of program.
EJCT	Begins new page.
DUMP	Selective dump. Three operands, specifying (1) beginning of dump, (2) end of dump, and (3) blank or zero. Program is terminated immediately after dump.
PDUMP	Like DUMP, except that control returns to program after dumping.
FILE	Four operands; each like the corresponding FORTRAN DEFINE FILE parameter. Seven words used.

D–11. FORTRAN–ASSEMBLER EQUIVALENTS

From the program logic manual (no tracing)

FORTRAN	Assembler		
I = J	LD	L	J
	STO	L	I
A = B	LIBF		FLD
	DC		B
	LIBF		FSTO
	DC		A
A = I	LD	L	I
	LIBF		FLOAT
	LIBF		FSTO
	DC		A
I = A	LIBF		FLD
	DC		A
	LIBF		IFIX
	STO	L	I
I = J + K	LD	L	J
	A	L	K
	STO	L	I
A = I + B	LD	L	I
	LIBF		FLOAT
	LIBF		FADD
	DC		B
	LIBF		FSTO
	DC		A
A = B + I − J	LD	L	I
	LIBF		FLOAT
	LIBF		FADD
	DC		B
	LIBF		FSTO
	DC		GTI
	LD	L	J
	LIBF		FLOAT
	LIBF		FSBR
	DC		GTI
	LIBF		FSTO
	DC		A
I = J*K	LD	L	J
	M	L	K
	SLT		16
	STO	L	I
A = B*C	LIBF		FLD
	DC		B
	LIBF		FMPY
	DC		C
	LIBF		FSTO
	DC		A
I = J/K	LD	L	J
	SRT		16
	D	L	K
	STO	L	I

(Continued)

D-11. FORTRAN—ASSEMBLER EQUIVALENTS (Continued)

FORTRAN	Assembler		
A = B/C	LIBF		FLD
	DC		B
	LIBF		FDIV
	DC		C
	LIBF		FSTO
	DC		A
I = J**K	LD	L	J
	LIBF		FIXI
	DC		K
	STO	L	I
A = B**I	LIBF		FID
	DC		B
	LIBF		FAXI
	DC		I
	LIBF		FSTO
	DC		A
A = B**C	LIBF		FLD
	DC		B
	CAU		FAXB
	DC		C
	LIBF		FSTO
	DC		A
A = JOE(B+C,D) +E	LIBF		FLD
	DC		B
	LIBF		FADD
	DC		C
	LIBF		FSTO
	DC		GTI
	CALL		JOE
	DC		GTI
	DC		D
	LIBF		FLOAT
	LIBF		FADD
	DC		E
	LIBF		FSTO
	DC		A
DO 10 I = J,K	LD	L	J
	STO	L	I
	LABEL	....	
10 CONTINUE	MDX	L	I,1
	LD	L	I
	S	L	K
	BSC	L	LABEL,+Z
DO 10 I = J, K, M	LD	L	J
	STO	L	I
	LABEL	....	
10 CONTINUE	LD	L	I
	A	L	M
	STO	L	I
	S	L	K
	BSC	L	LABEL,+Z

D–11. (Continued)

FORTRAN	Assembler			
GO TO (111, 112, 113), I		LDX	I1	I
	ADR1	BSC	I1	ADR1+1
		DC		[address of 111]
		DC		[address of 112]
		DC		[address of 113]
If (I) 111, 112, 113		LD	L	I
		BSC	L	[111] ,+Z
		BSC	L	[112] ,+−
		BSC	L	[113] ,−Z
IF (A) 111, 100, 113		LIBF		FLD
		DC		A
		LD	3	+126
		BSC	L	[111] ,+Z
		BSC	L	[1B] ,−Z
100 CONTINUE				
PAUSE II		LIBF		PAUSE
		DC		(address of constant II)
READ (N, 101), A, I		LIBF		SRED
		DC		N
(nondisk linkage)		DC		(address 101)
		LIBF		SIOF
		DC		A
		LIBF		SIOI
		DC		I
WRITE (N, 101), A, I		LIBF		SWRT
		DC		N
(nondisk)		DC		(address 101)
		LIBF		SIOF
		DC		A
		LIBF		SIOI
		DC		I
		LIBF		SCOMP

SUBROUTINE

APPENDIX E

E-1. 1130 SUBROUTINE LIBRARY

Subroutine	Names	Other Subroutines Required
FORTRAN		
Called by CALL		
Loader Reinitialization (card only)	LOAD	None
Data Switch	DATSW	None
Sense Light On	SLITE, SLITT	None
Overflow Test	OVERF	None
Divide Check Test	DVCHK	None
Function Test	FCTST	None
Trace Start	TSTRT	TSET
Trace Stop	TSTOP	TSET
Integer Transfer of Sign	ISIGN	None
Real Transfer of Sign (E)	ESIGN	ESUB, ELD
Real Transfer of Sign (S)	FSIGN	FSUB, FLD
Called by LIBF (card/paper tape)		
Real IF Trace (E)	VIF	TTEST, VWRT, VIOF, VCOMP
Real IF Trace (S)	WIF	FSTO, TTEST, WWRT, WIOF, WCOMP
Integer IF Trace (E)	VIIF	TTEST, VWRT, VIOF, VCOMP
Integer IF Trace (S)	WIIF	TTEST, WWRT, WIOI, WCOMP
Integer Arithmetic Trace (E)	VIAR, VIARX	TTEST, VWRT, VIOI, VCOMP
Integer Arithmetic Trace (S)	WIAR, WIARX	TTEST, WWRT, WIOI, WCOMP
Real Arithmetic Trace (E)	VARI, VARIX	ESTO, TTEST, VWRT, VIOF, VCOMP
Real Arithmetic Trace (S)	WARI, WARIX	FSTO, TTEST, WWRT, WIOF, WCOMP
Computed GO TO Trace (E)	VGOTO	TTEST, VWRT, VIOI, VCOMP
Computed GO TO Trace (S)	WGOTO	TTEST, WWRT, WIOI, WCOMP
Trace Test–Set Indicator	TTEST, TSET	None
Pause	PAUSE	None
Stop	STOP	None
Subscript Calculation	SUBSC	None
Store Argument Address	SUBIN	None
I/O Linkage (E)	VFIO, VRED, VWRT, VCOMP, VIOAI, VIOAF, VIOFX, VIOIX, VIOF, VIOI	FLOAT, ELD/ESTO, IFIX
I/O Linkage (S)	WFIO, WRED, WWRT, WCOMP, WIOAI, WIOAF, WIOFX, WIOIX, WIOF, WIOI	FLOAT, FLD/FSTO, IFIX
Card Input/Output	CARDZ	HOLEZ
Printer-Keyboard Output	WRTYZ	GETAD, EBCTB
Printer-Keyboard Input/Output	TYPEZ	GETAD, EBCTB, HOLEZ
1132 Printer Output	PRNTZ	None
Paper Tape Input/Output	PAPTZ	None
Card Code-EBCDIC Conversion	HOLEZ	GETAD, EBCTB, HOLTB
Console Printer Code Table	EBCTB	None
Card-Keyboard Code Table	HOLTB	None
Address Calculation	GETAD	None
Called by LIBF (monitor)		
Real IF Trace (E)	SEIF	FSTO, TTEST, SWRT, SIOF, SCOMP
Real IF Trace (S)	SFIF	FSTO, TTEST, SWRT, SIOF, SCOMP
Integer IF Trace	SIIF	TTEST, SWRT, SIOI, SCOMP
Integer Arithmetic Trace	SIAR, SIARX	TTEST, SWRT, SIOI, SCOMP
Real Arithmetic Trace (E)	SEAR, SEARX	ESTO, TTEST, SWRT, SIOF, SCOMP
Real Arithmetic Trace (S)	SFAR, SFARX	FSTO, TTEST, SWRT, SIOF, SCOMP
Computed GO TO Trace	SGOTO	TTEST, SWRT, SIOI, SCOMP
Trace Test–Set Indicator	TTEST, TSET	None
Pause	PAUSE	None
Stop	STOP	None
Subscript Calculation	SUBSC	None
Store Argument Address	SUBIN	None
I/O Linkage (non-disk)	SFIO, SRED, SWRT, SCOMP, SIOAF, SIOAI, SIOF, SIOI, SIOFX, SIOIX	FLOAT, ELD/ESTO or FLD/FSTO, IFIX
Disk-I/O Linkage	SDFIO, SDRED, SDWRT, SDCOM, SDAF, SDAI, SDF, SDI, SDFX, SDIX	DISKZ
Disk Find	SDFND	DISKZ
Card Input/Output	CARDZ	HOLEZ
Disk Input/Output (part of supervisor)	DISKZ	None
Printer-Keyboard Output	WRTYZ	GETAD, EBCTB

E-1. 1130 SUBROUTINE LIBRARY (Continued)

Subroutine	Names	Other Subroutines Required
Called by LIBF (monitor)		
Printer-Keyboard Input/Output	TYPEZ	GETAD, EBCTB, HOLEZ
1132 Printer Output	PRNTZ	None
Paper Tape Input/Output	PAPTZ	None
Card Code-EBCDIC Conversion	HOLEZ	GETAD, EBCTB, HOLTB
Console Printer Code Table	EBCTB	None
Card-Keyboard Code Table	HOLTB	None
Address Calculation	GETAD	None
ARITHMETIC AND FUNCTIONAL		
Called by CALL		
Real Hyperbolic Tangent (E)	ETNH, ETANH	EEXP, ELD/ESTO, EADD, EDIV, EGETP
Real Hyperbolic Tangent (S)	FTNH, FTANH	FEXP, FLD/FSTO, FADD, FDIV, FGETP
Real Base to Real Exponent (E)	EAXB, EAXBX	EEXP, ELN, EMPY
Real Base to Real Exponent (S)	FAXB, FAXBX	FEXP, FLN, FMPY
Real Natural Logarithm (E)	ELN, EALOG	XMD, EADD, EMPY, EDIV, NORM, EGETP
Real Natural Logarithm (S)	FLN, FALOG	FSTO,XMDS,FADD,FMPY,FDIV,NORM,FGETP
Real Exponential (E)	EXPN, EEXP	XMD, FARC, EGETP
Real Exponential (S)	FXPN, FEXP	XMDS, FARC, FGETP
Real Square Root (E)	ESQR, ESQRT	ELD, ESTO, EADD, EMPY, EDIV, EGETP
Real Square Root (S)	FSQR, FSQRT	FLD/FSTO, FADD, FMPY, FDIV, FGETP
Real Trigonometric Sine/Cosine (E)	ESIN, ESINE, ECOS, ECOSN	EADD, EMPY, NORM, XMD, EGETP
Real Trigonometric Sine/Cosine (S)	FSIN, FSINE, FCOS, FCOSN	FADD, FMPY, NORM, XMDS, FSTO, FGETP
Real Trigonometric Arctangent (E)	EATN, EATAN	EADD, EMPY, EDIV, XMD, EGETP, NORM
Real Trigonometric Arctangent (S)	FATN, FATAN	FADD, FMPY, FDIV, XMDS, FSTO, FGETP
Fixed-Point Square-Root	XSQR	None
Real Absolute Value (E)	EAVL, EABS	EGETP
Real Absolute Value (S)	FAVL, FABS	FGETP
Integer Absolute Value	IABS	None
Real Binary to Decimal/Real Decimal to Binary	FBTD, FDTB	None
Called by LIBF		
Get Parameters (E)	EGETP	ELD
Get Parameters (S)	FGETP	FLD
Real Base to Integer Exponent (E)	EAXI, EAXIX	ELD/ESTO, EMPY, EDVR
Real Base to Integer Exponent (S)	FAXI, FAXIX	FLD/FSTO, FMPY, FDVR
Real Reverse Divide (E)	EDVR, EDVRX	ELD/ESTO, EDIV
Real Reverse Divide (S)	FDVR, FDVRX	FLD/FSTO, FDIV
Real Divide (E)	EDIV, EDIVX	XDD, FARC
Real Divide (S)	FDIV, FDIVX	FARC
Real Multiply (E)	EMPY, EMPYX	XMD, FARC
Real Multiply (S)	FMPY, FMPYX	XMDS, FARC
Real Reverse Subtract (E)	ESBR, ESBRX	EADD
Real Reverse Subtract (S)	FSBR, FSBRX	FADD
Real Add/Subtract (E)	EADD, EADDX, ESUB, ESUBX	FARC, NORM
Real Add/Subtract (S)	FADD, FADDX, FSUB, FSUBX	NORM, FARC
Load/Store FAC (E)	ELD, ELDX, ESTO, ESTOX	None
Load/Store FAC (S)	FLD, FLDX, FSTO, FSTOX	None
Fixed Point Double Word Divide	XDD	XMD
Fixed Point Double Word Multiply	XMD	None
Fixed Point Fractional Multiply (short)	XMDS	None
Real Reverse Sign	SNR	None
Integer to Real	FLOAT	NORM
Real to Integer	IFIX	None
Fixed Integer Base to an Integer Exponent	FIXI, FIXIX	None
Normalize	NORM	None
Real Arithmetic Range Check	FARC	None
DUMP		
Called by CALL		
Dump Status Area	DMP80	None
Selective Dump on Console Printer	DMTX0, DMTD0	WRTY0
Selective Dump on Printer	DMPX1, DMPD1	PRNT1

E-1. (Continued)

Subroutine	Names	Other Subroutines Required
INTERRUPT LEVEL		
Level 0	ILS00*	None
Level 1	ILS01*	None
Level 2	ILS02*	None
Level 3	ILS03*	None
Level 4	ILS04*	None
*These subroutines are not identified by name in the card and paper tape systems		
CONVERSION		
Called by LIBF		
Binary to Decimal	BINDC	None
Binary to Hexadecimal	BINHX	None
Decimal to Binary	DCBIN	None
EBCDIC to Console Printer Code	EBPRT	EBPA, PRTY
IBM Card Code to or From EBCDIC	HOLEB	EBPA, HOLL
IBM Card Code to Console Printer Code	HOLPR	HOLL, PRTY
Hexadecimal to Binary	HXBIN	None
EBCDIC to or from PTTC/8	PAPEB	EBPA
IBM Card Code to or from PTTC/8	PAPHL	EBPA, HOLL
PTTC/8 to Console Printer Code	PAPPR	None
IBM Card Code to or from EBCDIC	SPEED	None
EBCDIC and PTTC/8 Table	EBPA	None
IBM Card Code Table	HOLL	None
Console Printer Code Table	PRTY	None
DISK SUBROUTINE INITIALIZE (card/paper tape only)		
Called by CALL		
Set Pack Initialize Routine	SPIR0, SPIR1, SPIRN	DISK0, DISK1, DISKN
OVERLAY (monitor only)		
Called by LIBF		
Local Read-in	FLIP0, FLIP1	DISKZ or DISK0, DISK1 or DISKN
INTERRUPT SERVICE		
Called by LIBF		
Card	CARD0, CARD1	ILS00, ILS04
Disk (part of supervisor in monitor system)	DISK0, DISK1, DISKN	ILS02
Paper Tape	PAPT1, PAPTN	ILS04
Plotter	PLOT1	ILS04
1132 Printer	PRNT1	ILS01
Console Printer-Keyboard	TYPE0, WRTY0	HOLL, PRTY, ILS04

E-2. VERSION 2 SUBROUTINES

Subroutine	Names
Called by LIBF	
2501 Card reader	READ0, READ1, READZ
1442 Card punch	PNCH0, PNCH1, PNCHZ
1403 Printer	PRNT3, PRNZ
1231 Optical mark reader	OMPR1
32-bit binary converted to card code decimal	BIDEC
Card code decimal to 32-bit binary	DECBI
Conversion subroutine	ZIPC0

E-3. SUBROUTINES IN NAME CODE

0225	5103	BINDC	060D	6880	FCOS	1559	9500	NORM
0225	5227	BINHX	060D	6895	FCOSN	1694	5646	OVERF
0305	9129	CARDZ	060E	38A3	FCTST	1705	7142	PAPEB
0305	9130	CARD0	0604	2880	FABS	1705	7213	PAPHL
0305	9131	CARD1	0604	4100	FADD	1705	75D9	PAPPR
040C	2255	DCBIN	0604	4127	FADDX	1705	78D5	PAPTN
0406	3846	DATSW	0605	3587	FALOG	1705	78E9	PAPTZ
0451	7F30	DMP80	0605	90C0	FARC	1705	78F1	PAPT1
0451	7131	DMPD1	0606	3055	FATAN	1706	4885	PAUSE
0451	79F1	DMPX1	0606	3540	FATN	1758	9563	POINT
0452	3130	DMTD0	0606	54C0	FAVL	1765	58F1	PRNT1
0452	39F0	DMTX0	0606	70A7	FAXBX	1766	3A00	PRTY
0494	3212	DVCHK	0606	7080	FAXB	220C	14C5	SCALE
050C	8059	ECHAR	0606	7240	FAXI	220C	14C6	SCALF
050C	8649	ECHRI	0606	7267	FAXIX	220D	6517	SCOMP
050C	8667	ECHRX	061C	58D7	FGETP	221D	68D6	SGOTO
050D	6880	ECOS	061D	9244	FGRID	2210	1180	SDAF
050D	6895	ECOSN	0610	9940	FDIV	2210	1240	DSAI
0504	2880	EABS	0610	9967	FDIVX	2210	3594	SDCOM
0504	4100	EADD	0612	3080	FDTB	2210	6000	SDF
0504	4127	EADDX	0612	5640	FDVR	2210	6256	SDFIO
0505	3587	EALOG	0612	5667	FDVRX	2210	6544	SDFND
0506	3055	EATAN	0616	75C0	FEXP	2210	69C0	SDFX
0506	3540	EATN	0625	50C0	FINC	2210	9000	SDI
0506	54C0	EAVL	0626	7240	FIXI	2210	99C0	SDIX
0506	70A7	EAXBX	0626	7267	FIXIX	2211	9144	SDRED
0506	7080	EAXB	064C	4000	FLD	2212	6663	SDWRT
0506	7240	EAXI	064C	49C0	FLDX	2214	1640	SEAR
0506	7267	EAXIX	064C	95F0	FLIPO	2214	1667	SEARX
0508	38C2	EBCTB	064C	95F1	FLIP1	2214	9180	SFIF
0509	7040	EBPA	064D	5000	FLN	2218	1640	SFAR
0509	7663	EBPRT	064D	6063	FLOAT	2218	1667	SFARX
051C	58D7	EGETP	065D	35A3	FPLOT	2218	9180	SFIF
051D	9244	EGRID	0651	6945	FMOVE	2218	9580	SFIO
0510	9940	EDIV	0651	7A00	FMPY	2224	1640	SIAR
0510	9967	EDIVX	0651	7A27	FMPYX	2224	1667	SIARX
0512	5640	EDVR	0666	44C5	FRULE	2224	9180	SIIF
0512	5667	EDVRX	068A	35A7	FSTOX	2225	6046	SIOAF
0516	75C0	EEXP	068A	3580	FSTO	2225	6049	SIOAI
0525	50C0	EINC	068A	40A7	FSUBX	2225	61A7	SIOFX
054C	4000	FLD	068A	4080	FSUB	2225	6180	SIOF
054C	49C0	ELDX	068C	1548	FTANH	2225	6240	SIOI
054D	5000	ELN	068D	5200	FTNH	2225	6267	SIOIX
055D	35A3	EPLOT	0688	2640	FSBR	224C	98C5	SLITE
0551	6945	EMOVE	0688	2667	FSBRX	224C	98E3	SLITT
0551	7A00	EMPY	0688	91D5	FSIGN	225C	5144	SPEED
0551	7A27	EMPYX	0688	9540	FSIN	2255	9000	SNR
0566	44C5	ERULE	0688	9545	FSINE	2264	5100	SRED
058A	35A7	ESTOX	0689	8640	FSQR	228D	65C0	STOP
058A	3580	ESTO	0689	8663	FSQRT	2290	2255	SUBIN
058A	40A7	ESUBX	069D	7540	FXPN	2290	2883	SUBSC
058A	4080	ESUB	0716	3044	GETAD	2299	98C0	SWRT
058C	1548	ETANH	0859	3142	HOLEB	23A1	7169	TYPEZ
058D	5200	ETNH	0859	3169	HOLEZ	23A1	7170	TYPE0
0588	2640	ESBR	0859	34C0	HOLL	238A	3597	TSTOP
0588	2667	ESBRX	0859	35D9	HOLPR	238A	3663	TSTRT
0588	91D5	ESIGN	0859	38C2	HOLTB	238C	58A3	TTEST
0588	9540	ESIN	089C	2255	HXBIN	2388	58C0	TSET
0588	9545	ESINE	0904	2880	IABS	250C	8649	VCHRI
0589	8640	ESQR	0909	4C30	IBM00	260C	8649	WCHRI
0589	8663	ESQRT	0918	99C0	IFIX	2666	3A29	WRTYZ
059D	7540	EXPN	094F	2C30	ILS00	2666	3A30	WRTY0
060A	3100	FBTD	094E	2C31	ILS01	2710	4000	XDD
060C	8059	FCHAR	094E	2C32	ILS02	2750	4000	XMD
060C	8649	FCHRI	094F	2C34	ILS04	2750	4880	XMDS
060C	8667	FCHRX	0988	91D5	ISIGN	2789	8640	XSQR

E-4. CORE REQUIREMENTS

Arithmetic and functional subroutines

Standard precision		Extended precision	
FADD/FADDX⎫ FSUB/FSUBX⎭	102	EADD/EADDX⎫ ESUB/ESUBX⎭	98
FMPY/FMPYX	52	EMPY/EMPYX	46
FDIV/FDIVX	86	EDIV/EDIVX	78
FLD/FLDX ⎫ FSTO/FSTOX⎭	54	ELD/ELDX ⎫ ESTO/ESTOX⎭	46
FLOAT	10		10
IFIX	40		40
NORM	42		42
FSBR/FSBRX	24	ESBR/ESBRX	24
FDVR/FDVRX	28	EDVR/EDVRX	28
SNR	8		8
FABS/FAVL	12	EABS/EAVL	12
IABS	16		16
FGETP	22	EGETP	22
FARC	34		34
XMDS	28		
FIXI/FIXIX	68		68
XSQR	52		52
XMD	66		66
XDD	74		74
FSIN/FSINE ⎫ FCOS/FCOSN⎭	108	ESIN/ESINE ⎫ ECOS/ECOSN⎭	138
FATN/FATAN	130	EATN/EATAN	150
FSQR/FSQRT	70	ESQR/ESQRT	76
FLN/FALOG	136	ELN/EALOG	148
FEXP/FEXPN	118	EEXP/EXPN	140
FAXI/FAXIX	78	EAXI/EAXIX	82
FAXB/FAXBX	54	EAXB/EAXBX	54
FTNH/FTANH	54	ETNH/ETANH	46
FBTD (bin. to dec.)⎫ FDTB (dec. to bin.)⎭	420		420
DMTD0/DMTX0	412		412
DMPD1/DMPX1	520		520
DMP80	102		102
DATSW	34		34
DVCHK	16		16
FCTST	30		30
LOAD	138		138
OVERF	18		18
SLITE, SLITT	68		68
TSTOP	6		6
TSTRT	6		6
ISIGN	24		24
FSIGN	34	ESIGN	34

Card/Paper Tape Only		Card/Paper Tape Only	
WARI/WARIX	32	VARI/VARIX	32
WIAR/WIARX	36	VIAR/VIARX	36
WIF	26	VIF	26
WIIF	24	VIIF	24
WGOTO	22	VGOTO	22
WFIO/WIOI/WIOAI/ WIOF/WIOAF/ WIOFX/WCOMP/ WWRT/WRED/ WIOIX ⎬	854	VFIO/VIOI/VIOAI/ VIOF/VIOAF/ VIOFX/VCOMP/ VWRT/VRED/ VIOIX ⎬	864

Monitor Only		Monitor Only	
SDFIO/SDAF/SDAI/ SDCOM/SDF/SDFX/ SDI/SDIX/SDRED/ SDWRT ⎬	602		602
SDFND	60		60
SFAR/SFARX	32	SEAR/SEARX	32
SFIO/SIOI/SIOAI/ SIOF/SIOAF/SIOFX/ SCOMP/SWRT/SRED/ SIOIX ⎬	892		892
SFIF	26	SEIF	28
SGOTO	22		22
SIAR/SIARX	36		36
SIIF	24		24

Miscellaneous and ISS subroutines

CARD0		242
CARD1		246
PAPT1		254
PAPTN		294
DISK0		356 (1)
DISK1		620 (1)
DISKN		808 (1)
WRTY0		124
TYPE0		296
PLOT1		216
PRNT1		386
ILS00		18
ILS01		18
ILS02		18
ILS03		18
ILS04		30
SPIR0		48 (2)
SPIR1		62 (2)
SPIRN		62 (2)
FLIP0		72 (3)
FLIP1		48 (3)
PAUSE		12
STOP	Card/P.T.	8
	Monitor	12
SUBSC		30
SUBIN		32
TTEST/TSET		16
CARDZ		80
PAPTZ		202
PRNTZ		176
TYPEZ		82
WRYTZ		60
HOLEZ		54
GETAD		14
EBCTB		54
HOLTB		54

(1) Card/Paper Tape only, part of supervisor in Monitor.
(2) Card/Paper Tape only.
(3) Monitor only.

(Continued)

E-4. CORE REQUIREMENTS (Continued)

Conversion subroutines

BINDC	72
DCBIN	88
BINHX	44
HXBIN	66
HOLEB	134
HOLPR	100
EBPRT	102
PAPEB	246
PAPHL	244
PAPPR	192
SPEED	330
HOLL	80
EBPA	80
PRTY	80

E-5. EXECUTION TIMES

Arithmetic and functional subroutines

STANDARD		EXTENDED	
FADD/FADDX	460	EADD/EADDX	440
FSUB/FSUBX	560	ESUB/ESUBX	490
FMPY/FMPYX	560	EMPY/EMPYX	790
FDIV/FDIVX	766	EDIV/EDIVX	2060
FLD/FLDX	180	ELD/ELDX	160
FSTO/FSTOX	180	ESTO/ESTOX	170
FLOAT	330		330
IFIX	140		140
NORM	260		260
FSBR/FSBRX	650	ESBR/ESBRX	740
FDVR/FDVRX	1090	EDVR/EDVRX	2520
SNR	80		80
FABS/FAVL	50	EABS/EAVL	60
IABS	100		100
FGETP	330	EGETP	320
FARC	60		60
XMDS	260		--
FIXI/FIXIX	465		465
XSQR	550 av. (860 max.)		550 av. (860 max.)
XMD	520		520
XDD	1760		1760
FSIN/FSINE	3.0	ESIN/ESINE	5.4
FCOS/FCOSN	3.4	ECOS/ECOSN	5.9
FATAN/FATN	5.2	EATAN/EATN	8.9
FSQRT/FSQR	4.5	ESQRT/ESQR	10.4
FALOG/FLN	5.1	EALOG/ELN	8.0
FEXP/FXPN	2.0	EEXP/EXPN	4.4
FAXI/FAXIX	3.8	EAXI/EAXIX	4.7
FAXB/FAXBX	8.0	EAXB/EAXBX	13.3
FTANH/FTNH	4.3	ETANH/ETNH	8.1
FBTD (bin. to dec.)	40.0		40.0
FDTB (dec. to bin.)	20.0		20.0

E-5. (Continued)

Miscellaneous and ISS subroutines

Subroutine and Function	Times (μsec) (n = word count)
ILS00	112
ILS01	112
ILS02	112
ILS03	112
ILS04	148
CARD0	
Test	165
Read	$14930 + 38.5 (n)$
Punch	$763 + 185 (n)$
Feed	605
Sel. Stack.	290
CARD1	
Test	165
Read	$14972 + 38.5 (n)$
Punch	$800 + 190 (n)$
Feed	640
Sel. Stack.	325
WRTY0	
Test	165
Print	$228 + 734 (n)$
TYPE0	
Test	165
Read print	$685 + \epsilon (825 + 48.5y) + 390 a + 1595 b + 1224 c$
	ϵ = sum of char. times for each graphic
	y = no. char. skipped in table look-up
	a = EOM character
	b = re-entry character
	c = backspace character
Print	$344 + 920 (n)$
PAPT1	
Test	152
Read	$432 + 808* (n)$
	*add +112 if check
Punch	$480 + 680* (n)$
	*add +96 if check
PAPTN	
Test	176
Read	$408 + 952* (n)$
	*add +112 if check
Punch	$464 + 840* (n)$
	*add +64 if check
PLOT1	
Test	130
Print	418 = if char is 0-9
	472 = if char is A
	624 = if char is B
	$698 +$ 752 = if char is C
	224 = per dup. of previous pen motion

E-5. (Continued)

Miscellaneous and ISS subroutines

Subroutine and Function	Times (μsec) (n = word count)
PRNT1 Test Print	188 44142 + 5971.2 (n-1)* *subtract 11.4 for each word where 1 char. does not match; 22.8 where both char. do not match.
Print Numeric	25950 + 2736.8 (n-1) +268 x x = no. idle cycles before 1st numeric char. on wheels is reached
Control Single space Double space Triple space Skip to channel 12 Skip to channel 1	708 998 1288 676* 936* *add 208 for each channel crossed before correct one reached
DISK0 Test Read Write Without RBC With RBC Write Imm Seek 1 to center By addr	178 1492 1778 2050 1062 1076 1502
DISK1 Test Read	178 900 + 760 x + 478 y x = no. sectors y = no. seeks after 1st sector
Write Without RBC Write With RBC Write Imm Seek 1 to center By addr	1292 + 660 x + 822 y 1562 + 1098 x + 908 y 660 + 622 x + 476 y 1072 1468
DISKN Test Read	178 908 + 652 x + 1012 y x = no. sectors y = no. seeks after 1st sector
Write Without RBC Write With RBC Write Imm Seek 1 to center By addr	1516 + 610 x + 926 y 1728 + 1022 x + 1178 y 820 + 606 x + 282 y 1076 1478

E-5. (Continued)

Conversion subroutines

Subroutine	Initial- ization	Best	Worst Std. Set	Worst Extd. Set	Table Look- Up
BINDC	1130	–	–	–	–
DCBIN	1110	–	–	–	–
BINHX	620	–	–	–	–
HXBIN	760	–	–	–	–
HOLPR	430	211	2395	3533	45.5
EBPRT	420	207	2487	3675	47.5
HOLEB EBCDIC output EBCDIC input	550 550	159 161	2343 2441	3481 3629	45.5 47.5
SPEED Packed EBCDIC output Unpacked EBCDIC output Packed EBCDIC input Unpacked EBCDIC input	250 270 240 240	270 260 394 404	– – 1594 1604	– – 3914 3924	– – 80.0 80.0
PAPPR Per shift char. input Per graphic char. input Per control char. input	580	180 427 407	– 2707 2687	– 3895 3875	– 47.5 47.5
PAPHL PTTC/8 input Per shift char. input Per graphic char. input Per control char. input PTTC/8 output Per control char. output Per graphic char. output Per shift/graphic char. output	490 490	180 306 296 266 316 446	– 2482 2472 – 2492 2622	– 3870 3860 3830 3880 4010	– 49.5 49.5 49.5 49.5 49.5
PAPEB PTTC/8 input Per shift char. input Per graphic char. input Per control char. input PTTC/8 output Control char. output Per graphic char. output Per shift/graphic char. output	440 440	190 366 386 296 346 476	– 2542 2562 – 2522 2652	– 3930 3950 3860 3910 4040	– 49.5 49.5 49.5 49.5 49.5

E-6. INPUT/OUTPUT SUBROUTINES—CHARACTER CODES

Typical calling sequence, except for FORTRAN:

```
LIBF        (name)
DC          (control parameters)
DC          (address of I/O area)
DC          (address of error routine)
```

Subroutine	Input or output area	Characters/word in I/O area	Code assumed
ALL FORTRAN I/O sub-routines (end in Z)	121 words, beginning at/003C	One, lower eight bits	EBCDIC
CARD0 CARD1 (1442 Read-Punch)	Identified by second DC after LIBF. First word in this area contains the count of columns.	One, left-justified (bits 0–11)	Card code
DISK0 DISK1 DISKN	Identified by second DC after LIBF. First word: count of words to be transmitted. Second word: sector address where reading or writing begins.		Disk word and core word are identical
PRINT1	Identified by second DC after LIBF. First word in output area specifies the number of computer words to be printed.	Two	EBCDIC
TYPE0 WRTY0	Identified by second DC after LIBF. First word of area is number of characters.	Print: two	Console printer code
		Read-Print: one	Card code (card image)
PAPT1 PAPTN	Identified by second DC after LIBF. First word of area is number of computer words.	Two	Tape image (usually PTTC/8)
READ0 READ1	Identified by second DC after LIBF. (First word has count.)	One, left-justified (bits 0–11)	Card code
PNCH0 PNCHN	Identified by second DC after LIBF. (First word has count.)	One, left-justified (bits 0–11)	Card code
PRNT3	Identified by second DC after LIBF. (First word has count.)	One, left-justified (bits 0–11)	Card code

E-7. INPUT/OUTPUT SUBROUTINES—CONTROL PARAMETERS

(First DC after the calling LIBF.)

Subroutine	First hexadecimal digit (I/O Function)	Second digit	Third digit	Fourth digit
CARD0 CARD1	0 Test: Is previous operation completed? 1 Read 2 Punch 3 Feed a card 4 Select stacker	Not used	Not used	0

E–7. (Continued)

Subroutine	First hexadecimal digit (I/O Function)	Second digit	Third digit	Fourth digit
DISK0 (version 1 only) DISK 1 DISKN	0 Test 1 Read 2 Write without read-back check 3 Write with read-back check 4 Write immediate 5 Seek	Not used	*First digit=5.* 0 Seek cylinder with address in second word in In-put/Output area not 0; seek *next* cylinder	1 File-protect facility is used. 0 No file protect
PRNT 1 PRNT 3 (version 2 only)	0 Test 2 Print 3 Carriage control 4 Print numerical (PRNT 1 only)	Carriage control (first digit=3)	Carriage control after printing	Not used
		1 Skip to channel 1 2 Skip to channel 2 3 Skip to channel 3 4 Skip to channel 4 5 Skip to channel 5 6 Skip to channel 6 9 Skip to channel 9 C Skip to channel 12 D Space one E Space two F Space three		
TYPE0 WRTY0	0 Test 1 Read-print 2 Print	Not used	0	0 or 1
PAPTN PAPT1	0 Test 1 Read 2 Punch	0 Check word count 1 No check	Not used	Used with test function 0 Is reader ready? 1 Is punch ready?
PLOT 1	0 Test 1 Write	Not used	Not used	0
READ0 READ1 (both version 2)	0 Test 1 Read	Not used	Not used	0
PNCH0 PNCH1 (both version 2)	0 Test 2 Punch 3 Feed	Not used	Not used	0
OMPR1 (version 2)	0 Test 1 Read 3 Feed 4 Disconnect	1 Stacker selected 0 Not used	Not used	Timing-mark check test

Samples of Test Function in Input/Output Subroutines

Situation: Program is to loop until printer operation is completed.

```
TEST   LIBF   PRNT1
       DC     /0000    [The first digit is zero (indicates a test).]
       MDX    TEST
```

(Next instructions to be executed when printer operation is completed)

E-8. TYPES OF CONVERSIONS

CONVERTED FROM	CONVERTED TO								
	Binary	IBM Card Code (256)	IBM Card Code (Subset)	PTTC/8 (Subset)	EBCDIC (256)	EBCDIC (Subset)	Console Printer	Hex Equivalent (Card Code)	Decimal Equivalent (Card Code)
Binary								BINHX	BINDC
IBM Card Code (256)					SPEED				
IBM Card Code (Subset)				PAPHL		HOLEB	HOLPR		
PTTC/8 (Subset)			PAPHL			PAPEB	PAPPR		
EBCDIC (256)		SPEED							
EBCDIC (Subset)			HOLEB	PAPEB			EBPRT		
Hex Equivalent (Card Code)	HXBIN								
Decimal Equivalent (Card Code)	DCBIN								

E-9. CHARACTER CODE CONVERSION SUBROUTINES

IN—Address of first word of input area
OUT—Address of first word of output area
Where not specified, illegal characters are replaced by a space character

Name	Calling sequence		From	To	Comments
BINDC	LIBF DC	BINDC OUT	Binary number in accumulator	Card code (decimal) One per word	Six-word output—sign +5 decimal digits, beginning at OUT; no errors detected.
BINHX	LIBF DC	BINHX OUT	Binary number in accumulator	Card code (HEX)	Like BINDC, but to HEX; 4-word output; no errors detected.
DCBIN	LIBF DC	DCBIN IN	Card code (decimal) One per word, at IN	Binary word in accumulator	Reverse of BINDC; assumes 5 digits and sign in IN through IN +5; terminates on illegal character.
HXBIN	LIBF DC	HXBIN IN	Card code (hex) One per word, at IN	Binary word in accumulator	Four card-code characters in IN through IN+3 for input; output in accumulator; terminates on illegal character.

E–9. (Continued)

Name	Calling sequence		From	To	Comments
HOLEB	LIBF	HOLEB	Control digit	x = 0	
	DC	/000x	Card code	EBCDIC (subset)	
	DC	IN	One per word	Two per word	
	DC	OUT	Control digit	x = 1	
	DC	(No. of characters)	EBCDIC (subset) Two per word	Card code One per word	
SPEED	LIBF	SPEED	Control digit	x = 0	y = 0: Two EBCDIC characters per word
	DC	/00yx	Card code One per word	EBCDIC	y = 1: One left-justified EBCDIC character per word
	DC	IN			
	DC	OUT	Control digit	x = 1	(y is the third control digit)
	DC	(No. of characters)	EBCDIC	Card code, one per word	
PAPEB	LIBF	PAPEB	Control digit	x = 0	y = 0: Initialize case.
	DC	/00yx	PTT c/8 Two per word	EBCDIC (subset) Two per word	y = 1: Do not alter case.
	DC	IN			
	DC	OUT	Control digit	x = 1	
	DC	(No. of characters)	EBCDIC (subset) Two per word	PTTc/8 Two per word	
PAPHL	LIBF	PAPHL			Like PAPEB, but card code instead of EBCDIC.
	DC	/00yx			Card-code characters, one per word.
	DC	IN			
	DC	OUT			
	DC	(No. of characters)			
PAPPR	LIBF	PAPPR	PTTc/8,	Console printer code or 1403	y = 0: Initialize case;
	DC	/00yx			y = 1: Do not alter case.
	DC	IN	two per word	Printer code,	x = 0: Console printer code
	DC	OUT		two per word	x = 1: 1403 Printer code
	DC	(No. of characters)			
HOLPR	LIBF	HOLPR	Card code, one per word	Console printer code,	x = 0: Console printer code
	DC	/000x			x = 1: 1403 Printer code
	DC	IN		two per word	
	DC	OUT			
	DC	(No. of characters)			
EBPRT	LIBF	EBPRT	EBCDIC (subset),	Console printer code or 1403	x = 0: Console printer code
	DC	/000x			x = 1: 1403 Printer code
	DC	IN		Printer code,	
	DC	OUT	two per word	two per word	
	DC	(No. of characters)			
BIDEC (version 2)	LIBF	BIDEC	Two binary words in accumulator and accumulator extension	Card code (decimal)	11-word output: Sign and 10 decimal digits; no errors detected.
	DC	OUT			
DECBI	LIBF	DECBI	Card-code characters of a decimal number	Two binary words in accumulator and accumulator extension	First word input area is 0001; no errors detected.
	DC	IN			
	DC	(Address of no. of characters)			

E-10. ERRORS DETECTED BY THE ISS SUBROUTINES

ERROR	CONTENTS OF ACCUMULATOR		Contents of Extension (if any)
	Binary	Hexadecimal	
Card			
*Last card	0 0 0 0 0 0 0 0 0 0 0 0 0 0 0 0	0 0 0 0	
*Feed check *Read check *Punch check	0 0 0 0 0 0 0 0 0 0 0 0 0 0 0 1	0 0 0 1	
Device not ready Last card indicator on for Read	0 0 0 1 0 0 0 0 0 0 0 0 0 0 0 0	1 0 0 0	
Illegal device (not 0 version) Device not in system Illegal function Word count over +80 Word count zero or negative	0 0 0 1 0 0 0 0 0 0 0 0 0 0 0 1	1 0 0 1	
Printer-Keyboard			
Device not ready	0 0 1 0 0 0 0 0 0 0 0 0 0 0 0 0	2 0 0 0	
Device not in system Illegal function Word count zero or negative	0 0 1 0 0 0 0 0 0 0 0 0 0 0 0 1	2 0 0 1	
Paper Tape			
*Punch not ready	0 0 0 0 0 0 0 0 0 0 0 0 0 1 0 0	0 0 0 4	
*Reader not ready	0 0 0 0 0 0 0 0 0 0 0 0 0 1 0 1	0 0 0 5	
Device not ready	0 0 1 1 0 0 0 0 0 0 0 0 0 0 0 0	3 0 0 0	
Illegal device Illegal function Word count zero or negative Illegal check digit	0 0 1 1 0 0 0 0 0 0 0 0 0 0 0 1	3 0 0 1	
Disk			
*Disk overflow	0 0 0 0 0 0 0 0 0 0 0 0 0 1 0 0	0 0 0 4	
*Seek failure remaining after ten attempts	0 0 0 0 0 0 0 0 0 0 0 0 0 0 1 1	0 0 0 3	Effective Sector Id
*Read check remaining after ten attempts Data Error Data overrun	0 0 0 0 0 0 0 0 0 0 0 0 0 0 0 1	0 0 0 1	Effective Sector Id
*Write check remaining after ten attempts Write select Data error Data Overrun	0 0 0 0 0 0 0 0 0 0 0 0 0 0 0 1	0 0 0 2	Effective Sector Id
Device not ready	0 1 0 1 0 0 0 0 0 0 0 0 0 0 0 0	5 0 0 0	
Illegal device (not 0 version) Device not in system Illegal function Attempt to write in file protected area Word count zero or negative Word count over +320 (0 version only) Starting sector identification over + 1599	0 1 0 1 0 0 0 0 0 0 0 0 0 0 0 1	5 0 0 1	
1132 Printer			
*Channel 9 detected	0 0 0 0 0 0 0 0 0 0 0 0 0 0 1 1	0 0 0 3	
*Channel 12 detected	0 0 0 0 0 0 0 0 0 0 0 0 0 1 0 0	0 0 0 4	
Device not ready or end of forms	0 1 1 0 0 0 0 0 0 0 0 0 0 0 0 0	6 0 0 0	
Illegal function Illegal word count	0 1 1 0 0 0 0 0 0 0 0 0 0 0 0 1	6 0 0 1	
Plotter			
Plotter not ready	0 1 1 1 0 0 0 0 0 0 0 0 0 0 0 0	7 0 0 0	
Illegal device Device not in system Illegal function Word count zero or negative	0 1 1 1 0 0 0 0 0 0 0 0 0 0 0 1	7 0 0 1	

NOTE: The errors marked with an asterisk cause a branch via the error parameter. These errors are detected during the processing of interrupts; as a consequence, the user error routine is an interrupt routine, executed at the priority level of the I/O device.

All other errors cause a branch to location 41. The address of the LIBF in error is in location 40.

E-11. SUBROUTINE ACTION AFTER RETURN FROM A USER'S ERROR ROUTINE

Error Code	Condition	Subroutine Action
Card 0000	If function is PUNCH Otherwise	Eject card and terminate Terminate Immediately
0001*	If Accumulator is 0 Otherwise	Terminate immediately Loop until 1442 is ready, then reinitiate operation
Paper Tape 0004, 0005	If Accumulator is 0 Otherwise	Terminate immediately Check again for device ready
Disk 0001, 0002, and 0003	If A Reg. is 0 Otherwise	Terminate immediately Retry 10 more times
1132 Printer 0003, and 0004	If Accumulator is 0 Otherwise	Terminate immediately Skip to channel 1 and then terminate

*Assumes operator intervention.

E-12. SUBROUTINE ERROR INDICATORS

The three-word error indicator is just below the floating point accumulator. Hence the words are 122, 123, and 124 more than the value in index register 3, and their meaning is indicated in the following table.

Subroutine	Error	Error indicator word	Is set to	Comment
All real arithmetic	Overflow	1	= 1	FAC set to maximum
	Underflow	1	= 3	FAC set to zero
Floating point divide	Zero divisor	2	= 1	Dividend not changed
Square root	Negative argument	3	1 in bit 13	$\sqrt{}$ of absolute value
Natural logarithm	Zero argument	3	1 in bit 15	FAC set to maximum
	Negative argument	3	1 in bit 15	Absolute value of argument used
Sine and cosine	Absolute value of argument $\geq 2^{24}$	3	1 in bit 14	FAC set to zero
IFIX (floating point to integer)	Absolute value of argument $\geq 2^{15} - 1$	3	1 in bit 12	Largest possible signed result in accumulator
Integer base to integer exponent	Base = 0, exponent ≤ 0	3	1 in bit 11	Zero result
Floating point base to integer exponent	Base = 0, exponent ≤ 0	3	1 in bit 10	Zero result
Floating point base to floating point exponent	Base = 0, exponent ≤ 0	3	1 in bit 9	Zero result
	Base = 0, exponent $\neq 0$	3	1 in bit 15	Result is absolute value of base

The error indicators can be interrogated by:

1. CALL OVERFL (J):   J set to the value of indicator word one (J = 2 if no overflow or underflow).
2. CALL DVCHK (J):   J = 1 if indicator word two = 1; J = 2 otherwise.
3. CALL FCTST (I,J):   If indicator word three = 0, then I = 2 and J = 0.
                                   If indicator word three $\neq$ 0, then I = 1 and J = indicator word three.

MACHINE LANGUAGE

APPENDIX F

F-1. 1130 WORD FORMATS

		First word	Second word
		0 1 2 3 4 5 6 7 8 9 10 11 12 13 14 15	0 1 2 3 4 5 6 7 8 9 10 11 12 13 14 15
Data formats S = sign bit. Negative number in 2's complement form	Single precision integer	S	
	Double precision integer	S (Even address for leftmost word)	
Instruction formats F = 0 for short instruction T = tag bits (00, 01, 10, N) IA = 1 for indirect instruction	Short instruction	Op-code F T Displacement	
	Long instruction	Op-code F T IA Modifiers	Address
IOCC format See chart for function codes and modifiers		Address (Even address)	Device Func- Modifier tion

F-2. CORE STORAGE LOCATIONS

Address		Function
Decimal	**Hexadecimal**	
1	1	Index register 1
2	2	Index register 2
3	3	Index register 3
8	8	Interrupt branching address, level zero
9	9	Interrupt branching address, level one
10	A	Interrupt branching address, level two
11	B	Interrupt branching address, level three
12	C	Interrupt branching address, level four
13	D	Interrupt branching address, level five
32–39	20–27	1132 Printer scan field
	3C–B5	FORTRAN input-output area
50–144	32–90	In-core communications area (COMMA)
	38	Address of link to skeleton supervisor (version 1)
	276	Address of link to disk utility program (version 1)

Version 1	Version 2	
1C2	1C3	Beginning of FORTRAN or assembler core load (DISKZ used)
260		Beginning of FORTRAN or assembler core load (DISKO used)
370	2D6	Beginning of FORTRAN or assembler core load (DISKI used)
438	39E	Beginning of FORTRAN or assembler core load (DISKN used)

F-4. TAG BIT CODES

Instruction	Tag Bits	Register/Operation
Load Index Store Index	00	IAR
	01	XR1
	10	XR2
	11	XR3
Shift Left Shift Right	00	Disp.
	01	XR1
	10	XR2
	11	XR3
Modify Index and Skip		
F = 0	00	Disp. added to IAR
	01	Disp. added to XR1
	10	Disp. added to XR2
	11	Disp. added to XR3
F = 1; IA = 0	00	Disp. added to C
	01	Add. added to XR1
	10	Add. added to XR2
	11	Add. added to XR3
F = 1; IA = 1	00	Disp. added to C
	01	C added to XR1
	10	C added to XR2
	11	C added to XR3
Disp. = Contents of Displacement field of instruction		
Add. = Contents of Address field of instruction		
C = Contents of location specified by Add.		

F-3. INSTRUCTIONS ARRANGED IN ORDER OF OPERATION CODES

Mod bits (8–9)	Operation	Mnemonic	Function
	00001	XIO	Input-output
00	00010	SLA	Shift left accumulator
10	00010	SLT	Shift left accumulator and extension
11	00010	SLC	Shift left and count accumulator and extension
11	00011	RTE	Rotate right accumulator and extension
00	00011	SRT	Shift right accumulator and extension
	00100	LDS	Load status
	00101	STS	Store status
	00110	WAIT	Wait
	01000	BSI	Branch and store instruction address register
(Bit 9) 0	01001	BSC	Branch or skip on condition
(Bit 9) 1	01001	BOSC	Branch or skip on condition (resets interrupt level if branch or skip occurs)
	01100	LDX	Load index
	01101	STX	Store index
	01110	MDX	Modify index and skip
	10000	A	Add
	10001	AD	Add double
	10010	S	Subtract
	10011	SD	Subtract double
	10100	M	Multiply
	10101	D	Divide
	11000	LD	Load accumulator
	11001	LDD	Load double—accumulator and extension
	11010	STO	Store accumulator
	11011	STD	Store double—accumulator and extension
	11100	AND	Logical AND
	11101	OR	Logical OR
	11110	EOR	Logical exclusive OR

All other operation codes function as WAIT

F-5. EFFECTIVE ADDRESS COMPUTATION

	F = 0 (Direct Addressing)	F = 1, IA = 0 (Direct Addressing)	F = 1, IA = 1 (Indirect Addressing)
T = 00	EA = Disp + IAR	EA = Add	EA = C/Add
T = 01	EA = Disp + XR1	EA = Add + XR1	EA = C/Add + XR1
T = 10	EA = Disp + XR2	EA = Add + XR2	EA = C/Add + XR2
T = 11	EA = Disp + XR3	EA = Add + XR3	EA = C/Add + XR3

Disp = Contents of Displacement field of instruction.

Add = Contents of Address field of instruction.

C = Contents of Location specified by Add or Add + XR.

F-6. EFFECTIVE ADDRESS COMPUTATION—MACHINE LANGUAGE

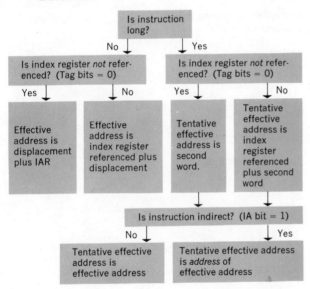

F-7. MDX INSTRUCTION

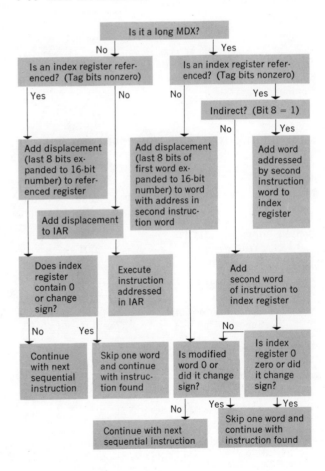

F-8. AND, OR, AND EOR OPERATIONS

Memory bit	Corresponding accumulator bit	Resulting accumulator bit		
		AND	OR	EOR
0	0	0	0	0
0	1	0	1	1
1	0	0	1	1
1	1	1	1	0

F-9. CARRY AND OVERFLOW INDICATORS

Instruction	Overflow	Carry
Add	On after the instruction if sum is too large for accumulator (ACC)	ON if there is a carry-out of the high-order bit position of ACC. Reset anew by each add instruction.
Add double		
Subtract	Like add	ON if there is a borrow in high-order bit position of ACC.
Subtract double		
Divide	ON 1) dividing by zero ON 2) quotient too large for ACC	Not affected
Shift left ACC Shift left ACC and EXT	Not affected	ON if the last position shifted out of the accumulator contained a 1-bit. OFF if a 0-bit.
Shift left and count	Not affected	ON if shift is terminated by 1 in high-order ACC bit; OFF if ACC is decremented to zero, even if 1 is in the high-order bit of ACC.
Any other command other than "status" command	Not affected	Not affected

F-10. INPUT/OUTPUT FUNCTION CODES AND MODIFIERS

Input/output device (code) instruction	Function code	Modifier bits		
		Bit number	Bit	Function
Console printer (00001)				
Write	001			
Sense device	111	15	1	Reset interrupt level 4 indicator
Console keyboard (00001)				
Read	010			
Control (interrupt)	100			
Sense device	111	15	1	Reset interrupt level 4 indicator
1442 Card read punch (00010)				
Read	010			
Write	001			
Control	100	8	1	Stacker select
		13	1	Initiate read
		14	1	Feed cycle
		15	1	Initiate punch
Sense device	111	14	1	Reset interrupt level 4 indicator
		15	1	Reset interrupt level 0 indicator
1134 Paper tape reader (00011)				
1055 Paper tape punch (00011)				
Read	010			
Write	001			
Control	100			
Sense device	111	15	1	Reset interrupt level 4 indicator

F–10. (Continued)

Input/output device (code) instruction	Function code	Modifier bits		
		Bit number	Bit	Function
Disk storage (00100)				
Initiate write	101	13–15		Sector
Initiate read	110	13–15		Sector
		8	0	Read operation
		8	1	Read-check operation
Control	100	13	0	Move access forward
		13	1	Move access backward
Sense device	111	15	1	Reset interrupt level 2 indicator
1627 Plotter (00101)				
Write	001			
Sense device	111	15	1	Reset interrupt level 3 indicator
1132 Printer (00110)				
Read emitter	010			
Control	100	8	1	Start printer
		9	1	Stop printer
		13	1	Start carriage
		14	1	Stop carriage
		15	1	Space carriage
Sense device	111	15	1	Reset interrupt level 1 indicator
Console entry switches (00111)				
Read	010			
2501 Card reader (01001)				
Initiate read	110			
Sense device	111	15	1	Reset bits 3 and 4 in Device Status Word (DSW)
1403 Printer (10101)				
Initiate write	101			
Control	100			
Write	101			Bits in address (4–15); control carriage skips to channels 1–12. DSW and channels 9 and 12 indicators are reset.
Sense interrupt	011			
Sense device	111	15	1	
1231 Optical mark page reader (01000)				
Read	010			
Sense interrupt	011			
Sense drive	111	15	1	Reset DSW
2310 Disk storage				
Drive 1—10001				
Drive 2—10010				
Drive 3—10011				
Drive 4—10100				
Sense interrupt	011			
Control	100	13	0	Arm moves toward center.
			1	Arm moves away from center. (address: number of cylinders to move)
Initiate write	101	13–15		
Initiate read	110	13–15		Sector (0–7) to be used
		8	1	
Sense device	111	15	1	Reset DSW

F-11. DEVICE STATUS WORD

Device	Console Printer	Keyboard	1442	1134 1055	1627	Disk Storage	1132	Console
Device Code	1	1	2	3	5	4	6	7
Interrupt Level	4	4	0, 4	4	3	2	1	5
Bit Position								
0	Service Response		Read Response		Response	Data Error	Read Emitter Response	Program Stop Key
1		Response	Punch Response	Reader Response		Operation Complete	Skip Response	Interrupt Run Mode
2		Request	Error Check			Busy, Not Ready	Space Response	
3		0 – Keyboard Entry 1 – Console Entry	Last Card	Punch Response		Busy	Carriage Busy	
4	Printer Busy		Operation Complete	Reader Busy		Carriage Home	Print Scan Check	
5	Printer Busy, Not Ready			Reader Busy, Not Ready			Forms Check	
6		Keyboard Busy		Punch Busy			Printer Busy	
7				Punch Busy, Not Ready				
8							Carriage Control Tape Channel No. 1	
9							2	
10							3	
11							4	
12							5	
13							6	
14			1442 Busy		1627 Busy	Sector Counts	9	
15			1442 Busy, Not Ready		1627 Not Ready		12	

F–12. INTERRUPT HANDLING

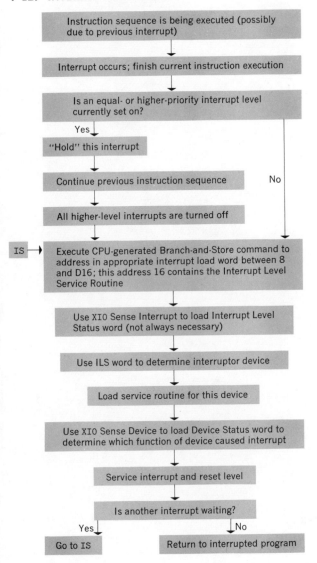

Instruction sequence is being executed (possibly due to previous interrupt)

↓

Interrupt occurs; finish current instruction execution

↓

Is an equal- or higher-priority interrupt level currently set on?

Yes ↓   No

"Hold" this interrupt

↓

Continue previous instruction sequence

↓

All higher-level interrupts are turned off

↓

IS → Execute CPU-generated Branch-and-Store command to address in appropriate interrupt load word between 8 and D16; this address 16 contains the Interrupt Level Service Routine

↓

Use XIO Sense Interrupt to load Interrupt Level Status word (not always necessary)

↓

Use ILS word to determine interruptor device

↓

Load service routine for this device

↓

Use XIO Sense Device to load Device Status word to determine which function of device caused interrupt

↓

Service interrupt and reset level

↓

Is another interrupt waiting?

Yes ↓   No ↓

Go to IS   Return to interrupted program

F–13. INTERRUPT CONDITIONS

Single disk storage interrupts   Level 2

Read
Read-check when operation completed
Write
Control (arm access)

Console interrupts   Level 4

Character printed
Control function completed
Interrupt request (INT REQ) key on keyboard pressed
Key on keyboard pressed (when keyboard is in select status, with keyboard select light on)

1442 Card read punch

Column of data ready to be entered into core   Level 0
Request for transmission of information to punch a column   Level 0
Operation completed (column 80 past read station or card past punch station)   Level 4
Card read errors

1132 Printer

The eight words of the print-scan field have been scanned and one character printed   Level 1
Punch in channels 1, 2, 3, 4, 5, 6, 7, or 12 of paper tape in printer

Console controls   Level 5

PROGRAM START button on console pushed
Mode switch is on INTERRUPT RUN, and execution of an instruction has just been completed.

2501 Card reader

Operation completed   Level 4

Paper tape reader

Character available for core   Level 4

Paper tape punch

Punching completed   Level 4

Plotter

Specified action completed   Level 3

1403 Printer

Transfer complete (120-position buffer full)   Level 4
Printing completed   Level 4

PROCEDURES

APPENDIX G

G–1. TURNING THE COMPUTER ON

1. Turn on the main switch on the central processor, located slightly above and to the right of the keyboard.
2. If the Disk File UNLOCK light (to the left of the keyboard) is on, then open the front right side of the cabinet and turn on the FILE switch. Turn on other disks if present.
3. Turn on the 1132 line printer, using the switch on its control panel. Also press the START button on the printer. Check that the printer has paper and reload if necessary.
4. Hold down Non-Process Runout (NPRO) on the card reader for a few seconds to clear cards from the reader.
5. The computer will be ready to operate when the FILE READY light on the console turns on. It may be necessary to read a cold start card (see Appendix G–2) to establish communication with the supervisor, although it is sometimes possible to return to the supervisor by means of the console entry switches (see Appendix G–3).

G–2. COLD START PROCEDURE

When a program misbehaves and destroys the connecting link with the supervisor program, one must use the cold start procedure. Sometimes this is also necessary when the machine is first turned on. This procedure requires a cold start card, which is supplied by IBM. The computer center will usually have a number of such cards available.

1. Hold down Non-Process Runout on the card reader for a few seconds.
2. Place a cold start card in the card hopper, face down, 9-edge in.
3. Place your program, if you plan to run one, on top of this card in the hopper. The cold start card may also be entered by itself for a program to be run later.
4. Place the card weight on top of the stack of cards.
5. Press START on the card reader, holding it down until the READY light on the reader comes on.
6. Press IMM (immediate) STOP, RESET, and PROGRAM LOAD on the console (keys to right of keyboard).

G–3. RETURN TO SUPERVISOR PROGRAM AFTER TROUBLE

The procedure which follows is based on the assumption that the skeleton supervisor is in core. If the procedure fails, use cold start procedure.

1. Press PROGRAM STOP. If this is not effective, and if the computer is not engaged in input-output, press IMM STOP.
2. Set console mode switch to LOAD position.

3. Enter core address 0038_{16} ($0000\ 0000\ 0011\ 1000_2$) in the console switches (up for 1, down for 0).
4. Press LOAD IAR on the console. (IAR is the instruction address register. You are placing the address of the next instruction to be executed, 0038, in the IAR.)
5. Set mode switch to RUN.
6. Press PROGRAM START.

The same procedure, with a different address in the console entry switches, is followed for branching to some point in a program currently in core. For example, if you load a FORTRAN program's "execution address" (from your listing) in the IAR, you will begin the program again, provided the program has not already destroyed itself.

G–4. DISPLAY CONTENTS OF A WORD IN MEMORY

1. Press PROGRAM STOP, if program is running. (If you wish to continue execution after display, note the address in the IAR.)
2. Set console mode switch to LOAD position.
3. Enter in the console switches the address of the word to be displayed.
4. Press LOAD IAR.
5. Set mode switch to DISP.
6. Press PROGRAM START.
7. Read the Storage Buffer Register (SBR) on the console; this is the word desired.
8. Pushing PROGRAM START again will display the next word in core, whose address will be one greater than that of the word displayed first.

G–5. DISPLAY INDEX REGISTERS

A variant of the general display procedures can be used conveniently to display the contents of three index registers, since these are in fixed positions in memory; index register 1 is in word 1, index register 2 in word 2, and index register 3 in word 3. We give the procedure fully, although a reading of the general display procedure would be sufficient.

1. Press IMM STOP and RESET.
2. Set console mode switch to LOAD position.
3. Turn off (down position) all the console entry switches.
4. Press LOAD IAR.
5. Set mode switch to DISP.
6. Press PROGRAM START *twice*. The storage buffer register now shows the contents of index register 1. Pressing PROGRAM START again will cause the contents of index register 2 to be shown in the SBR, and then pressing it once more will give index register 3.

G–6. ENTER WORDS IN CORE MEMORY

1. Press PROGRAM STOP, if program is running.
2. Set console mode switch to LOAD position.
3. Enter address, in binary, into the console switches. The address identifies the word to be changed.
4. Press LOAD IAR.
5. Enter word, in binary, into the console switches.
6. Press PROGRAM START.
7. Continue entering more words, each word in sequence, into the console entry switches and push PROGRAM START after each entry. The IAR is incremented by one each time, so each word entered is in one higher place in memory.

G–7. EXECUTE A PROGRAM FROM WORKING STORAGE ON DISK

In the method which follows, it is assumed that the supervisor program is in control, and that the card reader is being used for input.

1. Load a //bXEQ card in the card reader hopper.
2. Press START on card reader and hold until READY light comes on.
3. Press PROGRAM START.

A second method is available for procedure under supervisor control but with input from the console keyboard.

1. Type //bXEQ

A third method is used whenever the skeleton supervisor is in core.

1. Set 8038 (hexadecimal) in the console entry switches.
2. Set console mode switch to LOAD position.
3. Press RESET and LOAD IAR.
4. Set mode switch to RUN.
5. Press PROGRAM START.

G–8. STORE A FORTRAN OR ASSEMBLER PROGRAM ON DISK

1. Prepare the following two cards:

```
1              13  17  21      (Card columns)
|              |   |   |
//bDUP
*STORE         WS  UA  (up to 5 characters, left-
                        justified)
```

2. Place these cards after the program cards.
3. Follow with an XEQ card if program is to be executed.

G–9. EXECUTE A PROGRAM STORED ON DISK

Use an XEQ card with the program name left-justified in columns 8 to 12:

```
1      8
|      |
//bXEQb[name]
```

A JOB card may need to precede the XEQ.

G–10. CORE DUMP AFTER TROUBLE

1. Press IMM STOP and RESET.
2. Press NPRO on card reader and enter appropriate program in hopper:
   a) One-card program (supplied by IBM) for console dump; set the starting address in the console entry switches.
   b) Four-card program (supplied by IBM) for printer dump; ready printer. Dumps in hexadecimal from 00A016 to the end of core. Core address at the beginning of each line.
3. Press START on card reader and PROGRAM LOAD on console.

For dump subroutines in the system library, callable within programs, see IBM 1130 Subroutine Library descriptions of DMP80, DMTX0, DMTD0, DMPX1, and DMPD1.

G–11. MALFUNCTIONS OF CARD READER

The card reader subroutines check for error conditions. (See table of error conditions on following page.) If read or punch difficulties occur, the computer is put in a WAIT state (lights 2 and 3 on in the operation register) or goes into a loop (assembler and monitor especially). The error indicator on the card reader comes on, and the particular error is also displayed on the card reader control panel. The following action should be taken:
1. Lift up the remaining cards in the hopper and place them elsewhere.
2. Press NPRO, being careful to collect the cards ejected from the machine by this operation. The ejected cards are placed at the bottom of the hopper stack, so that they will be read first. (In the TRANS error the first card should not be placed in the hopper, but only the second and third ejected cards. If READ REG occurs *after* long wait, just as reader tries to pull in next card, enter only second of two NPROD. Otherwise on READ REG (i.e., during continuous reading), reenter both. See the following table for a discussion of these error conditions.
3. Place cards in the hopper.
4. Press READER START on the card reader to bring the first card into the reader.
5. Press PROGRAM START on the console if necessary.

Type of error	Indicator	Reason	Special notes
Hopper misfeed	HOPR	Card did not enter card reader from hopper	If card has been damaged, particularly in central area facing inward, it may need to be repunched. (But try to repeat operation before repunching.)
Feed check (punch)	PUNCH STA	Card improperly positioned in punch station	No special comment
Transport	TRANS	Card failed to pass into the stacker	No special comment
Feed cycle	FEED CLU	Cards advanced in position without a request	No special comment
Feed check (read)	READ STA	Card stuck in read station	No special comment
Read registration	READ REG	Incorrect read registration	Repeated errors of this type may indicate that cards are badly punched (misregistered) or that 1442 is badly timed, needs service.
Punch check	PUNCH	Improper punching	Correction of card to pre-punched state may be necessary before reentry into the hopper

G-12. ENTERING MATERIAL FROM TYPEWRITER

The procedure of entering numbers and letters from the typewriter is controlled not only by the typewriter keys and computer circuitry, but by the programming support of the computer. The following description applies to FORTRAN-used subroutines.

1. The computer expects material from the typewriter keyboard when the KB SELECT light, just to the left of the keyboard, is *on*. A WAIT (lights 2 and 3 on) shows in the operation register.

2. The two keys which control numeric or alphameric status are at the lower left and the lower right of the keyboard; the keyboard stays in either status until the other status key is depressed.

3. Numbers and/or letters must be entered according to the format specification in the program that is in control. It is convenient to write programs so that a message giving specifications for the data is typed just before they are entered. The following special points should be noted.

　a) The use of the space bar is equivalent to typing a zero.

　b) If the places indicated in the format statement for an integer number are not all typed, the subroutines consider the "missing" spaces to be zero. (For example, if one has an I3 format and types 20, the number will be considered as 200.)

　c) If the decimal point is explicitly entered in a real number, it is not necessary to fill in the end of the number with zeros. The format count of places includes both the decimal point and the sign. If no decimal point is entered, the additional missing spaces in the format will be considered as zeros, as above, before the program inserts a decimal point at the place indicated in the format statement. The common procedure is to type the decimal point, overriding the program format specification.

　d) Entering information contrary to the format specification, such as letters for an I or F format, leads to a FORTRAN I/O error. The computer will be placed in a WAIT state, with the accumulator showing the nature of the error. (See FORTRAN I/O error codes, Appendix A–7.) Pressing START returns control to the monitor and thus to the next program if one is waiting in the card hopper.

4. If it is desirable to retype a line without entering the typed information, the ERASE FIELD key should be pressed (to the right of the keyboard). The carriage will

be returned, and typing can commence once more.

5. After the full information has been typed, control is returned to the computer by pressing the EOF (End of Field) key on the right-hand side of the keyboard.

G-13. REMOVING AND INSERTING A DISK

1. Power must be turned on.
2. Turn off file switch (inside door on right-hand side).
3. Wait (about a minute) for unlock light to come on.
4. Pull down handle in front of file (inside door).
5. Slide out the old disk carefully.
6. Press down disk cover to protect against dust.
7. Slide in the new disk and put handle up.
8. Turn on file switch.
9. Wait for file ready light to come on (about $1\frac{1}{2}$ minutes)

G-14. EXECUTION ADDRESS

To find the absolute execution address of a FORTRAN or assembler program currently in core, display the word with address 007F (in the in-core communications area). See Appendix G-4 for details. If the FORTRAN input/output routines have been used, this word will have been overlaid with input/output information and so will no longer be the execution address.

The execution address, along with subroutine addresses, can be obtained by the use of an L in column 14 of the //bXEQ card. Alternatively, a simple assembler subroutine can be written to type the execution address at the beginning of a FORTRAN program.

G-15. PRINTER CARRIAGE CONTROL IN FORTRAN

Unlike the programming for other output devices, that of the 1132 printer assumes that the first character in a line is the carriage control character. The characters used and their meanings are as follows:

Blank, or any other character not mentioned here
   — Single space before printing
0 — Double space before printing
1 — New page before printing (depends on using the proper carriage tape)
+ — Data to be printed on the same line that the previous material was printed on

If the line begins with an alphameric message, set off, either with single quotes or with explicit H specification. The first letter in this message should be the carriage control symbol or the control character symbol in single quotes.

G-16. IBM MANUALS CONCERNING THE 1130

The ultimate source of information governing the 1130 is the collection of manuals published by IBM concerning this computer and its available programming languages. These manuals are often revised, both with Technical Newsletters and with new editions, and thus may reflect changes made since this book was written. The serious user will find it essential to consult the manuals, so it is advisable to have sets in the library and computer room.

The following list describes some of the available IBM literature on the 1130.

IBM 1130 System Summary (A26-5917)
Brief description of the 1130 components and programming language.

IBM 1130 Functional Characteristics (A26-5881)
Description of the general structure of the 1130 system, its machine language, and its input/output facilities.

IBM 1130 Assembler Language (C26-5927)
Brief definition of the assembler language.

IBM 1130 Subroutine Library (C26-5929)
Discussion of IBM-supplied subroutines, including those used in FORTRAN. Discussion of subroutines for input/output.

IBM 1130/1800 Basic FORTRAN IV Language (C26-3715)
Definition of the basic FORTRAN language for the 1130.

1130 FORTRAN Programming Techniques (C20-1642)
Advice on writing efficient FORTRAN programs. Very readable.

Core Requirements for 1130 FORTRAN (C20-1641)
Estimate of core storage needed for FORTRAN programs.

IBM 1130 Disk Monitor System Reference Manual
    (C26-3750)
Monitor and disk utility programs, including monitor control for FORTRAN and assembler.

IBM 1130 Disk Monitor System, Version 2 (C26-3709)
System introduction.

IBM 1130 Program Logic Manual (Y26-3752)
Description of the programs in the monitor system, including FORTRAN and assembler. Restricted distribution.

*1130 Continuous System Modeling Program Application
    Description* (H20-0209)
A program for simulating an analog computer, representing the problem in a way similar to an analog flow diagram.

1120 Continuous System Modeling Program (H20-0282)
Program reference manual.

*1130 Continuous System Modeling Programming System
    Manual* (H20-0284)
Programming logic of CSMP.

*Civil Engineering Coordinate Geometry (COGO) for IBM 1130
    Model 2I User Manual* (H20-0301)

Guidance for solving geometrical problems from surveying and related areas.

Civil Engineering Coordinate Geometry (COGO) System Manual (Y20–0064)
Programming logic of COGO.

IBM 1130 Scientific Subroutine Package, Programmer's Manual (H20–0252)
FORTRAN subroutine written by IBM for use in scientific programs.

IBM 1130 Data Presentation System Application Description (H20–0235)
Programming packages for the plotter.

IBM 1130/1800 Plotter Subroutines (C26–3755)
FORTRAN and assembler subroutines for plotting curves and characters.

IBM 1130 Bibliography (A26–5916)
List and descriptions of IBM publications for the 1130. The accompanying *SRL Newsletter* (N20–1130) also lists the descriptions of application programs.

INDEX

654